Labor and Desire

Women's Revolutionary Fiction

Labor & Desire

n Depression America

Paula Rabinowitz

The University of North Carolina Press

Chapel Hill & London

The paper in this book meets the guidelines for permanence and durability of the Committee on Production Guidelines for Book Longevity of the Council on Library Resources.

95 94 93 92 91   5 4 3 2 1

Library of Congress Cataloging-in-Publication Data
Rabinowitz, Paula.
  Labor and desire : women's revolutionary fiction in depression America / by Paula Rabinowitz.
     p.   cm. — (Gender & American culture)
  Includes bibliographical references (p.   ) and index.
  ISBN 0-8078-1994-8 (cloth : alk. paper). — ISBN 0-8078-4332-6 (pbk. : alk. paper)
     1. American fiction—20th century—History and criticism. 2. Feminism and literature—United States—History—20th century. 3. Women and literature—United States—History—20th century. 4. Revolutionary literature, American—History and criticism. 5. American fiction—Women authors—History and criticism. 6. Women intellectuals in literature. 7. Working class in literature. 8. Depressions in literature. 9. Radicalism in literature. 10. Desire in literature. I. Title. II. Series.
PS374.F45R33   1991   91-50259
                                                                            CIP

"Last Night," by Martha Millet, is used by permission of the author.

Portions of the Prologue and Chapter 3 were first published as "Ending Difference/Different Endings: Class, Closure, and Collectivity in Women's Proletarian Fiction," in *Genders* 8 (Summer 1990).

Portions of Chapters 2 and 3 were published as "Maternity as History: Gender and the Transformation of Genre in Meridel LeSueur's *The Girl*," in *Contemporary Literature* 29 (Winter 1988).

To Jacob and Raphael

Contents

Preface

As a child of suburbia growing up in the 1950s, I did not fully realize how the 1930s represented an important, though unspoken, episode in the lives of my parents, grandparents, and ultimately myself. I was made to understand that my middle-class life was a direct result of the poverty that had controlled my parents' childhoods, and that I was to be grateful for FDR and the NRA, for CCNY and a range of alphabetic institutions. Still, not much was actually said about the past. School proved little help; American history classes never managed to take us past the first world war. It was not until I entered college and became involved with the New Left that the idea of an old Left, of another era of radical ferment, could be explored in any depth. This study owes its beginnings to two unrelated sources: an offhand comment Fredric Jameson made, in a lecture at the 1982 Midwest Modern Language Association meeting, that we should "reinvent" the 1930s, and the revelation by my grandmother of a shame-filled memory she had from the Depression. To earn money to buy a chicken for Sabbath suppers, she told me, she would on Fridays sit in the butcher's shop and, for a nickel a chicken, perform the service of plucking feathers for those customers who could afford this small luxury. Her embarrassment about this was profound; it declared to the whole community that her husband could not provide for his family and, more significantly, that she was an incompetent Jewish mother because poverty had led her to work in public. The image of my grandmother's hands, covered with blood and feathers, has haunted me since she secretly related the scene to me before her death.

Jameson had suggested that, as radical scholars, we need to rewrite the narrative of the 1930s. My grandmother's story seemed to suggest how. It was the absence of almost any women's names from Daniel Aaron's *Writers on the Left* that led me to begin this study. I knew from my own family and from films

ix

like *Union Maids* (1974) that women had marched on the picket lines, challenging not only the boss's authority but also that of their husbands and fathers. Surely, there must have been women writers on the Left who had told stories as powerful as my grandmother's.

When I began working on this study, almost none of the texts I discuss were in print. The Delacorte Press had once again silenced Tillie Olsen; *Yonnondio*, so recently published, was out of print, thus going the way of so many works by women, especially those multiply marginalized by class or race. The Feminist Press had plans to reissue a series of novels from the 1930s, but as yet only Agnes Smedley's *Daughter of Earth*, one of their first reprints, was available. Since that time Feminist Press, Monthly Review Press, Naiad Press, Virago Books, and some university presses and commercial houses have begun to publish new editions of these lost works. Thus a new context for my study has developed as I have written it.

Now I can have a dialogue with the editors and reviewers of these various editions. Then I had only the memories of some friends and acquaintances who had been active in the 1930s Left (yes, they remembered reading *I Went to Pit College*) and materials deposited in the Labadie Collection of the University of Michigan library, in the Tamiment Collection of New York University's Bobst Library, and in the archives of the New York Public Library to provide clues about women's participation in 1930s literary radicalism. Consequently my goals have changed as I have written this work, developing with the new theories of gender and sexuality generated by feminist studies. My process of reinventing the 1930s began as an archaeological recovery of the lost novels by women who wrote out of a radical, rather than a romantic or gothic, tradition but developed into a re-vision of the prevailing scholarship of the 1930s.

As I read the novels, some of which survive only in the copyright depository of the Library of Congress, the material spoke a challenge to the conventional wisdom that the 1930s were an era dominated by class consciousness and that feminism as an ideology ended (temporarily) in the 1920s.[1] Even that second "reinvention" has now largely given way to an examination of the ways in which women authors create narratives of class-conscious female subjectivity and, in so doing, produce theories about the interrelationship of class and gender. The "powers of desire" that moved women to revise narrative as they searched for gaps through which to enter history mirror my desire to empower these narratives to rewrite history.[2] In this way, I believe this study makes a contribution to what Elaine Showalter calls the "third phase" of feminist criticism: implementing various theories and practices of gender as a category of knowledge to reconstruct cultural history.[3]

The 1930s need to be reinvented for their significance to American cultural studies. The marginalization of the 1930s within dominant literary history has been reproduced within feminist and Marxist critical communities because the prescriptions and economism of much 1930s literary and political analysis seem naive at best and vulgar at worst. Nevertheless, radical women's writing of the period elaborated female subjectivity as the site where desire and history (e)merge, thereby challenging both Marxist and feminist criticism by its insistent reminder of the material bases of sexuality, gender, race, ethnicity, and class—the complex factors that both unite and divide women from each other and from men.

Many people have contributed to this study and, although none of the errors present here are their fault, much of the credit must go to them. Christy Brown, Herb Eagle, June Howard, Beth Spencer, Martha Vicinus, and Alan Wald read early drafts of the work and provided helpful criticisms of it. Between 1982 and 1986, Anne Herrmann, Janis Butler Holmes, Laura Kipnis, Margaret Lourie, Anita Norich, Margot Norris, Sandra Silberstein, and Domna Stanton nurtured me with invaluable insights about the relationship between feminist practice and literary theory through our feminist critical theory study group. My colleagues and friends in the University of Michigan Women's Studies Program, Alice Echols and Ruth Bradley, struggled with me through the day-to-day grind of writing. Their humor, encouragement, and brilliance added considerably to my understanding of the relationships among politics, sexuality, and culture.

My friend and coeditor, Charlotte Nekola, graciously permitted me the use of materials collected for our anthology, *Writing Red.* Our on-going discussions about women's literature and politics formed the germ of this study. Conversations with Nancy Armstrong, Constance Coiner, Maria Damon, Barbara Foley, Melanie Hawthorne, Paul Lauter, Meridel LeSueur, George Lipsitz, John Mowitt, Tillie Olsen, Marty Roth, Con Samaras, Leonard Tennenhouse, and Harvey Teres have clarified my readings of history, theory, and fiction.

My parents, Shirley and Samuel Rabinowitz, and family members—Len and Mark Rabinowitz, Sheri Stein, and Rae Bernstein—were always willing to listen to my ideas even when they were paying for our frequent long-distance phone calls. Financial assistance for researching and writing the book came from the Horace H. Rackham School of Graduate Studies, the Program in American Culture, and the Committee for Gender Research at the University of Michigan and from the Graduate School, the College of Liberal Arts, and the English Department of the University of Minnesota. My research assistant, Judith Halberstam, aided me in innumerable ways; her wit, energy, and intellect ensured that this book was completed more or less on time. My editors at the University of North Carolina Press, Iris Tillman Hill, Kate Torrey, and Pam Upton, guided me throughout the process of transforming manuscript to book.

Paradoxically, I must thank the defunding of the arts and the Left, which meant that David Bernstein, ex-calculus teacher, actor, and organizer, remained unemployed while I finished this book, leaving me to benefit from his sympathetic yet critical editing; I feel lucky to have had his love and support over the years. Finally, this book is dedicated to Jacob Bernstein and Raphael Rabinowitz, who have lived their entire lives with this study. Their remarkable joy, patience, and creativity have given me the necessary time and energy to work.

Labor and Desire

Prologue

On the Breadlines and the Headlines

When Elizabeth Leonard, the expatriate artist of Tess Slesinger's 1934 novel *The Unpossessed*, decides she must return home, she quotes a letter from her cousin Bruno, who intones that the "country's on the breadlines, the headlines, the deadl——." This chain of signifiers, leading from hunger to its printed description, from the class of people that filled the breadlines to the class that wrote about them, from those whose bodies were marked by poverty, hunger, and labor to those who earned their living through the written word (intellectuals, journalists, and artists), mirrors the trajectory of this study. Literary radicalism developed out of specific historic events of the 1930s—the Depression and fascism—but it also produced a discursive field that marked off certain political issues as acceptable for print, delimiting the boundaries of political discourse. Literary radicalism produced a discourse of the working class and a location for intellectuals in America, a nation that has traditionally resisted acknowledging the work and words of either group.

In the quote above, Elizabeth never finishes her sentence because, to a large extent, the claims of the intellectual laborer who was ruled not by the time clock but by the deadline appeared lifeless to the arbiters of leftist culture during the 1930s. Nevertheless, because "all writing is propaganda" (as another character reminds us), the production of a language to speak of class deprivation and struggle was important to the Left's organizing efforts during the 1930s. It is precisely the contradiction between the power of intellectuals' words and the inefficacy of their actions that fueled much of the debate among literary radicals. To interpret the ways in which different bodies encoded class differently, this study examines their texts.

I

Although writers worked in every genre, using a variety of stylistic and formal techniques, their common urge to document, to record, to report, and ultimately to change the world fired much of the political culture of the 1930s. The "documentary expression" of many writers has been the focus of numerous critical studies of 1930s aesthetics, and virtually every anthology of literature from that decade includes a section on reportage.[1] By creating a rapport between the direct experiences of those who suffered and struggled and the writers who came into contact with them, reportage served to link the breadlines to the headlines. Furthermore, because of its peculiar formation—the direct rendering of (class) struggle through carefully detailed (individual) analysis—reportage also linked the genres of personal narrative and political economy; in so doing, it connected traditionally feminine forms of writing to more conventionally masculine ones. Moreover, as the dominant literary innovation of the decade, it affected a number of other forms. Thus fiction, poetry, and drama all sought to re-create the immediacy and power offered by the direct testimony of reportage. The claims of history on the literature of the 1930s re-formed the generic boundaries of writing itself. These boundaries—between classes and genres—ultimately shaped the gendered narratives of both political and literary history.

In "Women on the Breadlines," Meridel LeSueur's first piece of reportage for the *New Masses*, the writer, an unemployed mother of two, places herself among the "women you don't see": those who are single, out of work, and hungry. She was criticized for her "defeatism" by the editors, who were annoyed that such women were not joining the organizations of the working class and that this writer was not striking a more hopeful note. Implicitly, her stance suggested that narratives about the breadlines needed modification when it was women who stood on them.[2] Because the hungry woman had no place on the breadlines, she rarely figured in the headlines either. And so, by the end of the decade, Meridel LeSueur was positing another story for the working-class woman: her politics was "written in the book of the flesh." As a worker and a woman, the radical working-class woman was inscribed both by her labor and by her desire; thus, according to LeSueur, an analysis either of the bodies of women or of their texts will lead us inevitably to the other.[3]

As a narrator of working-class women's lives, Meridel LeSueur theorizes the relationship of bodies and texts, of labor and desire, suggesting that we need to understand the working class as both embodied and textualized. Moreover, she insists that we read both bodies and texts as gendered. For

LeSueur, the differentials between male and female bodies are located in the belly. The body of the working-class man of the 1930s—and to an extent its text—is hungry, an empty space once filled by its labor; the body of the working-class woman, as well as her text, is pregnant with desire for "children," for "butterfat" to feed them, and, most significantly, for "history" to change the world for them. Even though LeSueur's vision ultimately reinforces gender polarities, her radical insistence that texts and bodies, desire and labor, be read as gendered and classed elaborations of each other has been pivotal to my writing.

More recently, Jeanne Westin's *Making Do: How Women Survived the '30's* recounts the memories of lower-middle-class and working-class women whose experiences were only tangentially connected to the great labor struggles taking place among male farmers and workers. Westin argues that the private sphere to which many women were confined during the 1930s, when legislation was passed prohibiting the employment of married women in order to make a place for the male breadwinner, left "the women who learned to make do or do without . . . literally and historically invisible."[4] Like many feminist critics and historians, Westin assumes a distinction between the public sphere of (male) power and the private sphere of (female) powerlessness. Yet as Nancy Armstrong suggests, the cultural work of the two spheres is mutually affirming because each ratifies the other.[5]

Despite the efforts of LeSueur and others to place women on both the breadlines *and* the headlines, women have remained invisible in standard accounts of the 1930s, particularly those written by literary radicals both then and now. Rather than continue the trend of decrying women's absence from the public sphere, however, my study argues—through an analysis of the context, content, and form of white women's "revolutionary" fiction—that a rich selection of women's voices and visions circulated during the decade.[6] These women's varied descriptions of world-historical events and domestic intimacies indicate the interpenetration of both spheres. Ultimately, their differently gendered narratives of class struggle necessitate a rethinking of both class and gender as conceptual categories.

By engendering class through writings that were markedly influenced by the documentary tradition, in which the observer of history becomes a participant in it, American literary radicalism ultimately embodied texts. Adapting the conventions of realism and the innovations of modernism, 1930s revolutionary fiction revealed the gendered narratives in and of class relations in

America and thereby provided a grammar with which to speak of both radicalized workers and intellectuals as historical subjects. Just as LeSueur and Westin corrected the androcentrism controlling the imagery and memory of the Depression by presenting the stories of women, so women's revolutionary fiction expanded the terrain encompassed by literary radicalism to produce a history of female subjectivity. In so doing, such fictions helped to develop a theory of the embeddedness of class, gender, and sexuality in our bodies and our texts.

These novels, read as a genre, provide access to a gendered history of 1930s literary radicalism that revises many of the accounts already written about this period and explains why women have been occluded in most of them. Because gender was not recognized as a salient political category by the Left—although it figured as a metaphoric one—few have thought to look for the women's voices among those recorded. Even many women's historians have accepted the characterization of the 1930s as irrelevant to feminist issues because of the predominance of class struggle, and so for the most part they have ignored women's struggles during the period. These omissions are related, and they develop from the tendency of both Marxist and feminist theories to assign primacy to one category of difference—class on the one hand, gender on the other. But once class and gender are read as mutually sustaining discursive systems dependent upon re-presenting each through the other, the divisions that have resulted in the partial histories of the Left and of women disappear. Leftist women's fiction of the 1930s rewrites women into the history of labor and workers into the history of feminism. By encoding classed gender and gendered class in narrative, it presents alternative sites for theorizing the interrelationship of class and gender. Narrative itself then becomes both the form and the content of new histories and new theories about women, literature, and politics in 1930s America.

Thus a study of women's revolutionary fiction must begin with two sets of revisions. The first requires a revision of the prevailing scholarship on 1930s literary radicalism to include a discussion of women's participation. Much of the scholarship of literary radicalism has been institutional; it has focused on what Josephine Herbst characterized as the "head boys" who edited journals, wrote criticism, and prescribed the ideological and aesthetic content of the movement.[7] The reasons for this are entangled within the political and literary debates generated during the 1930s that have set the tone for most subsequent work on the period. As I will demonstrate in the following chapter, most histories of literary radicalism have emphasized the correlation between the shifting political pronouncements of the Communist Party of the United States (CPUSA) and the changes in literary values expressed by Marxist critics. Such a rendering of literary history, besides being profoundly undialectical, is also profoundly gendered. It reproduces culturally ascribed values of masculinity and femininity by failing to register the ways in which binary oppositions reinvoke gendered hierarchies. Because scholarship about the 1930s has reproduced the conditions of 1930s criticism, which inscribed gender by maintaining its absence, gender has not figured in the literary history of the period.[8]

Another series of reconsiderations that must occur to rectify the silencing of women's voices from the 1930s requires scrutinizing and challenging the notions of the feminine (literary) tradition in much feminist historiography. Conventional histories of the American women's movement have, for the most part, contributed to the lack of information about women's writings of the 1930s by depicting the decade as a step backward for feminism.[9] When the "first wave" ended in 1920, so the story goes, women's concerns were put on the back burner until *The Feminine Mystique* (1963) spurred what eventually became the women's liberation movement of the late 1960s. Yet within both liberal and leftist discourses, women's concerns were voiced and acted upon during the 1930s. Roosevelt's New Deal helped advance women into (symbolic) positions of power in government, while separate women's journals, councils, and organizations challenged "male supremacy" within the CPUSA. In fact, there was a lively debate between feminists and Communists about autonomous women's organizations, the relations of production and reproduction in the home and the workplace, protective legislation, the importance of free abortion and birth control for working-class women, and the power of gender ideology to define capitalist and fascist societies.

For example, Mary Inman's *In Women's Defense* (1940) and Grace Hutchins's *Women Who Work* (1934) explored the implications of the double day for the working-class woman. By arguing that the sexual double standard represented the "code of a class," producing a classed sexuality through gender asymmetry, Inman challenged Popular Front conventions that reaffirmed bourgeois conceptions of maternity and female sexuality for the working-class woman.[10] By insisting that working-class women labored as producers and reproducers of goods, services, and workers, Hutchins claimed that working-class mothers, even when they were not engaged in "productive labor" outside the home, were still constituted as proletarians by the "double burden."[11] Nevertheless, despite their feminist overtones, both authors reinscribed the body of the working-class woman within classed arrangements that repressed gender differences. Working-class women may well have been "the pivot of the system," but that system was understood to be "capitalism": that is, an economic relationship between (primarily ungendered) classes.[12]

If 1930s Marxist-feminism subordinated gender to class, most American feminists failed to register class differences among women at all. During the 1930s, feminist organizing receded after suffrage, although the National Woman's Party continued to push for the Equal Rights Amendment (ERA) to the Constitution. Debate over the ERA, however, pointed up the tensions between working-class and middle-class women. Many working-class women believed that the ERA would benefit only a handful of business and professional women, at the expense of the vast numbers of working women who gleaned a measure of security from the minimum wage and other protective legislation. A few feminist organizations like the Women's Trade Union League or Margaret Sanger's movement for birth control crossed class lines, acknowledging class differences among women. For the most part, though, feminist organizations spoke to and for only a handful of women.[13] Thus the "woman question" remained as marginal within the 1930s Left as it was within the nation as a whole, while the class struggle failed to penetrate feminist politics.

Marginality has defined the terrain of feminist literary criticism; it has served to outline a field of inquiry—women's literature—yet it has also limited that field. In the *Norton Anthology of Women's Literature*, subtitled *The Tradition in English*, Sandra M. Gilbert and Susan Gubar establish an alternative canon. Yet their anthology excludes most women's political writing. Few works of feminist literary criticism have analyzed women writers as political theorists, in part because the cultural and historical analyses that established a gendered division between public and private spheres have implied a certain closure regarding the form and content of women's writings. Women's literature, like woman's place, is viewed as private and extrahistorical, providing a particularistic vision in contrast to the universalized stance of masculine discourse. Of course, the concept of masculine universality needs to be challenged by women's private considerations. But we also need to understand how women's lives, however private, nevertheless construct political history, and how women's writings engage in debates that extend into the so-called public arena.[14]

In *No Man's Land: The Place of the Woman Writer in the Twentieth Century*, Gilbert and Gubar skirt the 1930s altogether, jumping from the 1920s to the 1940s and 1950s to make their case for a "war of words" between modernist men and women—a war that entailed sexual and linguistic struggle but precluded class conflict.[15] Nevertheless, as Deborah S. Rosenfelt has argued, a socialist-feminist literary history can be written.[16] It would include works by women (and by some men) that narrate a theory of gendered subjectivity built upon the differences within and among women—differences of race, class, sexuality, region, ethnicity, age, and so forth—thereby producing a discourse that politicizes literary history and so resists gendering it. What Rosenfelt and Judith Newton call "materialist-feminist criticism" demands an elaboration of multivalent subjectivities through narrative.[17] Such a narrative would, for instance, re-present the various combinations of class and racial differences through gender and sexual differences and vice versa.[18]

Classed female subjectivity, then, might be found at the moments in narrative when ideology "transpierces" the body, to use Julia Kristeva's term.[19] Leslie Rabine calls this "feminine historicity . . . the desire on the part of a feminine character to enter the historic process."[20] While this desire remains submerged for the middle-class heroines of the romances and domestic novels Rabine surveys, in revolutionary fiction by women of the 1930s it constructs a narrative of female class consciousness out of the woman's body, providing us with another theoretical framework for understanding the mutual embeddedness of the discourses of class and gender.

Women's revolutionary narratives of the 1930s have, by and large, been ignored or disparaged by the Marxist critics of the period for remaining too feminist, and they have been excluded from contemporary feminist reconstructions of literary history because they transgress the gender lines dividing men from women by investigating class, racial, and geopolitical differences among women. In fact, the writings of women on the Left actually produce a third configuration. These writings neither depend directly on Marxist theory (like that of Inman and Hutchins and many contemporary socialist-feminists), which views gender as an add-on to class, nor do they emerge from radically feminist separatism (of Alice Paul and the National Woman's Party and most contemporary cultural feminists), which adds class onto its dominant gender analysis in order to rectify its own middle-class bias. The narratives by women literary radicals construct a classed female subject whose textual elaboration develops from the (maternal) body of the (fraternal) working class. Thus women's revolutionary fiction of the 1930s narrates class as a fundamentally gendered construct and gender as a fundamentally classed one and so enables the beginnings of a theory of gendered classed subjectivity.

During the 1930s, class struggle in the United States was metaphorically engendered through a discourse that re-presented class conflict through the language of sexual difference. The prevailing verbal and visual imagery reveled in an excessively masculine and virile proletariat poised to struggle against the effeminate and decadent bourgeoisie. Thus the potentially revolutionary struggles of the working class were recontained within the framework of the eternal battle between the sexes found in domestic fiction. The discourses of the 1930s represent one historically specific instance of the "deep connection between how relationships [of class and gender] are represented and how they are implemented."[21] As categories of differences, gender and class are not mutually exclusive but instead remain fundamentally implicated as "re-presentations" of themselves and each other in narrative. It is for this reason that Nancy Armstrong argues for reading the gendered subject of literature as history.[22]

"History," according to Louis Althusser, "is a process without a telos or a subject"; that is, history refuses narrative. Through what Fredric Jameson calls "master narratives," the historiography of narrative itself, or through what Hayden White refers to as "emplotment," however, history slides into its other—a story with subjects, causes and effects, and endings.[23] Narratives insist upon (well-)constructed subjects and a telos that traces their temporal and spatial patterns to an inevitable conclusion. Nevertheless, the subjects constructed through narrative are not as unified, nor are their movements as teleological, as Althusser's distinctions between history and narrative would have us believe. Despite attempts to cover over the gaps among them, the various subjects deployed through narrative—dispersed among readers, writers, and characters—split away from each other, deferring an ending. As the subjects of narrative break apart, so too do the claims for a difference between narrative and history.

In fact, "the work of narrative," says Teresa de Lauretis, "is a mapping of differences, and specifically, first and foremost, of sexual difference into each text; and hence, by a sort of accumulation, into the universe of meaning, fiction and history, represented by the literary-artistic tradition and all the texts of culture."[24] Thus, in de Lauretis's view, history could be understood as "a sort of accumulation" of the narratives of (sexual) difference. The super-imposition of differences onto each text is but one instance of the larger process by which history plots its own narrative, which in turn also maps (sexual) difference.

De Lauretis's reading of the maps of sexual difference in narrative (and history) owes much to Althusser's theory of ideology and the subject but pushes his theory to account for gender.[25] To explain his axiom "ideology interpellates individuals as subjects," Althusser demonstrates the process of ideological interpellation by recalling the experience, common to all of us, of reflexively turning our heads when someone on the street yells "Hey, you!"[26] The interpellation process produces the narratives by which history is (mis)understood as the result of individuals acting. Actually, the (ungen-dered) subject (that is, the individual) is an *effect* produced by the ongoing process of history rather than being the *cause* of historical events. Althusser's model needs some refinement, however, because ideologies of gender read the markings of sexual difference on an individual body and interpellate the subject as male or female. The interpellated subject is also the gendered and embodied subject; that is, when someone yells "Hey, lady!," only those pedestrians who identify themselves as female will pause. Yet this difference goes un(re)marked in Althusser's work. Thus unspoken, femininity also remains uninterpellated, exceeding the subject as Althusser theorizes it. It is this (sexual) difference that de Lauretis sees as the foundation of narrative—and ultimately of the "universe of meaning, fiction and history."

Once gender becomes recognized within subjectivity, the differences sepa-rating narrative and history collapse because, in Joan Scott's words, "sexual difference is simultaneously a signifying system of differentiation *and* a histor-ically specific system of gendered differences." Gender, like class, is both "a concept and a practice" and as such is both constitutive of and constituted by the social meanings of narratives.[27] The only way we know history is through the retelling of accumulated stories that are narrated, either literally or metaphorically, by and through the bodies of gendered subjects. So it is to narrative as history (or, more precisely, it is to the gendered narratives of classed history and the gendered history of classed narratives) that we must look for outlines of a (theory of) classed, gendered subjectivity.

A brief discussion of two key works of women's revolutionary fiction will serve to begin laying out the terms of my argument. Agnes Smedley's *Daughter of Earth* (1929) and Mary McCarthy's *The Company She Keeps* (1942) act as brackets for this study of the classed female subject in 1930s women's literary radicalism.[28] These two works historicize the gendered classed subject and, as such, they are emblematic texts for reading the white working-class woman and the white female intellectual—two subject positions that have proved resistant to both Marxist and feminist theories of culture.

In many ways, *Daughter of Earth* represents the Ur-text of women's proletarian fiction of the 1930s. According to many contemporary and subsequent critics, its publication in 1929 signaled the beginnings of proletarian realism as a literary movement in the United States. The novel recounts the personal and political life of Marie Rodgers through a framed narrative, which uses a thinly veiled autobiography to authenticate itself.[29] The framing device provides the illusion of distance between the coextensive narrator and subject, Marie Rodgers, a woman whose recovery from a breakdown sends her back to her past. Smedley's frame sets up dual spaces, times, and classes: America and Denmark; past and present; middle-class writer and working-class organizer. What happens to the working-class woman when she decides to write out the "fragments of [her own] life and make a crazy-quilt of them" is the subtext of this novel. The text itself enunciates the "ruins of life" of the woman worker (4). The device of the framed narrative highlights the seeming incommensurability of the narratives of class and gender differences within traditional realist plots.

Moreover, despite its central proletarianism, *Daughter of Earth* violates the very generic conventions it establishes. Within the main body of the narrative, two other discourses are established and set into combat: the dual narratives of desire (of the gendered body) and history (of class and anti-imperialist politics). These two opposed narratives are, of course, interrelated and in fact inseparable; it is the attempt to separate them that drives Marie crazy. Smedley's strategy of representing both narratives in one classed and gendered body connects them to each other, breaking the conventional plot patterns of each; ironically, it also renders the working-class woman unscripted. Hence the crazy quilt, and hence Marie's craziness.

Rachel DuPlessis has identified these dual narratives within nineteenth-century fiction as "the quest plot" and "the plot of romantic thralldom."[30] She argues that twentieth-century women's narratives often subvert the distinctions between the two by joining these incompatible and gender-marked plots, resulting in novels that are misread because they break generic (and gender) conventions. For instance, Zora Neale Hurston's *Their Eyes Were Watching God* (1937), another framed narrative, was castigated by Richard Wright for lacking a "basic idea or theme. . . . Hurston had no desire to write serious fiction. The sensory sweep of her novel carries no theme, no message, no thought."[31] Hurston's novel was illegible to an African American Communist critic (in fact, he accused her of pandering to white racists' fantasies of African American life by staging a minstrel show in fiction); similarly, Smedley's novel was dismissed by Walt Carmon, another critic also writing in the *New Masses*, as being "marred as a class novel because it owes its bias to the bitterness of a woman."[32] For both reviewers, the combination of terms animating each novel—African American woman on the one hand, woman worker on the other—was incommensurable.

Marie is always simultaneously aware of her gender and class differences; and it is the simultaneity, the sense that both narratives are undifferentiated, that sets up the tensions for the protagonist and the reader. The attempt to overcome, inscribe, erase, and understand the ways that a woman worker cannot have a history marks Marie and fuels her story. What Marie's differences (and her different narratives) signify is a looming contradiction because a form cannot be found to narrate the combination effectively. Hence the framed narrative, in which the now-educated, politically active, psychoanalyzed writer can reflect back on her deprived and brutalized past. The frame effectively transforms Marie the worker into a middle-class woman by reinscribing the class differences between narrator and character.

Yet her transformation is not really convincing given the skeletal frame and the enormous text(ure) of the narrative. Moreover, Marie's narrative is itself fractured. The early years of conflict with her family—a rebelliousness enacted against her abusive mother (who presents the horrific image of a woman wasting away from overwork and too many childbirths) and against a violent and hypocritical father (who beats her mother and abuses her prostitute aunt, whose body supports his family)—comprise most of the first part of the novel.

Marie insists that she is her father's daughter—a storyteller of the earth; yet increasingly it is her mother's ruined body, victim of an overdetermined (re)productive labor (as mother and launderer), that inhabits the story Marie retells through her litany of beatings, her fears of sex and pregnancy, and later her political development.

The second half of the novel finds Marie increasingly involved in the Indian anticolonialist movement, in which the tensions caused by her gender and class powerlessness are replaced for a time by a feminized image of the mass movement and its non-Western, non-working-class men. The vision of this feminized mass movement appears briefly as a possible container for the narrative contradictions of class and gender differences. For example, Marie's involvement in the Indian independence movement places her in a new relationship to history and politics. Marie remains marginal to the movement because she is a woman and white and the lover (eventually the wife) of one of the revolutionaries, but her body becomes the contested terrain of a power struggle among the Indian nationalists. Nevertheless, despite the male dominance of the independence movement, the Indian men do not threaten her as her father did. They are femininized, possessing soft, gentle hands and quiet voices. Yet one of her comrades rapes her, marking her as a perpetual outsider to the movement and estranging her from her husband.

Marie careens into madness in part because of the violation of her body, in part because Indian nationalist Juan Diaz enters her apartment wearing the turquoise belt buckle her father had worn when she was a girl. Clothed in this garb of Western masculinity, Juan Diaz breaks forever Marie's illusion of the nurturing, feminine, collective space of the Indian movement, much as her mother's abusiveness and her abused body destroyed Marie's desire to mother. Exchanging America and politics for Denmark and psychoanalysis, Marie resituates herself and her story within the frame of middle-class narrative authority, marked by distant, bleak vistas, fragmented memories, and competing desires. By framing Marie's story, Smedley encloses her difference as a working-class woman writer—that is, as an anomaly—but demarks class and gender within distinct narrative zones.[33]

Even within the fragments of the modernist novel, however, the representation of class and gender remains problematic for a female subject who is positioned by political allegiances. *The Company She Keeps*, Mary McCarthy's narrative about Margaret Sargent, weaves six satirical episodes based on the author's young adulthood as a leftist intellectual in New York into another morality tale. Meg figures as a peripheral character in her own first-person narrative when she describes the sleazy business operations of her antique-dealing employer. Even when "she" is the focus of a vignette, she is observed from without by an intimate, knowing narrator and some contemptuous lovers whose ironic tone distances her story from its teller. If the middle-class intellectual does not need to frame her story as Smedley's heroine did, she nevertheless needs to disclose to her readers in a foreword that "the home address of the self, like that of the soul, is not to be found in the book" (x). The self may not live in the book, but, McCarthy's novel finally tells us, it does survive somewhere: perhaps in the bohemian world of Greenwich Village writers, artists, and politicos Margaret Sargent inhabits; perhaps in the reconstruction of the disparate strands of her narrative.

Meg's body is clearly not (de)formed by the hunger that molded Marie's childhood; in her world there is sumptuous eating and drinking. Like Marie, however, Meg is figured by the desire her body both seeks and inspires in others. Her story is revealed through a series of encounters with other characters: her soon-to-be-former husband, her new lover, the proprietor of "Rogue's Gallery," the "Man in the Brooks Brothers Shirt," the "Genial Host," and the intellectual from Yale. In each story, Margaret Sargent at first appears in command of herself, her men, and her social situation; however, she is quickly overwhelmed by forces that reposition her from powerful "Young Divorcee" to fragile and easily manipulated little girl. To pass some time between Omaha and Sacramento, she sets out to flirt with the business-man sharing her Pullman car. By the end of a long night of drinking and slightly perverse sex, though, she is more properly under the sway of his fantasies of her in silk underwear. He resists her desire that he desert his middle-management position at Little Steel for the glamour of fighting in Spain; but she accepts his gifts. Much in the way that the political tables turn for Meg, so too does she mistake her "sexual freedom" for "a passport conferring on her the status of citizeness of the world" (20).

In a seemingly reverse chronology, it is not until the final section of the narrative that we learn Margaret Sargent's story. As she reenacts her own analysis by her not-too-bright psychiatrist, she reveals that she is a motherless child. Despite her claims to "reject this middle-class tragedy, this degenerated Victorian novel where I am Jane Eyre or somebody in Dickens or Kipling or brave little Elsie Dinsmore fainting over the piano," in fact, to "reject the whole pathos of the changeling, the orphan, the stepchild," her modern(ist) "disunity" is undermined. It is precisely to the domestic fiction of the nineteenth century that Meg and the reader must turn to find the textual antecedent of the middle-class woman, albeit usually one of a less sexual nature. Meg's final disclosures on the couch return her to the modern form of domestic enclosure—analysis.[34]

As a writer for the *Liberal*, a weekly modeled roughly on *The Nation* or the *New Republic*, Margaret Sargent's life is dominated by deadlines rather than by the breadlines of the earlier years of the Depression. In intellectual New York circles of the late 1930s, the struggles of the working class have become abstracted and degenerated into sectarian debates among increasingly despairing fellow travelers of one political stripe or another. These intellectuals, like the Yale man, either slide into complacent support for Stalin's horrors in Moscow and Barcelona or else move into more lucrative positions (as Jim Barnett does when he resigns, for "political" reasons, from the *Liberal* to take a job with the newly formed slick publication, *Destiny*, roughly modeled on *Fortune*). Others shrilly defend Trotsky and lapse into wounded self-pity at their ostracism by former comrades. Riven with splits, the Left fractures because of its own contradictions rather than those within capitalism; it is divided and increasingly disembodied. Meg's voice runs through the Yale man's mind like the voice-over in cinema and haunts him as he struggles simultaneously to resist her body and her politics.[35]

In a political climate dominated by the New Deal and the CPUSA-sponsored Popular Front, politics for the supporters of Trotsky consists of "an ill-assorted group of nervous people [who] would sit in a bare classroom in the New School or lounge on studio couches in somebody's apartment listening to Shachtman, a little dark lawyer, demolish the evidence against the Old Man in Mexico." Because they are cut off from the proletariat, these dissenting intellectuals "wore an expression of injury, of self-justification, a funny, feminine, 'put-upon' look" (218). For Meg, politics does not emanate from the flesh, as LeSueur argued, but rather from a sense of exhibiting one's "allegorical possibilities" in a grand "morality play" in which sexual freedom and Trotskyism become the protagonists allied against motherhood and the Loyalist defense of Spain (151). After an impassioned defense of Trotsky's decision to publish a critique of the Soviet Union in a Hearst paper, Meg reveals: "I'm not even political. . . . I do admire Trotsky. He's the most romantic man in modern times" (194). Thus politics begins to reenact the forms of the domestic novel, and the erasure of the working class in Margaret's narrative reinforces the emasculation of the political intelligentsia. They, like Pflaumen, the genial host, possess an "androgynous" air, "something not pansy, but psychically hermaphroditic" (149).[36]

It appears that the female intellectual, whose structural position within the sexual economy of capitalism (as outlined by literary radicals) is doubly alienated, cannot reclaim a maternal identity in the way that, however fleetingly, Marie Rodgers could within the Indian independence movement. Like Marie, Meg Sargent retreats to the couch and recounts her memories of a damaged childhood in order, one feels, to justify her sexuality. Marie's narrative becomes increasingly sketchy after she leaves the subjects of her childhood poverty and developing class consciousness and moves on to New York and her work for a socialist newspaper. The spaces she cannot fill in her story reveal her inability to produce the narrative of her developing sexuality. Silenced about sex, Marie cannot fully claim her (middle-)class identity. Paradoxically, Meg's relatively open narrative of her desires precludes an awareness of her own class identification. Yet hers is the story of a middle-class sexuality. As the political woman becomes the psychoanalyzed woman, Meg's body is confined within the domestic spaces of therapist's office, husband's apartment, lover's bed, and her narrative itself.

The "fragments" of Marie's sexual life could be precariously contained by maternal collectivity and then recontained by a framed narrative. The "disunity" of Meg's political life fits into a different, more modernist, and equally middle-class narrative—psychoanalysis. In the case of each woman, retracing the past by describing a childhood full of psychological and physical privation becomes the means of encoding (middle-class) white female subjectivity in narrative. Ultimately, each narrative relies on the conventions of domestic fiction to contain the unruly textual/sexual politics embodied by the radical working-class or intellectual woman. Within the bourgeois psychological narrative of domesticity, gender supplants class; but within women's revolutionary fiction, the narrative fragments of a working-class woman or a female intellectual interdepend upon gendered class and classed gender. In effect, white women's revolutionary fiction reads both gender and class (and in some cases race) as simultaneously determining and undermining the subject as a cause and effect of (hi)story.

The differing pulls of class and gender, history and desire, body and text in Smedley's and McCarthy's pivotal novels bring into focus a range of issues that form the basis of this book. Chapter 1 regenders the history of literary radicalism. The discursive field created by literary radicals as they interpolated the political languages of history into literary criticism was dominated by large events—the Depression and the rise of fascism—but it was articulated through internecine debates among a few (male) editors and writers. Their rhetoric of class struggle and antifascism masked (or, more precisely, relied upon) metaphors of gender embedded in it.

In Chapter 2, I argue for a reading of women's revolutionary novels as a genre marked by the relationships of gender, class, and sexuality in its narratives. This genre enables the understanding of an alternative history of 1930s literary radicalism because the texts and bodies of women resisted the categories offered by American Marxism to explain literature and politics. The two novels discussed above figure as representative types within the genre in that they tell different (though compatible) tales of a classed and gendered subject embedded in the narratives of history and desire. The final two chapters of this book provide readings of some examples of both working-class and intellectual women's narratives that, to varying degrees, de-form the classic proletarian novel. My hope is that the very insularity of this study will produce clear evidence of the ways in which literary genres historicize and theorize class and gender.

The narratives of subjectivity that reveal a body marked by history and desire—by productive and reproductive labor—neither begin nor end with women's revolutionary novels of the 1930s. As we enter the 1990s, the headlines register disbelief that women have been forced onto the contemporary breadlines forming at churches and community centers across the nation. This "feminization of poverty," which appears to be unprecedented in the United States, actually has a historical antecedent in the generation of hungry women LeSueur and other female writers of the Depression era documented. Historical amnesia has erased their stories from our memory, but the (classed and gendered) subject continues to write itself.[37] Perhaps when we understand that the work and words of women create different political and literary histories, then the walls separating literature from history, women from men, bourgeoisie from proletariat, can be torn down and the world remade.

Labor and Desire

A Gendered History of Literary Radicalism

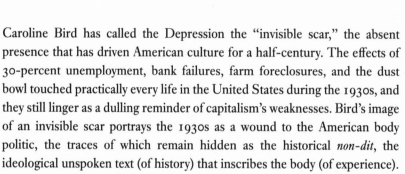

Caroline Bird has called the Depression the "invisible scar," the absent presence that has driven American culture for a half-century. The effects of 30-percent unemployment, bank failures, farm foreclosures, and the dust bowl touched practically every life in the United States during the 1930s, and they still linger as a dulling reminder of capitalism's weaknesses. Bird's image of an invisible scar portrays the 1930s as a wound to the American body politic, the traces of which remain hidden as the historical *non-dit*, the ideological unspoken text (of history) that inscribes the body (of experience).

It is not only the Depression that has left its invisible scar on the body politic. The history of American radicalism is largely a forgotten one, easily overcome by the "infection" of anticommunism that plagues American cultural history.[1] The ascendancy of the Left during the 1930s explains why the decade has been the victim of historical amnesia.[2] During that time there were abrupt shifts in line among leftists as the Communist Party of the United States (CPUSA) instituted its own version of Stalinism, with the result that loyal Party members frequently found themselves biting their tongues. Yet countless memoirs have recalled what Harold Clurman has referred to as "the fervent years" of the 1930s with vitriolic bitterness, wild enthusiasm, or sentimental nostalgia, until it seems that nothing new can be said of America's turn leftward. The "invisible scar" of the Left serves as a point for obsessive rumination—for worrying over, the way one fingers an unseen blemish unconsciously, almost ritualistically, until it erupts into prominence. Thus, paradoxically, the 1930s appear simultaneously as the most remembered and most forgotten decade in American cultural history.

As a trope both of damaged bodies and of hidden texts, the invisible scar of the 1930s can be found on the bodies and texts of women and literary history as well as in histories of labor, radicalism, intellectuals, and popular culture. Its contours alter the histories of women, literature, and radicalism in the United States and reveal the markings of each on the others. Thus a study of women's literary radicalism entails a revision of three histories—women's, literature's, and radicalism's—in order to trace how the invisible scars have in each case both determined and erased those of the other two.

This chapter examines the relationship between the decade's leftist political field, marked primarily by the CPUSA, and its cultural field, dominated by literary radicalism. Most critics present the history of 1930s literary radicalism as a corollary to the history of the Communist movements of the decade. I argue that the absent presence of gender in these two fields alters the shape of both the political and the literary history of the Left and recasts their relationships to one another. Gender is figured in culture even when it remains unspoken. My purpose in the chapters that follow is to articulate how gender was constructed within the rhetoric of the literary Left during the 1930s and what effects that (gendered) construction had on the fiction of radical women. To do this, it is necessary simultaneously to look at the works and words of women, which are usually coded as gendered, and at those of men, which although resisting gender coding are nevertheless also gendered.

Politics and the History of Proletarianism

In his "political autopsy" of American literary radicalism, Philip Rahv stressed that it is impossible to understand the movement without also addressing the power of the American Communist Party as institution and experience in the lives of 1930s writers.[3] Because many of the writers and critics influential in leftist literary circles were Party members, "fellow travelers" (those loyal to, but unaffiliated with, the CPUSA), or dissenting anti-Stalinists, they tended to be personally involved in Party politics. In addition, the Party believed during the decade that one of its roles was as creator of apparatuses that would foster a new aesthetic in American arts. The powerful imagery of the Depression helped turn the attention of intellectuals leftward, and this in turn made intellectuals a focus of Party policy. From its Third Period early in the decade, when its ultraradical politics limited its broad appeal by emphasizing a proletarian culture, to its later years, when the rhetoric of working-class militancy was tempered by appeals to the American people during the Popular Front era, the CPUSA engaged intellectuals in aesthetic and political debates in support of the working class and against fascism.

Literary radicalism never represented the primary focus of Party work. The CPUSA's emphasis during the early 1930s was on organizing industrial workers, the unemployed, and minorities and later on fighting fascism. However, among intellectuals, who had access to both the left-wing journals and the pages of the bourgeois press, literary radicals assumed a power to shape both the rhetoric of the 1930s Left and its subsequent (literary) history. In a sense, this was also true for the CPUSA in general during the 1930s; it acquired a disproportionate ability to shape the ideological and economic concerns of the decade. The gap between American culture as a whole and the subculture of the Left needed to be rhetorically stitched over, and in their ability to accomplish this lay the power of radical intellectuals to shape both the 1930s Left and its subsequent history, even though they were but a small minority of the larger culture or even of its leftist subculture.

Rahv's analysis, coming on the heels of the Stalinist terror culminating in the Moscow trials, the defeat by Franco's fascists of the Loyalists in Spain, and the spread of nazism, correctly rings a note of "I told you so." Rahv accuses the Party of manipulating its intellectuals into constructing a "strategic mystification" of policy by cloaking political discussions as literary criticism. Because of his central position among the New York intellectuals, as Alan Wald calls them, Rahv set the tone for most subsequent scholarship about 1930s literary radicalism. His model became the basis for a variety of studies of both the CP-affiliated literary radicals and their anti-Stalinist critics.[4] This model, ironically, proceeds out of the "mechanical materialism" for which Rahv had criticized most Party-affiliated critics a few years before and, I would add, reproduces the gender relations of middle-class culture.

The image of writers who follow the correct line—Max Eastman's "artists in uniform," who march in lockstep to the call of the Party—relies on two assumptions. First, it implies that the Party was a monolith that affected everyone who came into contact with it in exactly the same way. Second, it reads literary (and critical) writings as epiphenomena of political doctrine. By giving precedence to the political over the literary, this reading of literary radicalism represents another version of the base/superstructure model. In its most vulgar form, Marxist theory reduces the dialectical play of material and ideological forces in history to a simplistic, unidirectional narrative wherein the base (material needs) determines the superstructure (ideological illusions). Although this model usually posits the base as purely economic, consigning the political to the superstructure, one can easily see that Rahv's analysis depends on extending the chain of linkages from the economic to the political through the literary-critical and finally to literature itself.[5]

Because power is supposed to reside in the determinants of history, economics and politics are privileged as sites of causality; literature, associated with the private renderings of the writer's mind, becomes merely an ideological effect. The realm of history—signified by political parties and their policies—controls the realm of literature. Put another way, the external world of objects produces effects on the internal world of subjects. A schematic drawing of Rahv's analysis might look like this:

Rank and File	Correct Line	Literature
↑	↑	↑
Communist Party	Party Ideologues	Critics
↑	↑	↑
The Depression	Communist Party	Correct Line
ECONOMIC →	POLITICAL →	LITERARY

In each category and across categories, effectivity can be plotted in only one direction. But each category is not equally weighted. Thus the hierarchically organized system of democratic centralism is reproduced in critical works whose purpose is to describe the writings of selected authors.

From my brief outline, it is easy to see that this model of analysis is profoundly gendered even as it erases gender as a salient category for organizing thought. Power flows from the public spheres of history (controlled and determined by men) to the private spheres of literature (produced and consumed by women). Clearly this is a wildly reductive reading; a few women, such as Elizabeth Gurley Flynn, sat on the central committee of the CPUSA, and many men read and wrote radical literature. But as we shall see, the gendered implications of this model were not lost on either male or female writers. Moreover, the invisible scar of gender on the model has meant that women's voices have rarely been heard by either contemporaneous or subsequent critics of literary radicalism. Even as gender was put into discursive practice in the field of 1930s criticism, its theoretical articulation was repressed.

Daniel Aaron mentions some women as signatories of various petitions, and Walter Rideout even analyzes some women's novels, though without giving attention to their inscriptions of gender. Their key texts for the study of literary radicalism, written in the "dark ages" of the late 1950s and early 1960s, are remarkable for their even-keeled discussions of communism; they excavated dozens of authors who had burrowed underground during the cold war. Aaron and Rideout cannot be faulted for lacking insights as feminist literary critics, as our history had been effectively erased also. By writing intellectual and social histories and collective biographies of those most visible within the institutions of literary radicalism—the editors of *New Masses* and *Partisan Review* and the members of the John Reed clubs and the League of American Writers—they charted in detail the "political history" of literary radicalism begun by Rahv. Their focus was on the "head boys," the men who pronounced political theory and translated it into critical and literary practice.[6] They simply could not see the radical women; or, if they noticed them, they either read such women as ungendered (that is, as if they were male) or else dismissed their work as "more about sex than politics."[7]

The "political history" of proletarian literature actually predates the 1930s by several decades. When Joseph Freeman noted in his introduction to the anthology *Proletarian Literature in the United States* (1935) that the term "proletarian literature" had been used by the socialist editors of *The Comrade* as early as 1901 and that Floyd Dell used it in connection with John Reed and Jack London in *The Masses* in 1919, he was arguing for a new literary genre with its own political history. The political history Freeman was creating for the CPUSA-sponsored volume ironically included bohemian (and feminist) critics like Floyd Dell, who by 1935 had been officially discredited by the Party. Despite the sympathy Freeman displayed for a wide range of writings (including a number by women), however, the anthology ultimately codified the diverse definitions of proletarian literature into a unified but restricted field. This field had earlier been mapped in *The Liberator* in 1921, when Michael Gold declared that he had discovered a new path for American literature that would lead it "toward proletarian art," just as William Foster had declared that the CPUSA would proceed "toward Soviet America." Gold argued that the modernist literary experiments of the early years of the twentieth century were degenerating into mere stylistic self-indulgence, losing much of their radicalizing effect as their content became increasingly obscure. He sought a realistic prose that would capture the working-class experience in America, and almost a decade later he put his critical call into practice with his autobiographical novel, *Jews without Money* (1930). Originally published in sections in the *New Masses* and *Menorah Journal*, Gold's novel, which consists of a series of vignettes about growing up poor and tough on New York's Lower East Side, became a road marker to guide the proletarian literature that followed.[8]

In 1929, shortly after Gold took over full editorship of the *New Masses*, he published an editorial calling on working-class writers to document their lives in fiction, drama, and poetry—to "write . . . your life" for others to read.[9] Gold's new direction for authors led to the "mines, mills and farms" of America, challenging the bourgeoisie from the alleys of a radicalized working class rather than from bohemian MacDougal Street. Though these two roads crossed at various points (for example, the *New Masses* partly identified with its forerunner, the bohemian *Masses*, published by Max Eastman, John Reed, and others), Gold's primary identification with working-class concerns reflected the politicization of art that occurred as the effects of the 1929 stock market crash became apparent. The economic devastation could not be ignored; it provided a concrete illustration of the economic and social *op*pression inherent in the American system, which had previously been seen by many of these same writers as cultural and sexual *re*pression.

But it was Gold's infamous 1930 attack on Thornton Wilder in the *New Republic*, in which he branded the author as the "prophet of the Genteel Christ," that launched "proletarianism" into the discourse of American literary criticism. Gold objected to the language of the "pansy" *poseurs* of modernism. He declared Wilder's theology of "Jesus Christ, the First British Gentleman, . . . a daydream of homosexual figures in graceful gowns moving archaically among the lilies."[10] The current American economic crisis demanded a "vigorous" literature to unite the hunger-ravaged working class and forge it into a revolutionary proletariat. By constructing the proletariat and proletarian literature as masculine, Gold implicitly connected modernism with bourgeois decay and femininity. His call, in his review and in the pages of the *New Masses*, for a virile poetics and politics encouraged the explosion of proletarian writing that marked the first years of the decade. One author, praising Gold's literary criticism, put it this way: "The stale Bohemian writer, recognizing the vigor of the new proletarian literature, sadly contemplates his own wilted phallus, and howls that the Goddess of Pure Art is being raped by barbarians."[11] Gold's choice of metaphors ultimately set the tone for the homophobic and antifeminine rhetoric of literary radicals, situating female and gay writers of revolutionary fiction at a precarious angle to the official stance of the genre's institutions.[12]

When he articulated the position of the proletarian critic and author, Gold was writing partly as a literary critic and partly as a loyal (though sometimes maverick) member of the Communist Party. During the early years of the 1930s, the Party was still in its ultraleftist Third Period. Between 1928 and 1932, the CPUSA exhibited an excessively paranoid sectarian rigidity, during which the Party's membership shrank drastically after its leadership went underground. Because the Party saw major class warfare as imminent, no alliances could be made with any remnants of bourgeois democracy, including its intellectuals; even the socialists were branded "social fascists." Only a militant proletariat with its own culture could march "toward Soviet America." Thus proletcult, which had begun as an experimental force in the Soviet cultural explosion following the October Revolution, became a way to shore up the image of the revolutionary potential of the American working class. In fact, by the time "proletarianism" entered the vocabulary of most radical intellectuals, it had long since been abandoned by Stalinist Russia.[13] Nevertheless, the Party felt it imperative to establish organizations that would encourage and disseminate writings by and about proletarians.[14]

By 1933 proletarianism was firmly established within leftist literary circles. Even writers who were not committed to working-class movements were influenced by the form and content of the proletarian novel. For instance, Catherine Brody's *Nobody Starves* (1932) was based on union organizing at the Flint auto plants during the early years of the decade; however, it rejects the political position of the proletarian novel by twisting the classic revolutionary ending. The novel depicts a young, unemployed autoworker and his unemployed wife, who experience disastrous results from their refusal to join the demonstrating strikers. Out of desperation and hunger, the worker murders his wife but then does not commit suicide as he had planned. His arrest takes place against the background of the "Internationale," sung by a chorus of demonstrators marching to the plant gates. Brody's defeated hero stands as a critique of the fantasy of individual solutions, but also as a reminder that many workers resisted the mass movements of the Left.

By the mid-1930s, even murder mysteries displayed the influence of proletarianism: a second-rate radical journalist becomes a hard-boiled detective to uncover a fascist plot in *Murder in the W.P.A.* (1937).[15] Documentary collections of workers' and intellectuals' prose began to resemble the plots of the typical proletarian novel. A manuscript that emerged out of the Affiliated School for Workers, *I Am a Woman Worker* (1936), collected women's oral and written statements (primarily anonymous) describing their experiences as workers. The editors arranged the book under five subheadings that provided a narrative structure for the developing class consciousness of the women: "Getting a Job," "Life in the Factories," "Open Shops and Company Unions," "Trade Unions and Organized Shops," and "On Strike!" *I Am a Woman Worker* focuses on the special concerns of women workers—sex-segregated labor pools, sexual harassment, sexist unions, the double day—as well as on their differing senses of commitment to work, family, and each other; by doing so, the book discloses the unspoken content of a sector of the working class whose voices were not articulated by official Party or union organizations (or by literary history and criticism). In addition, by presenting an evolutionary model of working women's consciousness from innocence to militance—from alienation to collectivity—the volume reproduces the plots of many novels.[16]

Similarly, Henry Hart's collection of the speeches and debates from the 1935 American Writers' Congress reads like a version of the "collective novel" so important to proletarian fiction. In this case, however, the divergent voices represent various strains among leftist intellectuals, ranging from the back-to-nature mysticism of Waldo Frank to the Stalinist diatribe of Moishe Nadir.[17] Hart concludes the book with James T. Farrell's gesture of unity as he stood at the end of the meeting and urged the members to join in a rendition of the "Internationale." Thus, by the mid-1930s, the effects of proletarianism, particularly its novel form, seemed to be so overdetermined that any reconstruction of an actual strike or mass meeting could only be narrated within the framework of its fictional form. In effect, intellectuals produced and reproduced the narratives of class struggle by which we now remember the 1930s and in so doing could be said to have invented this period of radical (literary) history.

The Ham Sandwich Theory of Literature

Just as the history of proletarian literature was written in response to the CPUSA, so too were the attempts to define a theory of revolutionary aesthetics. In 1929, when Michael Gold asserted that "literature was no more mystic in its origin than a ham sandwich," he was attempting to wrest writing from the control of the elite and place it in the hands of common people. By identifying literature with food, he suggested that writing was a mundane activity of the body, not an exalted one of the mind. As the devastation of the 1929 crash took its toll, however, even a ham sandwich became a rarity. Left critical debates stressed "art as a class weapon" over the bohemians' "art for art's sake," but ultimately both positions were based on formalisms that appealed narrowly to specific audiences, and so the debates produced an effect quite the opposite of the one Gold had intended. Four central issues came to dominate these debates: the attitude, politics, and class of the author; the themes, plots, and characterizations of the text; the audience for whom the text was written; and the appropriate form with which to convey plot and politics to that audience. For example, in his address to the 1935 American Writers' Congress, entitled "What the Revolutionary Movement Can Do for a Writer," Malcolm Cowley outlined four ways that a connection with the proletariat could benefit a writer's output: the revolutionary movement provides an audience; it produces a new subject matter; it forces a new perspective on the self as "a social product"; and it allies the interests of intellectuals with those of workers.[18]

This last contribution clearly speaks to the question of the political efficacy of intellectual labor. An on-going crisis for American intellectuals has been their inability to define a space within the American landscape. By transforming the relationship of author to audience from an aesthetic to a political alliance and by foregrounding material experience in the form and content of writing, the new subject matter and the new perspective on self revised the relationship of politics to culture and of audience to art(ist). In a sense, 1930s literary radicalism provided an answer to the dilemma of the writer searching both for an appropriate voice to render the social as personal and the personal as social and for an audience for that voice. Literary radicalism, no matter how prescriptive, did present a model for forging a relationship between text and context, between author and audience, between self and collectivity, and between politics and culture. As such, it promised something new to both intellectuals and workers. In effect, literary radicalism produced a discursive field through which intellectuals could stake a claim in the political arena.

According to E. A. Schachner, "the coming of age of our literature" occurred on March 6, 1930, when over a million unemployed workers demonstrated for unemployment insurance. At that moment, writers discovered "the truth that literature and politics are welded together in the hot fires that are generated in the struggles between classes" and turned their attention to "new audiences—the revolutionary working class and the most progressive members of the professional and intellectual classes."[19] As official Party doctrine on proletarian literature, Schachner's "Revolutionary Literature in the United States Today" distinguished between proletarian and revolutionary literature, setting the stage, I suspect, for the changes in literary and political policy that were about to come. Despite his optimism in the early pages of his work, Schachner can find little evidence of truly revolutionary writing—a few poems and plays and only eight novels comprise his list. Interestingly, whereas he finds Michael Gold's *Jews without Money* steeped in sentimentality, he lauds three women novelists—Grace Lumpkin, Fielding Burke, and Myra Page—for their novels about the Gastonia textile mill workers' strike in which Ella May Wiggins, a young mother-worker-song-writer-activist, was killed by company goons. He argues that the history of southern white male culture, which constrained elite white women within the double standard, created a sensitivity among these privileged women to the plight of black and white workers. His analysis, in fact, echoes Grace Lumpkin's and Myra Page's own explanations of their conversions to communism.[20]

Despite his somewhat nuanced reading of the class-race-gender configurations operating in American culture, Schachner (and many CPUSA-affiliated critics like Granville Hicks and Gold) generally reduced Marxist criticism to discussions of an author's stand on a series of crucial issues, or on his or her class position, to determine literary merit. Although this focus on an author's class alignment was certainly reductive, it did result in a number of interesting experiments in collective writing, featuring a group of anonymous workers and usually one published author who met together to create a story or novel. These collective writings, whose purpose was to make the ham sandwich more palatable, provided a means for transcending the gender and class divisions within the Left. One such story was serialized in the 1935 volume of *Working Woman*. Coauthored by "A Group of Workers" and Jane Benton, "Stockyard Stella" concerns an incident of sexual harassment that provokes the victim's enraged fiancé into a fistfight with the floor manager. When he is dismissed, the other workers walk off the job and refuse to return to work unless he is reinstated. They are all fired, and a militant strike action forces both men and women to assume new (and differently gendered) responsibilities—the men cook, the women agitate. Naturally, the strikers are successful; everyone is reinstated and their union is recognized (though, strangely, nothing is said about the sexual harassment), so the workers can return to their proper gender roles. This story, which relies on the conventions of melodrama as well as proletarianism, was proclaimed "the first American proletarian love story" in the *New Masses*.[21]

In "We're Writing a Book," British author Naomi Mitchison describes her experiences writing a collective novel with a group of factory workers from both the Labor and Communist parties. The process involved meeting with a group of skilled workers and their wives (most of whom were "non-earning" women) to review her work. The workers talked among themselves about their lives, enabling Mitchison to glean their syntax, ideas, and emotions. Mitchison's Popular Frontist project reveals a condescension toward the workers that was repressed in its American proletarian counterpart; yet both display the utopian promise that collectivity offered to literary radicals during the 1930s. The divisions between workers and intellectuals, between writers and critics and audiences, seemed to melt away when intellectuals like Mitchison could "give these people a sense of their own importance and dignity . . . moving with purpose in a world that they and I together want to change."[22]

But did "these people" want to read about themselves? When Louis Adamic, writing in the December 1934 issue of the *Saturday Review of Literature*, asked, "What does the proletariat read?," he questioned the premise of leftist authors and critics that workers constituted the primary audience for proletarian literature. He claimed that workers were not reading proletarian novels and poetry because (notwithstanding the two works just discussed) proletarian literature was too innovative in form; it required too much work on the part of an already exhausted worker-reader. Furthermore, Adamic doubted whether any worker would spend the money to purchase such literature and, because the novels and journals were issued in such small numbers, they were rarely available in libraries.[23] He argued that even when a "proletarian" novel was accessible to workers, as with Catherine Brody's *Nobody Starves*, it was rejected by the very people portrayed within its pages, who felt it to be depressing and inaccurate. As one woman complained, "I got sore reading the book. We wear much nicer clothes than she says we do."[24]

The growing sectarian debates among political theorists following Stalin's consolidation of power in the mid-1930s ultimately were reproduced in literary debates among critics. One controversy involved the relationship of the content of the new revolutionary literature to the doctrines of existing political organizations like the CPUSA. Philip Rahv and Wallace Phelps addressed this question in their essay "Recent Problems of Revolutionary Literature." Influenced by Leon Trotsky's *Literature and Revolution* (1923), this essay cautioned against jettisoning all of bourgeois culture for a new proletcult. Yet Rahv and Phelps stressed the importance of developing a new form for revolutionary literature. In their view, the critical measure that counted only the proletarian content of a literary work without sensitivity to its form mirrored the mechanical materialism of vulgar Marxism. They differentiated their critical stance from the extreme "leftism" of Schachner, who, they argued, had repudiated a historical approach to literature when he claimed that the "new age" of writing began at a specific moment in 1930. Furthermore, they asserted that Schachner's emphasis on context blinded him to the necessity for formal analyses of the "imaginative assimilation of political content" that distinguishes literature from polemic. Finally, they celebrated the new revolutionary fiction as a form that more fully engages its audience, politically and emotionally, than the older genres of drama and poetry that appealed to Schachner.[25] Where Schachner had chided Granville Hicks for being a moralist, Rahv and Phelps felt that Hicks's criticism was tied too closely to content and so represented the right wing of revolutionary criticism. They considered both Hicks and Schachner (and Gold) too tightly bound to the "political program of Communism."

Rahv and Phelps's early challenge to the hegemony of the *New Masses* within American Marxist criticism was taken up more fully by James T. Farrell in his 1936 polemic, *A Note on Literary Criticism*. Accusing Gold of "revolutionary sentimentality" (as had Schachner) and Hicks of "mechanical materialism," Farrell tried to disengage the creation of literature from an allegiance to any political dogma.[26] His critique was a forceful call for developing a more complex analysis of the relationship of politics to culture by moving away from merely criticizing literature on the basis of its content or its author's allegiance to doctrine. Yet this work too reflected the sharp sectarianism that was coming into focus among literary radicals. Written after Farrell had distanced himself from the Party, *Note* tested Trotsky's theories of literature against the American scene.

As the preceding discussion indicates, the shape of literary critical debates among the "head boys" seemed to follow loyally the directions of the emerging sectarian debates among Marxists as the Party simultaneously contracted its diversity in support of Stalin and expanded its range with the Popular Front. On its face, Rahv's analysis appears accurate; critical discussions over the efficacy of proletarian literature reverberate with political meanings. But as demonstrated by the readers' response to *Nobody Starves* or the writers' themes in "Stockyard Stella," the direct connections between politics and literature were far more tenuous among working-class women readers and writers. The group of women workers who produced "Stockyard Stella" for *Working Woman* clearly understood that they were writing a "proletarian love story" because they could not imagine a literature that did not narrate desire. In this they were satisfying their own (and, one suspects, *Working Woman*'s readers') desires for a good story.

Farrell's piece, coming exactly at the moment when the Communist Party was stressing unity among progressives as part of the development of the Popular Front, called into question much Party rhetoric. Although Farrell was attacked as a "Trotskyite" in the pages of the *New Masses* shortly after his *Note* appeared, he was defended there as well by fellow traveler Josephine Herbst. For a variety of reasons, writers and critics were at odds among themselves even in a climate that was supposed to accommodate diverse progressive positions. Sectarian divisions exploded after Stalin's Moscow trials had found Trotsky, Grigory Zinoviev, and Nikolay Bukharin guilty of treason. More important, Communist-oriented writers shifted their literary focus from the working class to antifascism, in large part due to the experiences some had as journalists and soldiers on the front lines of the Spanish Civil War, but also because the Popular Front line emphasized containing militarism rather than celebrating workers' militance.

Contrary to the usual characterization of the Third Period as rigidly doctrinaire, during the early years of the decade the Party actually tolerated a wide range of heterodox opinions. Because of its outlaw status in mainstream American life, the minuscule CPUSA of the Third Period held a romantic attraction for many newly radicalized intellectuals who had recently graduated from 1920s Bohemia.[27] Although during the early 1930s the Party stressed action over intellection, denouncing modernists as "master masturbators," its search for the correct line stressed ideological purity rather than pragmatic policy and was thus primarily an intellectual struggle.[28] Not until the latter half of the decade, after the development of the Popular Front in 1937, did this broad diversity narrow. Although many writers remained aloof from the power centers, and thus relatively autonomous, others experienced searing effects from the shifts in the Party line. For example, Richard Wright described his anger and frustration at the sudden dissolution of the John Reed clubs that had helped nurture his career. His attempts to keep the Chicago chapter alive, rather than "organize a committee against the high cost of living" as the Party directed, were futile, and *Left Front*, the organ of the Chicago John Reed Club, ceased publication.[29]

The contributors to the collection from the second American Writers' Congress, entitled *The Writer in a Changing World* (1937), spoke with a more unified voice than did those participating in the first congress. Although the congress reached out to a wider group of writers—including established authors like Archibald MacLeish, who previously had come under attack for expressing a "fascist unconscious"—most of the talks repeatedly decried the barbarism of fascist regimes in Italy, Germany, and Japan and the spread of war in Spain, Ethiopia, and China. These internationalist themes belied a closure among official literary radicals. That lack of unity was reflected in Michael Gold's savaging of "renegades" in the editor's notes of the *New Masses* as well as in the denunciations mounted by the anti-Stalinist Left against those henchmen who mimicked Moscow's line more closely than before. If novels from the beginning of the decade seemed to end with a chorus of marching strikers, novels from the late 1930s tended to end with the lone intellectual packing for a stint as a radical journalist in Spain. A shift in plot and theme had occurred, though structural and formal elements remained consistent. The anarchist critic David Lawrence answered his own query, "Who Slew Proletcult?" by blaming the appointment of writers sympathetic to the CPUSA to positions of power in the Federal Writers' Project of the Works Progress Administration (WPA), an action that tempered their radicalism.[30]

Lawrence's economistic explanation for the demise of proletarian literature during the latter years of the 1930s sums up the ways in which the polemicism of Party-affiliated critics (regarding authorial intention and class alignment) and the formalism of the anti-Stalinist literary Left precluded the development of a sophisticated American Marxist criticism that could address the hegemonic functions and counterhegemonic subversions of literature. Critic Mary Papke points to the relative intellectual isolation of American Marxists during the 1930s to explain the naive polemicism of these critical debates. Many of Marx's early works on ideology were not yet available in translation, nor were the debates on Marxist aesthetics among Georg Lukács, Walter Benjamin, and Bertolt Brecht or Antonio Gramsci's theories of hegemony.[31]

Papke argues that the "extrinsic criticism" that focused heavily on the connection between authorial politics, class, and literature relied on a simplistic use of the base/superstructure model. Essentially a reflection theory, this extrinsic criticism considered the content of a work to be a direct expression of an author's political allegiance, in much the same way that mechanical Marxism considers culture and society to be direct reflections of the economic structure. Even as they railed against the cultural "barbarism" of fascism, the Party aesthetes were, unfortunately, increasingly influenced by the barbaric events occurring within the Soviet Union after Zhdanovism emerged as the cultural policy of Stalinism.[32] At the other extreme, members of the anti-Stalinist Left often rephrased the formalist arguments of the modernists by stressing the autonomy of literature, using an elitist reading of Trotsky's theories on literature that denied the possibility of an authentic proletarian culture.

In effect, Papke anticipates my argument; but she too follows the critical debates without reference to the literary works involved. Curiously, as the sides were drawn more sharply among the critics and their polemics grew shriller, many creative writers evolved a dialectical relationship between political content and literary form in their works, thus developing a more complex theory of literary production than their critics.

Within the hierarchies of leftist culture, critics inhabited a space between artists and workers, their criticism being neither art nor propaganda. Implicitly (and occasionally explicitly) they expressed ambivalence about their position vis-à-vis both creative writers and political organizers. This middle ground not only left them without clearly defined class markers but stranded them in the "no man's land" outside of gender boundaries as well.[33] Thus the role of the revolutionary critic became a favorite topic of literary radicals. The usual questions predominated: For whom did one write—workers, revolutionary authors, bourgeois critics? What single element identified revolutionary criticism—theme, politics, form, author, or audience? What did one make of clearly revolutionary writing by a bourgeois author? Or, conversely, how did one judge a truly proletarian work that failed to draw a revolutionary conclusion (for example, *Call It Sleep*, which had precipitated a minor controversy in the *New Masses*)? Various answers filled the reviews, critical essays, and letters to the editors of radical journals as critics sought to justify themselves. "After all," wrote the editors of the *New Masses* rather plaintively, "revolutionary criticism, quite as much as revolutionary fiction, is a weapon in the class struggle."[34]

Once, in "Authors' Field Day," the *New Masses* provided a forum for a number of writers whose work had been treated roughly by their reviewers' "weapons." Many authors stressed their dissatisfaction with the dogmatic and prescriptive readings their works had received. Lauren Gilfillan and Josephine Herbst argued that, because they were "American bourgeois, traditionally white-collar," they were writing for "the intellectuals, those people so beautifully designated as swamp people, who in the final disintegration have no place of their own, who must throw their forces with the proletariat or perish."[35] As female intellectuals, they were under no illusions about their class position. Rather than posture as tough proletarians (like Michael Gold, whom Herbst criticized for his vitriolic and personal attack on James T. Farrell), they preferred to propagandize, to use Kenneth Burke's term, within their own boggy backyard. By the 1950s, these arguments had grown to melodramatic proportions. For instance, in testifying before the McCarthy committee, writer Grace Lumpkin declared that the Party had blackmailed her into including material that followed the Party line under the threat of poor reviews, which "would 'break' her literary career."[36]

Notwithstanding the paranoia of the recanting Communist, this kind of critical censure had an insidious effect on writers. In her 1968 memoir, "Yesterday's Road," Josephine Herbst recalled her visit to the Soviet Union as a guest of the 1930 Kharkov writers' conference. Her recollection of the debates differed markedly from the accounts given by "the Faithful" delegates—A. B. Magil, Harry Potamkin, and William Gropper—in the *New Masses*. Herbst remembered one female representative of the Comintern insisting that literature should be more than "workers' correspondence." Echoing Trotsky, this woman argued that because literature, like revolution, was fermented in the culture of the bourgeoisie, the middle class could not be ignored by writers. Her critique of proletarianism, coming at the very moment when Gold was heralding its emergence, was never conveyed to the readers of the *New Masses*. At the time, Herbst never mentioned the discrepancies between her memories and those of the others, thereby censoring herself in support of the Party even though she was not a member.[37]

These Third Period excesses were supposedly tempered during the Popular Front years, when spaces opened up for radical intellectuals in the WPA and in the popular presses (as they had for Mary McCarthy's "Yale man"). In reality, though, the pressures to conform to acceptable political and literary positions continued unabated. Writers who stepped out of line were denounced as "thugs," "enemies," or "renegades." The situation was not without irony for both Party-affiliated and anti-Stalinist critics. Herbert Solow set out to document the "Minutiae of Left-Wing Literary History" for *Partisan Review* by examining the contributors to the *New Masses* from 1926 to 1938. He found numerous instances in which people who were currently considered "enemies" for criticizing the Popular Front, the Moscow executions of intellectuals, or the Communist Party's actions in Spain had once been valued contributors. Tracing the revisions in Michael Gold's critical stance, Solow jabbed sarcastically at the contortions achieved by Party-affiliated critics during the years of his study. He noted that Hemingway had gone from being as "heartless as a tabloid" in 1928 to being lionized as a supporter of the Spanish People's Front a decade later. In 1926 Gold had declared that "the spirit of Revolution works and ferments in Trotsky," but by 1938 that same person had become the "enemy of mankind."[38]

But even the Stalinist *New Masses* could demonstrate a self-reflexive irony on occasion, as it showed in printing the "Ballad of a Slightly Addled Cultural Worker on the United Front":

I used to be redder than any rose—
    My novels and plays never failed to extol

The embattled worker (in a Gellert pose)
    As he mounted the System's slick greased pole.
    But I've drifted far from that open shoal
Where sectarian banners waved high, unfurled;
    Today I *conceal* the proletarian soul:
I'm of much more use in the bourgeois world.[39]

The shifts in line that were supposed to pass unnoticed by the "artists in uniform" whom Max Eastman denounced were very obviously commented upon within leftist journals. Apparently, as these sectarian debates show, not everyone could fix a literary "ham sandwich." Its correct preparation depended upon precise recipes and select ingredients known to only a few chefs. Despite the ever-shifting ideological debates of the Left, though, Max Eastman's claim seems unsubstantiated in America. Many authors, particularly women, changed the menu when they tired of the internecine warfare raging in the left-wing journals.[40] As Kenneth Burke argued in 1935, it was novels, plays, and poems that would produce the "revolutionary symbolism" needed to convince "the people" of socialism's benefits, not the critics' internal and often esoteric sectarian debates.[41]

Love and Hunger

Because the history of 1930s literary radicalism has been defined by the prescriptions and debates of the (male) critics of the decade, it remains skewed and incomplete. Women, as both subjects and authors, occupy an especially precarious position in this history. Yet women did produce radical literary works. Throughout the decade, Josephine Herbst continued to write the trilogy of bourgeois decline that she had begun in the early years of proletarianism, while Meridel LeSueur continued to revise the proletarian plot to accommodate women's experience.[42] In fact, Ruth McKenney's proletarian saga *Jake Home*, based on the life of William Z. Foster, was not published until 1943.

In one sense, the women involved in literary radicalism constituted a colony within the movement. Often they reviewed one another's novels, implying a ghettoization within the pages of male-dominated leftist journals but also suggesting that they read, and were influenced by, each others' work.[43] This review process forms yet another example of the sexual division of discursive labor that kept women out of positions of authority: sending them to report on a particular strike rather than allowing them to develop strategic pieces on union organizing; for the most part excluding them from editorial boards and opportunities to write literary criticism or theory and instead consigning them to review or write poetry and fiction.

In another sense, however, women helped redefine the entire field by locating the political subject as much in language and the body as in history. In this sense, their works often provided a fuller analysis of the economic, social, and political history of American capitalism than those of either the *New Masses* or *Partisan Review* critics. White middle-class women writers like Josephine Johnson, who were attracted to literary radicalism later in the decade (during the Popular Front period), actually produced some classic proletarian novels. Because many of the female authors who were able to pursue careers as writers were not working class, much of their work, even when it was "proletarian," examined the relationship of the (female) intellectual to the working-class movement. They often explored the position of the social worker, teacher, or nurse—those female appendages of the state who mediate between the working-class family and government bureaucracy. Thus, as Herbst noted in her refusal to contribute to David Madden's anthology *Proletarian Writers of the Thirties*, what was prescribed by the "head boys" did not always describe what those on the periphery, like herself, wrote.

What all this suggests is the need to write a regendered history of literary radicalism. Another story emerges from the novels, poems, stories, plays, and reportage by women literary radicals that have been recently unearthed by feminist scholars. It too constitutes a political history of literary radicalism, but it casts its net wider by incorporating the history and ideology of gender and sexuality into political culture. A gendered history of literary radicalism proceeds from two sources. As the foregoing discussion has demonstrated, the critical and scholarly works marking the field have repressed gender as a political category, yet the very repression of the terms of the body—as gendered and sexed—becomes the basis for reading gender as an absence. Another source is the work and words of women who, although neither critical and institutional leaders nor feminist activists, produced a range of Marxist-feminist writings that tilts our perceptions of the 1930s.

As heirs to the feminist and avant-garde movements of the earlier twentieth century, radical women writers of the 1930s found themselves within a subculture that had already acknowledged gender differences and was now writing the story of class struggle. In Bessie Breuer's *The Daughter* (1938), for example, Katy realizes that because her mother's generation had fought for women's rights, she is free to sit all night in a bar with two strange men—a labor organizer and a striker—discussing the organizing strategy of the fishermen's strike in the South Florida resort she visits. But radical women were still constrained by the sexism that pervaded the Left no less than the rest of society. Even though the Communist Party had a vocabulary by which to name gender inequality, it never developed effective mechanisms for organizing against it. Moreover, the feminized position of the intellectual within the discourse of the Left effectively suppressed issues of gender and sexuality among literary radicals. This, then, is the invisible scar within the scar—the submersion of gender within class that was covered over in the "political history" of literary radicalism begun by Rahv.

One place to begin regendering the political history of literary radicalism might be Evelyn Scott's prefatory remarks to her saga of American bourgeois decline, *A Calendar of Sin* (1930). Scott declares that her novel is an attempt to "allow 'love and hunger' equal expression in the same book."[44] Her two-volume narrative tracks the history of both sexual desire and capital accumulation during the nineteenth century. The multiple narratives link economic, social, sexual, and geographic mobility to the histories of feminine desire and masculine acquisition. Scott argues that what the desiring woman wants—the goods of the free market, including not only commodities but labor itself—the acquiring man has because of his direct connection to economic power. A novel that gave equal expression to love and hunger, then, implied a narrative that inscribed both feminine desires (historicized in domestic fiction) and masculine economies (domesticated by historical fiction). It was a novel that stretched the conventions of domestic and historical fiction by self-consciously asserting the connections between the laboring and desiring bodies of men and women within the history of capitalism.

Scott's terms—*love* and *hunger*—signify the gender distinctions marking the bodies of men and women in American history. Her attempt to mobilize both sets of narratives appears to me as a strategic design to recast realist fiction to do the cultural work needed by literary radicalism. This work required a committed stance by the authors of fiction who were confronted with the new economic landscape of the Depression—a terrain that not only remapped the boundaries of fiction to include hunger as well as love but also recharted the field of American politics.

The devastating image of hunger in Depression-ravaged America gave intellectuals a structuring ground on which to figure their narratives. The hungry body, like the laboring body, was male—but a male body turned in on itself, emasculated, as historical forces worked inside it, depleting its power. According to Granville Hicks, the effects of unemployment on the bodies of working men produced a spectacle that could not be ignored by Depression-era writers: "We saw them on the street . . . standing dazed and bewildered . . . [or] sleeping on the stairs of subway entrances, covered with salvaged newspapers."[45] Whether witnessed or experienced, hunger lurked on the horizon of the American landscape during the first years of the Depression. Its image haunted the imagination of the decade's writers, in time becoming a fixed memory.

In his introduction to *The American Writer and the Great Depression*, Harvey

Swados recalls a childhood memory of the "dulled and shamed glances" of hungry men who came to his door to be fed. Joseph North introduces his anthology of writings from the *New Masses* with a memory of "the cold hell of hunger, the unparalleled assault of starvation" on the bodies of millions of Americans, which he sees as the central metaphor for the Depression experience. Similarly, Jack Conroy's introduction to his anthology of writings from *The Anvil* notes that, after the 1929 crash, many expatriate writers returned home to "unemployment and hunger," not only as experience but also as subject matter. For instance, H. H. Lewis begins his story "Down the Skidway" with a description of "Hunger—like the police dick who stalks by banks, luxurious hotels, jewelry stores, elite cafes, shadowing a *starved* American to catch him mooching—the hunger beast had stalked me . . . pounced upon me, chewed me up, digested the sweet juices of my egotism, and dumped me." For Richard Wright, hunger was the prevailing experience as well as the dominant image of the 1930s. His cynical memoir of his years in Communist organizations in Chicago, later entitled *American Hunger*, stressed this; though hunger, for him, meant "more than bread"—it was also a hunger for "human unity."[46]

For these and other male intellectuals, the image of lack—defined by the male body's deprivation of food and labor, the starving and idle bodies of unemployed men—signified a need not only for radically reconstructing the economy but also for revising the relationship of intellectuals to workers and to their work(s). The heroic worker, who labored all day and organized all night, became the model for revolutionary fervor. His virile pose contrasted sharply with pictures of the defeated, empty men standing on the breadlines and with the effete intellectual (epitomized by Marcel Proust), the "master masturbator" of modernism, who was content at best to sit and disparage capitalism rather than actively to fight it. At the same time, these powerful images contributed to the suppression of the female voice in both history and narrative, because literary radicals portrayed themselves in extremely masculine terms in order to combat their marginalizaton within both leftist and American culture by metaphorically identifying themselves with the masculine proletariat.

But portraying the effects of the Depression on the bodies of workers as the primary force shaping literary radicalism distorts literary history as much as focusing on the sectarian debates of leftist critics. Many other factors also shaped the leftward turn of intellectuals during the 1930s. The dramatic image of the militant worker promoted by the Wobblies, the legacy of Sacco and Vanzetti, and the enthusiasm of intellectuals returning from visits to the Soviet Union (such as Lincoln Steffens, who declared, "I have seen the future and it works") all fostered the romance of political radicalism. Among intellectuals, furthermore, turn-of-the-century political progressivism, coupled with philosophical pragmatism, led to an ascendancy of scientific or rationalistic theories to account for economic, social, and technological changes. The popularizations of Darwinian theories of evolution and Einstein's refinements of the Newtonian universe created a receptive audience for vulgar Marxist explanations of the economic crisis of 1929. The general public came to have a broader appreciation of different social and cultural systems through anthropologists' explorations of the range of human behaviors. In addition, the rise of sociological criticism as a model for relating literature to history and the culture of the small, independent ("little") magazine, which nourished avant-garde and leftist authors, helped legitimate a class-conscious literature.

Thus, many argue that literary radicalism in America began not in the hungry years of the 1930s but in the opulence of the 1920s, when American writers found little in their own society to nurture them and so ventured to Europe in search of a new literary culture. Jack Conroy claimed that the little magazines of the 1920s, whose literary elements consisted of a "rebellion . . . against the fetters of form and language taboos," were crucial to the 1930s political aesthetic. Josephine Herbst maintained that the "revolutions in language—sex" of the 1920s were as important as the economic crises of the 1930s for her generation of writers. Likewise, Granville Hicks's memories of the culture of the Depression begin in the 1920s with the revolt against what he terms "Victorianism" in literature. James Gilbert has remarked on the ways that the "three Bohemias" of Greenwich Village culture in the 1920s became the basis for American literary radicalism in the 1930s.[47]

These three Bohemias—for art, modernism; for sex, feminism and Freudianism; for politics, the anarcho-syndicalism of the Wobblies—suggest again that the histories of literature, women, and radicalism must be told as interlocking narratives. The migration of so many disaffected intellectuals to the Left was shaped by more than the turmoil of the Depression. It was also an inheritance from their earlier rebelliousness, given fresh form by the vision of a new culture and a new politics emerging simultaneously in the Soviet Union. Like Richard Wright, who hungered for more than bread, 1930s writers desired a literature that could do more, both politically and aesthetically, than the muckraking naturalism of the late nineteenth and early twentieth centuries and more than the psychological experimentation of early modernism.

Women's memories of the 1930s, like men's, are shrouded with the pall of hunger that ended the Roaring Twenties, but again there were many other reasons for their growing involvement with the Left. This was particularly true in the case of women intellectuals, for whom the Depression decade opened up a range of possibilities that enabled their entry into what Leslie Rabine has called "feminine historicity."[48] Of course, they too were affected by the economic devastation around them. Nonetheless, in women's memoirs the 1930s are remembered less as a decade of (male) lack than as one that mobilized and to some extent fulfilled (female) desires. In this respect, women's memoirs of the 1930s also are distinguished from women's personal writings of earlier generations. Thirties women speak of History—with a capital "H"—intervening into their lives and remaking them.[49] For Josephine Herbst, "yesterday's road" led from the "vagabond twenties" to Moscow through "the crossroads where my own history intersected the history of our time."[50] This is the theme of Vivian Gornick's oral history of the CPUSA—what she calls the "romance" of communism. As "Marian Moran" (Dorothy Healey) remembers the 1930s: "The years with the fruit pickers became a world within the world." She goes on to account for her tenacious adherence to the Party by suggesting that the experiences of the 1930s became emblems of the "great sweep of Marxist revolution. . . . Day by day people were developing, transforming, communicating inarticulate dreams, discovering a force of being in themselves. Desires, skills, capacities they didn't know they had blossomed under the pressure of active struggle. . . . It was my dream of Socialism come to life."[51]

Similarly, for all her criticisms of the Party, Peggy Dennis describes the early 1930s as a time when abstract theories penetrated her daily life: "For me personally, this world movement embracing millions took on a face and form as I lived and worked and studied in Moscow."[52] For Agnes Smedley, "the poverty of Asia" that she observed in 1930 Shanghai "presse[d] in upon [her] on every side," and she "more and more became political . . . with emotions being crowded completely, or almost completely, out of [her] life."[53] Jessica Mitford recounts that "major conflicts were brewing beyond the confines of the fortress," as she called her family estate, which would lead her to communism and her sister to fascism. She attributes their divergent paths somewhat to personality, but more significantly she felt "that we were somehow being swept apart by a huge tidal wave over which we had no control," which she later simply called "the *Zeitgeist* of the thirties."[54] The Zeitgeist of the 1930s, for women at least, meant that the content of their narratives could include the public field, supplementing if not supplanting the private sphere of personal confession.

The revolutions in language and sex that Herbst felt had marked the 1920s still reproduced a cultural split that owed its organization to gender divisions, in which literature and the body were coded as feminine while history and the body politic were masculinized. Revolutions in language and sex had already been produced by (middle-class) women's narratives even when it appeared otherwise.[55] What the 1930s signified for women writers was yet another change: revolutions in history, economics, and politics became immediate concerns for female as well as male writers, opening up a realm other than the personal for literary production. It seemed briefly during the 1930s that women could be more than the object of desire in American literature. They too could enter the field as subjects: riding horses to the Cuban sugar soviet Realengo 18; marching with the Red Army in China; digging trenches with the Loyalists in Spain; and picketing with striking longshoremen in San Francisco, truckers in Minneapolis, autoworkers in Flint, rubberworkers in Akron, and coalminers in Pittsburgh. With these women, as with an African American male writer like Wright, hunger could not fully account for their narratives. They cataloged lack, but they did so with a sense of the enormous possibilities now open to them as women intellectuals. Thus, despite the precarious class and gender tags that characterized the (male) intellectual as effete, and so politically suspect, women (and, in Wright's case, African American male) intellectuals tied their emotional stakes to historical circumstances.[56]

Evelyn Scott's claim for a narrative of love and hunger countered the rhetoric of literary radicals that engendered the proletariat as masculine. If the issues of the working class were solely economic and, as such, coded through hunger, then desire coded as love remained the narrative repository of femininity—that is, of the bourgeoisie. In *Anti-Oedipus*, Gilles Deleuze and Felix Guattari argue that the narratives of love and hunger, of body and economy, are interchangeable under capitalism. The "universe of subjective representation" produced by capitalism forces the splitting of social and psychological formations into the state and the psyche, when actually each is operating in and through the other. This "double alienation—labor-desire" produces the codes of representation under capitalism.[57] Scott's project hints at the historical and narrative links among each level of the split. What Scott required was a dual narrative to record both the history of hunger and the history of desire, both masculinity and femininity, both the working class and the bourgeoisie. She was, in effect, arguing for the multiple tracks that the three Bohemias had opened up for intellectuals, but which the masculine metaphors of proletarian realism made problematic for (women) intellectuals. Her dual trajectory became one strategy by which women writers reconstructed literary radicalism to accommodate their alienated position as female intellectuals.

Word-in-Deed

Indeed, as Scott's foreword to *A Calendar of Sin* suggests, one of the central developments in women's revolutionary literature of the 1930s was the incorporation of social events and political responses into the female body: hunger and labor became sexualized. For women writers, as for all leftist intellectuals, the Depression functioned as the political ground onto which the figure of personal aesthetic response was etched. This response dwelled in contradictions—between personal experience (the body) and political doctrine (the text), and between personal witness inscribed in the (narrative) urge to document and political commitment dramatized by the (historical) urge to act. Deborah S. Rosenfelt has argued that the Third Period's focus on workers acting in concert to create a revolutionary situation implied a corresponding dismissal of the ideas of intellectuals. Despite Marx's insistence that theory and praxis must remain inseparable, American Marxists, apparently acting on the Comintern's ideology and program, often could not reconcile the "life of the mind" with direct action.[58]

In *Silences*, Tillie Olsen obliquely describes her inability to disentangle her Party responsibilities from those necessary for her writing.[59] As a woman worker and writer, she was multiply pulled by the often dichotomized positions operating within the Left. More broadly, the institutions and apparatuses that the Party had fostered to encourage the proletarian aesthetic held within them this same (gendered) contradiction—between word and deed— for all its active participants, regardless of their class or gender. But for the women intellectuals who wrote about their working-class sisters, this dichotomized tension actually became the substance of their writing. Unable to find another image, Genevieve Taggard's poem, "Life of the Mind, 1935," posed the relationship between the writer and her times as that between "soldiers" and "their meat." Noting that "Necessity to eat, / Necessity to act, / And act aright, renews / The mind's link with the arm," Taggard can only figure the "act" in the prevailing terms of hungry men. Only "action like a sword" can "redeem the word" and win "the battle of the mind." However, she refuses to "relinquish" poetry and solves the writer's dilemma by combining "word-in-deed."[60] As she intones, "The words in the books are not true / If they do not act in you." The duality between word and deed was rectified by this word indeed, which appeared to overcome the differential between workers and intellectuals—that is, between virility and effeminateness— through a hybrid form that crossed genres, genders, and classes.

The vexing debate over the place of the intellectual within the working-class movements of the 1930s had a number of strands. Most outrageous were the anti-intellectual rantings of some Party members who denounced "the air-conditioned bourgeois word-manufacturers" as mouthpieces for the false consciousness of both popular and elite cultures in America.[61] Even the more staid analyses of the anti-Stalinist Left echoed these same sentiments, however, when they claimed for themselves an authenticity greater than that of CPUSA members and fellow travelers whose true selves were masked. The most notorious version of this conflict was the on-going suit by Lillian Hellman against Mary McCarthy after McCarthy denounced Hellman on television as a "dishonest writer," saying that even her "ands" and "thes" were lies. Robert Warshow asserts that the legacy of the thirties was the failure of intellectuals to maintain "the emotional and moral content of experience, putting in its place a system of conventionalized 'responses.'"[62] According to his retrospective, the insidious effects of Stalinism were most evident in "mass culture," which further debased the relationship of writer to experience.[63] These various readings of the intellectual's inability to deliver the authentic goods—Truth—look back nostalgically toward some lost moment before the total, universal, whole, complete speaking subject was declared by Louis Althusser to be an ideological construct.

This sentimentalized view of the intellectual as upholder of high culture suggests yet another manifestation of the intellectual's seemingly insecure place within American culture. That insecurity, Christopher Lasch has argued, arises primarily because "intellectuals were outsiders by necessity: a new class, not yet absorbed into the cultural consensus," whose "rebellion" took the form of cultural radicalism rather than political practice. Yet as the primary producers and consumers of liberal discourse—that is, as the "traditional intellectuals" of liberalism, to use Antonio Gramsci's term—all intellectuals perform within the arenas of the political and the popular. They remain frozen in the master-slave dialectic by authorizing themselves to speak for the Other(s), which, according to Julia Kristeva, sets the individual and the masses in opposition.[64]

The relationship of the intellectual to the state and to civil society has been theorized in various ways by Antonio Gramsci, Michel Foucault, and Raymond Williams. Their dualistic categories—organic, specific, and committed versus traditional, universal, and aligned—refer to the political organization of culture; but although they fail to register gender, they nevertheless implicitly inscribe it within political culture. The intellectual as codifier and disseminator of hegemonic ideas—Gramsci's traditional (vs. organic) intellectual, Foucault's universal (vs. specific) intellectual, or Raymond Williams's aligned (vs. committed) writer—functions in one of two ways depending upon his conscious or unconscious appropriation of hegemonic discourses.[65] As an authoritarian figure—a schoolmaster, clergyman, and so forth—he appears in the guise of stern father who controls the knowledge and actions of wayward sons. Even in his more benign garb of liberal journalist, professor, or critic, his politics are cloaked despite the transparency of his authority. The seamless fabric constructed out of the traditional intellectuals' writings strengthens the political hegemony, whether totalitarian or liberal.

In its liberal form, more than in its overtly dominating one, the intellectual figure assumes the disembodied voice of a conciliator, who smooths the rough edges of a regime like a mother soothing a child after its father's anger. In this guise, the intellectual appears to take on the maternal qualities and feminized forms so open to criticism by those on the Left. For instance, when Joseph North, in "College Men and Men," applauded some students in Mexico for possessing "enough masculinity . . . to defy the police and fly the red flag," he was implying that the traditional intellectual—the college man who is clearly not a *man*—could define his proper gender position after committing himself to the working-class struggle.[66] The traditional intellectual of liberalism is ambiguously gendered, displaying both patriarchal and maternal aspects. This gender confusion might have prompted Williams's call for an overt declaration of political commitment or Gramsci's insistence that organic intellectuals reassert their own masculinity by becoming the voice of the masses through the Party. Even Foucault's specific intellectual must assert local interests rather than claim status through a universalized position. This type of intellectual, who speaks for a particular position in opposition to the hegemonic, includes the female intellectual who defines herself by her gender.

When I speak of the female intellectual, I do so with the knowledge that by marking off gender I am implying that the term *intellectual*, when used alone, remains ungendered; actually, as feminist linguists have shown us, it signifies masculinity through its absence of gender ascriptions. To speak of the female intellectual, then, is to speak of an oppositional figure, a figure in opposition to itself, because the ideological function of the universal intellectual is to mask difference, to subsume dissent into consensus—to "propagandize" by invoking universal myths, as Kenneth Burke put it to the 1935 American Writers' Congress.[67] In other words, the (self-consciously) female intellectual becomes a "specific intellectual" of gender.

For committed women intellectuals, text is always "written in the book of the flesh" before it can be inscribed on the page. The female intellectual, if she is to speak both as female and as intellectual, defines a subcultural space that places her outside of the terrain of the traditional intellectual. Kristeva's characterization of the "new type" of intellectual as the dissident focuses on the place of woman as an "exile both by the general clichés that make up a common consensus and by the very powers of generalization intrinsic to language." According to Kristeva, woman, especially the mother, presents "a conflict—the incarnation of the split of the complete subject." Because "pregnancy is a threshold between nature and culture, maternity is a bridge between singularity and ethics. . . . A woman thus finds herself at the pivot of sociality—she is at once the guarantee and a threat to its stability."[68] The woman becomes the embodiment of the organic intellectual by virtue of her situatedness as a (re-productive) body. The definition of this new intellectual is revealed through manipulations of language and desire—through representation and reproduction. The intellectual works with words, displaying the power to contain others through disclosures of the self just as the pregnant woman contains another within her body. (S)he speaks for the body politic without necessarily speaking to it; in fact, in many cases, (s)he is not *of* it. Even without the epithets of femininity with which literary radicals laced their discussions of (universal) intellectuals, it appears (and Kristeva asserts it as the obvious) that the specific intellectual must also be a woman.[69]

The controversy between the powers of word and/or deed, of theory and/or practice, belies the hopelessly mechanical Marxism of 1930s American Communists who, in the wake of the visible devastations of the Depression, sought what Jessica Mitford called the "scientific" explanations that Marxism claimed for itself. By valorizing the act over its articulation, intellectuals were in effect consigning themselves to the dust bin of history, even as they were busy revising its narrative. However, by carefully defining a new type of (proletarian) writer—"a wild youth of about twenty-two, the son of working class parents, who himself works in the lumber camps, coal mines, steel mills, harvest fields and mountain camps of America"—Michael Gold and other literary radicals were distinguishing themselves from the feminized position of the traditional intellectual.[70] Proletarianism was the antidote for the intellectual as woman, because if the literary radical wrote like a worker, for a worker, and about a worker, he could in effect shift both class and gender inscriptions and become a (cultural) worker in the camps, mines, mills, and fields of America.[71] But this development still left no place for the woman worker or the committed female intellectual.

Revolutionary Girls and Partisan Mothers

"From 1930 on," wrote Henry Hart in 1935, "those whose function is to describe and interpret human life—in novel, story, poem, essay, play—have been increasingly sure that their interests and the interests of the propertyless and oppressed are inseparable."[72] As I have been arguing, the "interests" that intellectuals expressed both in and for the oppressed were expressed differently by male and female writers. Whereas the men were often preoccupied by metaphoric and actual inscriptions of lack on the bodies of unemployed and hungry men, the women, though no less sensitive to these horrors, also reveled in the opportunities afforded them. For women, the inscriptions of desire on the female body acted as links to history, and their "political history" of literary radicalism resonates differently than men's. With many people putting off marriage and childbearing because of the economy, middle-class women could continue their educations; in fact, until very recently, more women had earned Ph.D.'s during the 1930s than ever before or since.

Despite or because of the economic crisis, women made up over 25 percent of the labor force, and even married women entered the work force in greater numbers than before, although cultural (and sometimes legal) barriers proscribed hiring wives in many cases. With the advent of suffrage, many middle-class white women had expected to enter politics, but their gains in the public sphere were meager. However, because the Depression and later the threat of war had a financial impact on each household, women's "domestic" concerns took on new political meanings. With Eleanor Roosevelt, Frances Perkins, Molly Dewson, and others administering New Deal programs, women attained a degree of national political visibility.

Moreover, even if women's rights were continually shunted aside in favor of the apparently more pressing demands made by labor and minorities—both of which appeared monolithically male—the Left had a history of addressing "the woman question," which gave women both institutional and rhetorical avenues for organizing (or at least complaining) as women.[73] For example, a regular feature of the *Party Organizer*, an internal organ for CPUSA members, was "Work among Women," which often recounted the frustrations of women organizers and their constituents with the Party's tendency to dismiss women's grievances and distrust their political commitments. One correspondent complained that women were routinely assigned "technical work," that is, typing or copying leaflets that they had not been allowed to write. Rarely encouraged to take leadership positions, they were "organized in women's councils and mothers' leagues, instead of being drawn into the unemployed branches."[74]

A report from the girls' convention of the Young Communist League (YCL) called on boy comrades to discard their "male superiority." The girls also called on the YCL to train them for leadership, noting: "In the past we have often assigned girls only to routine jobs such as dues' secretaries, recording secretaries, etc." Finally, in calling for more interracial contact between girls and boys, the YCL girls admonished white boys to pay more attention to black girl comrades: "If our boy comrades claim that they do not know how to dance, we say that it's about time they learned."[75] (Apparently, racist attitudes about black women's innate rhythm persisted even among those who expressed sensitivity about and organized against racism and sexism.)

In its early years, *Working Woman*, the organ of the CPUSA Women's Commission, agitated unstintingly for free, safe, and legal birth control, including abortion, for all women. In so doing, the editors exposed the ways in which capitalism constructed the bodies of women differently than those of men; that is, capitalism stressed women's productive worth in terms of childbirth, men's in terms of labor. Because more workers meant lower wages and higher exploitation, the call for birth control was seen more as a class issue than a gender issue by the Party. Like the Third Period call for proletarian literature, this radically feminist position was out of step with events unfolding in the Soviet Union, where, despite the 1926 enactment of the Family Code, access to birth control and abortion had been severely curtailed by the implementation of Stalin's pronatalist policies during the 1930s.

During the years of its publication, 1929 to 1935, *Working Woman* also concentrated on such feminist issues as the relationship of white supremacy to sexual violence against African American women, the importance of organizing autonomous women's unions, the documentation of sexual harassment in the workplace, and the examination of the ideology of romantic love promulgated by popular culture. Soviet women wrote of their lives within a Communist society, and well-known labor journalists and organizers like Ella Reeve Bloor, Myra Page, Mary Heaton Vorse, and Grace Hutchins detailed the militant strike actions of women in America.

Nonetheless, most of these writings submerged gender within class and so were at best feeble attempts by the CPUSA to theorize the complex relationship of the two. *Working Woman* and the *Daily Worker*'s women's pages provide fascinating illustrations of this point. A typical page might feature an article on the position of women in the Soviet Union, suggesting not only that equality under the law had been achieved, but that economic and sexual equality had also become institutionalized. Another column might call for women to organize committees to fight against war and fascism. In addition, an article on birth control might feature a desperate woman pleading for "the knowledge" that would keep her from getting pregnant. Against these political pieces would be juxtaposed fashion tips, recipes for bean casseroles, or poems such as Pablo Neruda's "To the Mothers of the Dead Militia." In the *Daily Worker*, the women's columns were on the same pages as the cultural and entertainment news, indicating that women and culture occupied marginal positions compared with workers and politics, both in the pages of the paper and in the organization it represented. (I suspect, though, that this page and the sports page were the first ones most readers turned to.)

Editors exhorted their readers to submit letters or testimonials about their experiences as working women, farm women, or working-class housewives. In one case, a contest was held for the best response to a letter from a woman who complained that her husband would not allow her to attend meetings. Sixteen prizes were offered, ranging from a "Hamper of White Rose canned products" (first prize) to "Three large glossy photos of Lenin, Stalin and Marx" (sixteenth). Even in this one detects the centrality of hunger within the proletarian cultural discourse: food was certainly more valuable to the readers of *Working Woman* than hagiographical representations of the real "head boys."[76]

The range of concerns covered in *Working Woman* begins to outline the complex position of its eponymous anomaly within literary radicalism, but her figure becomes etched more precisely in women's literary texts. An examination of three women's poems from the early 1930s indicates the crude translation of bodies into texts that marked much proletarian art, whether by male or female writers. Paula Golden's ironic poem, "A 'Capitalist' Speaks," printed in the journal of the Detroit John Reed Club, uses a nursery rhyme scheme to convey the bourgeoisie's perceptions of workers. It begins:

> Those sweating masses,
> They're such asses—
> Always prating
> A-bout classes

and continues with the complaint that they

> Can't buy coal or pay their rent:
> Just a bunch of Down-and-Outers—
> Make good Soap Box Meeting Shouters—
>   Ain't even satisfied with "dole,"
>   A scrap of bread,
>   A lump of coal.[77]

Mary Lapsley's "Scaffolding," published in the independent Left journal *Modern Monthly*, figures the workers' bodies more concretely:

> Men's bodies, pared by hunger's knife,
> Still hug life.
>
> Furnace, shovel, derrick, crane
> Know their pain.

Steel, concrete: a bridge's net
Shows our debt.

Hard sure worlds these have encased,
Who are waste.[78]

In Golden's satiric rhyme, the capitalist refuses to see his workers as anything other than "sweating masses," undifferentiated bodies that are not only distastefully sweating but whose actions, as a mass, are as stupid as asses'. Lapsley's poem asks us to look directly at the men's "bodies" that make up the masses about which the capitalist speaks. Like the poem, the workers' bodies, "pared by hunger's knife," appear as scaffolding. Working at and worked by the machines, constructed out of "steel, concrete," their bodies become yet another tool of the labor process, so interchangeable with their machines that these alone can "know their pain." Yet their bodies are more than the merely physical evidence of their labor power; they "still hug life," those "who are waste." The imagist style makes a lyric of the labor process—in this case the building of a bridge—and celebrates the powers of the materials of construction while decrying the destruction of the workers themselves, whose bodies are articulated by the parings of hunger's knife, not engulfed in the sweating masses.

Whereas the first poem suggests an attempt at sarcasm, mocking the thoughts of the capitalist, the second falls pathetically into melodrama, enhanced by the simple rhyme scheme and short lines. These two approaches—sarcasm toward capitalists and sentimentality toward workers—marked much of the proletarian literature of the 1930s. A romantic naïveté interpreted the class struggle as a simplistic dualism pitting hungry (masculine) male workers against bloated (feminine) male capitalists and gave much proletarian poetry its cartoon-like feel. With the addition of female voices like that of Martha Millet, the (female) worker's desiring body is resurrected through the discourses of history and revolution:

Last night I heard a girl speaking
To a crowd; she was swift, fiery,
She uttered the word: Revolution.

I pace, aglow with the sounding of
Her simple phrases, reflect, shake
Hands with an imaginary man, a friend,

Calling him Comrade—the word
Lingers warm and confident on my lips.

We are parted, you and I, ghosts
Of the past—today having torn us
Apart—do not stare emptily.
I walk now free of you—
Free for the open day.

Last night I heard
The lips of a girl say: Revolution.
This morning I am alive.[79]

The speaker in this poem, moved by the political rhetoric of another young woman, has been transformed. She can now address a man as a "friend," a "comrade," free of the "ghosts / of the past." Thus hearing a girl say "revolution" signifies more than political or economic revolution for the speaker; it also transforms the relationships she has known between herself and a man as well as within herself, because separating "I" from "you" leaves her without the "ghosts of the past." This internalization of proletarianism links the passions of historical change, uttered in the "swift, fiery" words of the orator, with the romantic conceits of a private desire to be "free for the open day." Millet's poem evokes the same sensation as Mary Heaton Vorse's description of a gathering of the women's auxiliary in Flint's Pengally Hall, strike headquarters of the United Auto Workers (UAW): "The hall was packed with women, the men standing in a fringe at the back. The chairwoman of the meeting had never run a meeting before. All of the women were finding in themselves new powers and new strength, and they had found each other."[80] This feminized rhetorical power could work on the emotions of the male proletariat as well, as the unemployed "Joe" of one of Millet's short stories discovers. After speaking to a revolutionary girl, Joe feels "the impress of her strong fingers for a long time. Like a magnet that had drawn him back into life."[81]

The revolutionary girls that figured in Millet's writings were also stock characters in *Daily Worker* articles about Soviet women workers and American working-class women. Myra Page reported on this "new type of hero . . . with minds largely freed from all those petty household cares that hampered them in the past." One named "Proletarskaya," who was awarded the Order of

Lenin for "ten valuable suggestions for rationalizing production," claims when asked to speak about herself: "I don't know how to talk about myself. All I know is that I understand the masses and how to lead them to do their best."[82] These heroines had something in common with the spunky young women who populated Hollywood musicals and screwball comedies during the 1930s—for example, the three heroines of *Gold Diggers of 1933*, who demonstrate a class and gender solidarity when they conspire to "gold dig" the wealthy Bostonians who look down their noses at show girls.

This connection between popular culture and proletarian ideals was not lost on the Left (in fact, many screenwriters were themselves Party members or fellow travelers), as this report by the Hollywood correspondent to the *Daily Worker* illustrates: "Joan Crawford, Marion Davies, Helen Twelvetrees, Mary Pickford, Janet Gaynor and Joan Blondell have created another of those famous Hollywood 'revolutions' by publicly announcing their rejection of 'sex-appeal' as an implement in their artistic arsenal."[83] Like Page's "Women Heroes of Socialist Construction," the Hollywood stars were free to assert their power as working women. However, the more typical American version of these socialist heroes was neither a "shock brigader" nor a movie star nor a "gold digger," but a member of the Ladies' Auxiliary who could be found distributing strike relief when not busy "marching side by side with the men in the mass marches and demonstrations."[84] Genevieve Taggard's poem, "At Last the Women Are Moving," asks how "these timid, the slaves of breakfast and supper . . . these, whose business is keeping the body alive" have come to "stride . . . erect, bearing wide banners?" The women answer, "Not for me and mine only / For my class I have come / To walk city miles with many, my will in our work."[85] Thus the "Union Maid" of Woody Guthrie's song was not herself a proletarian; her access to class struggle was through marriage and family. If she did work, her femininity in a sex-segregated labor market meant that she was often seen as even more of a "slave" than her male counterpart, as the subject of Myra Page's article, "The Revolution Made a Person out of Me," asserts.[86]

Maxwell Bodenheim's "Revolutionary Girl," despite being "a revolutionist, a worker," is still merely "a girl" who "long[s] for crumpled 'kerchiefs, notes / of nonsense."[87] In H. H. Lewis's more bizarre rendering, "The American workingclass [*sic*] is a big-boned charmaid / Muscled like a man / Direct, simple-hearted and vulgar: / An Amazon / With great passionate dugs and a potent womb, / Whew! / A real man's woman!" This twist on the gendered proletariat portrays the working class as a virile woman. She is preyed upon by a variety of effeminate male theorists who have "been fixed," "never did know how," "petered out and went haywire," or are "dress-suited and manicured / and nice, nice." Liberals, socialists, anarchists, and Trotskyists fail to consummate heterosexual intercourse—marrying theory to practice—because as either castrated, inept lovers, premature ejaculators, or homosexuals they cannot rise to the enormous task of stimulating the mass(ive) working-class body. But this vision of female sexual insatiability has distinctly masculine features: she is "muscled like a man," "vulgar," "potent."[88] So only the "Man from Moscow" is sufficiently virile to impregnate this Amazon with revolutionary fervor. Whew! What a confused vision of female dread and homosexual anxiety! According to Guthrie, Bodenheim, and Lewis, the revolutionary woman has access to history as a handmaid of the (male) class struggle (through marriage or heterosexual intercourse). These diverse early 1930s representations of the working-class revolutionary woman have one thing in common: they figure the working-class female subject, whether as fiery speaker, abject slave, or "passionate charmaid," through a body that differs from the hungry, lacking body of the male worker.

By now, the outrageously sexist (and heterosexist) remarks of Michael Gold and other literary radicals are commonplace knowledge.[89] Less commonly known are the various ways that women writers sought to undo the effects of Gold's analog (worker is to intellectual as male is to female). Because his model effectively excluded the possibility of a working-class woman and denied credibility to a radical woman intellectual, women writers resorted to satire, melodrama, and exhortation to convince him and the rest of the "head boys" that they too could participate in the movements of the 1930s. For example, in response to Gold's classic definition of the proletarian writer as "a wild youth," this 1930 letter to the editor of the *New Masses* challenges Gold to find a place for her in his landscape:

> I am by birth a bourgeois, by conviction proletarian. Having escaped from a puritan, middle-western home, I now find myself plunged into the environment of a no less bourgeois university and without hope of salvation. I have tried certain neighborhood socialist leagues but for one whose interests are centered in modern literature, the labor problem, the regeneration of the theatre, etc., these socialist clubs are little more than non-religious prototypes of Christian Endeavor. What can I do? Where

can I go? Must a bourgeois be born, live and die, pretending to believe in the hypocrisies of his class, measuring his happiness by ownership of a chevrolet and radio set? Your letter says "No one who hasn't put his sweat, gall blood and fury into a piece of unpopular writing, while wondering at the same time how the room rent would be paid, can understand the drama of a proletarian writer's role." My scholarship meant that the rent would be paid, while I could do all the unpopular writing I pleased; it also meant that I could equip myself with an educational background which would permit me to beat the self-righteous babbits in their own language of academic culture—but now, I find myself isolated from the tragedies and comedies of the corporation stenographer, elevator-boy, or office clerk—and not a proletarian sympathizer to talk with.

Just what can I do?[90]

The author of this tongue-in-cheek plaint, Helene Margaret, spotlights a serious dilemma facing all radical intellectuals during the early years of the 1930s. However, her letter suggests that the position of the female intellectual is even more fraught with contradictions because of the pleasures she derives from her education. Although she phrases her dilemma as one that is class based, her problems clearly stem from her femininity, which will not allow her to produce "sweat, gall blood and fury." She cannot write "in jets of exasperated feeling," as Gold had claimed his new writer would. Although Helene Margaret does not explicitly address the issues arising from being female, her doubly feminine moniker and the tone of her advice-column letter, as well as her inference that the only labor open to her is office work, mark her concerns as more gendered than classed.

On an even more desperate note, Zelda Leknorf wrote the *New Masses*—after their publication of Meridel LeSueur's "I Was Marching," a story about the entrance of a middle-class intellectual woman into the workers' movement—that she "wanted to scream and tear at my face which shrieked guilt" at the sight of striking mill workers in New Bedford because she was not part of their movement. "The cowardice that lay beneath my flabby indolence and intellectual luxuriance" left her "gaping and superciliously discussing and criticizing tactics and maneuvers of the Party" because the "ghastly futility of our plight is overwhelming."[91] Just as the editors had earlier criticized LeSueur's portrait of unemployed women in "Women on the Breadlines" for its bleak and "defeatist" picture of poor women, they now admonished this "intellectual fellow-traveler [not] to indulge in hysterical self-flagellation," a characteristic of bourgeois women.[92] It is remarkable how often radical intellectuals relied on the vocabulary of that most decadent of theories, psychoanalysis, to effect their most biting critiques. Denouncing works as "neurotic" or "febrile" or "hysterical" or "homosexual" or "masturbatory" marked them as degenerate—as dangerously feminine and bourgeois.

If the markings of hunger and labor on the bodies of male workers inscribed the proletariat as masculine, then Helene Margaret's plight as a bourgeois intellectual woman was inscribed, like the body of the hysteric, by the text of her neurosis. Hopelessly outside of the working class because she was not hungry, the female intellectual was ideologically inscribed rather than materially determined. Given the hostility of most 1930s American Marxists to ideas (as opposed to action), their valuing of deed over word, the bourgeois woman represented the epitome of false consciousness. Her body was pure text. In effect, Helene Margaret and all bourgeois women on the Left were permanently estranged from historical change, which could be effected solely by the struggles of hungry and laboring bodies. This attitude partly explains Leknorf's more desperate note as she contemplates disfiguring herself when confronted with the vision of the proletariat in action. Her position as the feminine within the movement—by virtue of both her sex and her class—requires a self-deformation for her to become effective. Only by disfigurement, by tearing her face like a page of text, can she overcome the "flabby indolence" caused by discussing Party theory rather than actively placing her body in the struggle.

Leknorf's solution is one used by many revolutionary women writers to open a space for the woman intellectual as activist. The female protagonist of women's revolutionary fiction often conceives of herself as a "foreigner," a "grotesque figure," a "dragon," a "beast," a "creature," because she continues to think of herself as a woman rather than identifying herself completely with the (male) working class.[93] Disfigurement might have transformed the female body, gaining it entry into the proper revolutionary class, but it also pointed to the predicament of the female intellectuals' double alienation; pointing out gender differences in either the working class or the middle class implied a critique of the gendered understandings of class that undergirded proletarianism. This left the writer open to condemnation as being "still a suffragette."[94] Thus the gendered discourses of proletarian cultural practices during the Third Period reproduced the CPUSA's stance on women by mirroring the hostile relationship between "the woman question" and feminism.

As the Party shifted its political line from the Third Period's emphasis on working-class revolution to the Popular Front's struggle against fascism, however, literary radicals maintained their renderings of class through gender. As proletarianism gave way to populism, revolutionary girls became partisan mothers. In the political arena, this shift was exemplified by Earl Browder's 1936 presidential election slogan, which asserted that "Communism Is Twentieth-Century Americanism," a clear signal to wavering liberals that an alliance with the Party against fascism would not threaten their middle-class identification. In addition, literary radicals were beginning to accept Kenneth Burke's prophetic suggestion that *people*, rather than *worker*, better described the audience and subject of American revolutionary literature (although Burke was widely criticized when he made this observation at the first American Writers' Congress).

A similar shift governed the ways gender figured in Party rhetoric. As the Party sought to fit itself into mainstream American culture, it promoted images of stable family values anchored by the working-class woman as sacrificing mother. The "rebel girl" of the Wobblies had become Bodenheim's dubious "revolutionary girl," but by the late 1930s Lauren Gilfillan's claim that "when Woman is a Communist today she has been driven to it by her Motherly Instincts" was only partly sarcastic.[95] As early as 1933, Ella Winter had argued that mothers were natural antifascists; as such, their "job today is to protect all children from the cruel deaths and maiming decreed for them by a fascist world."[96] Genevieve Taggard found women joining the masses by marching directly out of their kitchens still "carr[ying] bundles."[97] This maternal Communist was popularly depicted in Jane Darwell's Oscar-winning performance as Ma Joad in the 1940 film version of *The Grapes of Wrath*. The hero of King Vidor's *Our Daily Bread* (1934), who improvises a cooperative farm by allowing people displaced by the dust bowl and the Depression to stay on his land, announces that he "feels like a mother" after the seeds of their collective labor begin to sprout. If women became Communists out of their maternal instincts, men could become mothers out of their communistic experiences.

By the middle of the decade, the Roosevelt administration had enacted many of the CPUSA's programs—unemployment insurance, social security, the right to independent unions—leading to an explosion of CIO-sponsored strikes in the coal, steel, maritime, rubber, and auto industries. The proletariat appeared to be rising from its state of lack—hunger and unemployment—into one of militant power. This change was coupled with a new rhetorical shift in which the celebration of the workers' collective strength was supplanted by the twin concerns of defending the Soviet Union and fighting fascism. At the same time, discussions of feminist issues receded from view as *Working Woman* was replaced by *Woman Today*, a publication modeled on popular women's magazines, and women's issues became centered around defending maternal values at home and in Spain. As the Comintern grew obsessed with rooting out its "enemies"—that is, Trotskyists—the rhetoric of Communists took on a military tone. After Franco launched his assault on Spain to topple its democratically elected government, Italy invaded Ethiopia, Japan marched on China, and Germany annexed the Sudetenland, the language of *workers'* militance gave way to calls for *people's* militarism. This language of war no longer referred to class struggle in the gendered rhetoric that had organized the early 1930s into virile workers and effeminate intellectuals. With "people's democracies" assuming the traditional feminine (and intellectual) role as defenders of culture against the invading "barbarians," the language of military defense appeared to make a space for femininity. But this reversal of gender positions still maintained the dualistic polarities embedded in cultural constructions of gender differences.

The new rhetoric found a place for the feminine, but that place was motherhood. Suddenly, maternity became a powerful political force. During the early 1930s, the condition had been viewed as draining, debilitating, and ultimately dangerous for the workers' struggle: because perpetual motherhood consigned a family to greater poverty, the woman-as-mother might not be consistently militant in her class solidarity. For example, she might urge her striking husband to return to work as a scab in order to feed her children. Even before motherhood became the dominant metaphor for the Left, however, the Party was described by Fielding Burke as a "great mother." (The call to defend Mother Russia from the brutal invading forces of the German Fatherland was enormously important inside and outside the Soviet Union, both before and after the 1939 nonaggression pact between Hitler and Stalin.)

When Beth McHenry reported on "The Nation's Finest—Those YCL Girls," she noted that some of "these pretty kids in the neat clothes" had joined because the Young Communist League had helped buoy the spirits of striking cigarmakers during their nine-week sit-in with "Easter flowers they sent the women sitting in at the National Cigar Co." At the 1937 YCL convention, the girls elected "the model American mother. That was Comrade Mother Bloor."[98] The following day, McHenry reported, there was a demonstration to honor Mothers' Day for Peace, a "mothers' movement" dedicated to changing the character of the traditional holiday from one of "sentimentalism and commercialism to a day devoted to the interests of peace." Sponsors for the rally included two members of Roosevelt's government—Secretary of Labor Frances Perkins and Elinore M. Herrick of the National Labor Relations Board—as well as a range of Popular Front organizations.[99] When women's brigades organized by the Workers' Alliance of America (WAA), a Popular Front mass organization, marched on Washington to demand expansion of the WPA, they planned to stand as "mute reminders" of the "needs of men, women and children for decent food, clothing and shelter," said Roy Cook, secretary of the WAA.[100] By stressing maternal values, Communists found a way to work with the New Deal Democrats they had formerly attacked as fascists.

In addition to realigning the CPUSA's domestic policies, pronatalist rhetoric became a powerful focus of internationalist concerns as well. For example, the Girls' Commission of the YCL, citing the "special problems" of women and girls, made the following proposals at their 1937 convention:

> Marriage and a happy family life are problems facing almost all girls. We would be doing a great service if we sought to get a law passed granting a bonus to all couples desiring to get married. Birth control information and education should be made legal; a system of child guidance and prenatal clinics must be made available to all. . . . When fascism attacks Spanish women and children it also attacks American women and girls. It is our duty to do everything in our power to help the people of Spain. We propose that girls in the Y.C.L. adopt Spanish babies and protect them from the fascist baby killers.[101]

Not only did motherhood shape the Popular Front focus on Spain, but Spain helped recast mothers into fellow travelers. Beth McHenry described her mother's conversion from anticommunism to support for the Spanish Loyalists after learning that both her priest and the local newspaper had lied about the war's disastrous impact on mothers and children.[102]

The celebration of maternity reached its apex in the popular imagination with the birth of the Dionne quintuplets in 1934. A popular cultural rendering of this pronatalist ecstasy, Preston Sturges's 1944 film *Miracle of Morgan's Creek*, depicts not only the fertile powers of working-class womanhood, but links them to the war effort: Betty Hutton delivers six babies after a one-night stand with a soldier. Thus, by the 1940s, the fecundity of North American womanhood was matched by the virility of its armed services, whose joint war efforts would defeat European fascism. However, it is important to realize that 1936, the year in which Genevieve Taggard watched working- and middle-class mothers march out of their kitchens, was also the year in which Franco mobilized against the government of Spain and the Kremlin began its show trials of Stalin's "enemies." The benign face of Mother Russia masked Stalin's brutal purges at home and abroad; and in Spain, posing as a savior of the Madonna, the fascist Franco murdered peasants.

Nineteen thirty-six was also the year that Dale Carnegie's *How to Win Friends and Influence People* and Margaret Mitchell's *Gone with the Wind* were bestsellers in the United States. Despite the radicalized discourse of intellectuals during the decade, many Americans' deeply ingrained xenophobic suspicion of radical politics continued unabated. In this respect, the 1930s differed little from preceding or subsequent eras. Thus, when the CPUSA decided to seek alliances with liberal supporters of Roosevelt, it needed to find an acceptable rhetoric that would seem comfortably American. The Popular Front's turn to icons of popular culture—Hollywood, Mom, the Dodgers, Abe Lincoln—enabled Marxism, which had previously been coded in the public imagination as European and Jewish, to display a wholesome American face.[103]

For these reasons, the rise of the Popular Front depended upon a corresponding pronatalist rhetoric. Once again the situation posed conflicts for the radical woman intellectual. On the one hand, the CPUSA's membership soared during the Popular Front years because the Party recruited women as never before (women comprised over 40 percent of its membership); on the other hand, it was only as mothers that women could find expression as historical subjects. Because many female intellectuals were themselves childless (how else could they roam the world, write, and organize?), they were again viewed as anomalous. The gendered class struggle that had privileged the virile proletariat had given way to an antifascist struggle of mothers, but a (gendered) rhetoric still overlaid the (ungendered) policy of the Left.

As the growing world crisis took shape, the resulting sectarian fights and shifts in Party line began to unravel the seams of Popular Frontism, including the simplistic transposition of political postures into maternal forms that dominated leftist culture. The year 1939 was pivotal for many CPUSA-aligned intellectuals who formally abandoned or informally withdrew from the Party after the Stalin-Hitler pact. Once the war in Europe was underway, a new set of problems emerged for the writer, and literary radicalism appeared dead. By the end of the decade, Trotskyists and anarchists were blasting Communist literary radicals for adapting to liberalism and popular culture. But they now blamed the Party's adherence to Stalinism as much as they did the success of Communist writers within the WPA writing projects. In the midst of all this, many women writers who had remained outsiders to the most heated debates continued to write revolutionary novels. By so doing, they were defying not only the various sectarian shifts in the Left but also the concerns of both popular and elite culture. For many of these authors, revolutionary fiction continued to provide a means for describing the complexity of American social relations even after the United States had entered World War II.

Women's writings provide an alternative reading of the theories and practices of 1930s literary radicalism. Because women rarely published major works of criticism or theory in the pages of leftist journals, their (re)construction of the 1930s has for the most part been ignored.[104] Women's literary talents were used primarily for fiction, poetry, and reportage. Many accounts of strikes that appeared in the *New Masses* or *Crisis* were written by those same women, who felt an exhilarating joy in becoming part of a wider struggle for justice. Rarely, however, did women contribute to what little political or aesthetic theory the leftist journals produced. A woman might be a reviewer—often of other women's books—because she had written a novel, but she was not expected to attempt to analyze the formal or ideological concerns of proletarian writing. (Mary McCarthy claimed she became the *Partisan Review*'s theater critic because she was married to an actor.) Serious criticism was left to men, such as Granville Hicks, Alan Calmer, Edwin Seaver, and Michael Gold in the *New Masses*, Philip Rahv and Dwight Macdonald in *Partisan Review*, or W. E. B. DuBois in *Crisis*. We must look to the literary works by women themselves for another theory of the history of literary radicalism—a history that will in many ways resemble those already written but will also recast the era and its debates to accommodate the desires of feminine historicity.

Because of the ingrained hostility toward radicalism in American culture, which contributed to its small membership and its sectarian factionalism throughout the decade, the Left remained a small subculture within 1930s America. Nevertheless, it achieved a relatively wide influence in a number of areas. As the primary force behind organizing industrial workers, the unemployed, and minorities as well as fighting war and fascism, it enjoyed considerable political influence during the Roosevelt years. Similarly, within cultural circles the aesthetics of "social significance," no matter how toughly contested they were within the Left itself or by those outside the Left, gained wide adherence among writers, critics, and readers. During the 1930s, the Left was responsible for setting the terms of debate within the political and artistic cultures of the United States, even as it remained marginal to state politics and to popular and elite cultures.

This curious combination of subcultural marginality and wide cultural and political influence produced a counterhegemonic discursive field that often exceeded the Left's own contradictory policies and programs. The simultaneous inclusion in and exclusion from dominant American culture that the Left experienced was recapitulated in the experiences of women within the Left, many of whom were attracted to the CPUSA because it offered a program for organizing oppressed industrial workers, farmers, and minorities while standing for democratic values. Yet, although the Party advocated equality for women, gender and sexuality—unlike race and class—were not recognized as sites for the construction of the political subject. Gender and sexuality served as metaphors rather than as historically determined and determining structures of oppression. This process of conflating class and gender deeply affected the women in the movement. The metaphors of gender skewed the writings of radical women intellectuals, which in effect transformed the contours of revolutionary literature. Politically, this contradiction found expression in "the woman question," which in practice was viewed as more or less extraneous to the class struggle but which ideologically committed the Left to sexual equality. Party theory stressed the importance of complete freedom for women, but the Party gradually constricted the range of women's roles within its organization and its rhetoric. The 1930s began with the CPUSA proclaiming every woman's right to free contraception and abortion, but the decade ended with the Party declaring that the fight against fascism in Spain was a fight to save Spanish motherhood.

Both literary theory and literary history proceed out of limited discourses and political practice is contained within specific institutions, almost all of which have been produced and recorded by male writers and/or activists. Thus, within the traditional framework of literary radicalism, neither do the novels by women produce literary theory or history nor do the institutions of sex and gender produce political practices. Because women did not participate as leaders of the movement—either as critics or as ideologues—the concerns considered crucial to 1930s (literary) radicalism are based almost entirely on the memoirs, critiques, and reviews of male authors. Within Party-dominated literary circles, the development of proletarian literature codified masculine metaphors for the working-class struggle; later, the shift to Popular Front concerns invoked maternal metaphors to fight fascism. Among the Trotskyists, a shift from proletarianism to formalism also tempered the emphasis on a virile poetics by focusing on the dilemma of the radical intellectual. In both cases, the move away from an emphasis on workers' stories rephrased the hysterical misogyny and homophobia of early 1930s criticism into a discourse that reinvoked the (maternal) powers of writers as the traditional intellectuals of liberal humanism.

A close look at the fiction that women on the Left were writing throughout the decade, however, indicates another site for the production of a literary history of the 1930s. The proviso to "write your life" suggested that areas previously exempt from literary exploration were now open to anyone daring enough to put them into print, including women. These writers recognized the female body as one contradictory site of sexual, gender, race, and class conflict in American society, and they used this understanding to rechart the terrain of literary radicalism. By redefining the narrative of desire as a means by which the female subject entered history, they repositioned both the female intellectual and the working-class woman in literature and history. In particular, women's revolutionary writings foregrounded the need for contraception and abortion, the terrors of forced sterilization and rape, and the repression of sexuality as primary determinants of class consciousness among working-class women. Similarly, because the female intellectual and the working-class woman occupied problematic (or nonexistent) places in the discourses that engendered class, the relationship of the intellectual to the working class provided a core for women's revolutionary fiction from its earliest moments into the 1940s.

Moreover, despite alterations in official policy and rhetoric toward both women's and aesthetic issues, there is a surprising continuity among the fictions written by women. No significant shift occurs in this literature throughout the decade. Rather, despite wide variations in style, form, plot, and politics among the authors, there is a remarkable coherence of thematic and structural elements among women's writings. From Agnes Smedley through Mary McCarthy—that is, from a Communist-aligned working-class woman constructing an identity using a proletarian narrative to a quasi-Trotskyist intellectual woman deconstructing self and narrative—women's revolutionary fiction is bound together by the ways it links class and gender, even if these ways are as radically different from one another as they are from the ways imagined by Gold or Rahv. Read together, women's novels challenge the critical convention that links literary radicalism, through a narrow reading of the narrative of history, to the Party's political shifts from the Third Period to the Popular Front. Instead, by tracing the narrative of desire as history that produced the differently classed and gendered subjects of women's texts, the novels suggest that those women occluded in the central discourses and institutions of the CPUSA negotiated continuous revisions of line, whether as organizers of needle-trade workers or as authors of novels about those same workers.[105]

When gender is registered as a category in the political history of literary radicalism, differences other than those between the Third Period and the Popular Front or between the Communist and anti-Stalinist Left appear. The differently gendered political subjects of women's revolutionary fiction have other stories to tell. The remainder of this book provides us with the means to begin to hear their voices.

The Contradictions of Gender and Genre

2

If feminist critical theory is to address the differences within and among women's and men's bodies and texts, then we, as feminist critics, must read within the constraints of genre and period while radically questioning the ideological assumptions of those formations. Each of us is only provisionally positioned by gender, because the cultural meanings of race, class, age, sexuality, ethnicity, and so forth are in constant flux as they modulate our gender ascriptions; one's subject position is always located on contested terrain. Just as we needed to reconsider the ways gender rewrites literary history, so, too, must we examine the ways gender inscribes genre. The novels by 1930s women literary radicals comprise another genre different from, yet indebted to, both proletarian realism (or any of the other names literary historians have given to the works of literary radicals) and the traditional woman's domestic narrative.

Nancy Miller has noted that women's texts seem "extraordinary"; they are filled with "implausibilities" that call attention to themselves because they transgress the boundaries between public and private discourses. The fiction written by radical women during the 1930s at once conforms to and yet cannot be contained by conventional readings of literary radicalism. What emerge again and again in these novels are the gaps produced by the difficulty of narrating a class-conscious female subjectivity, that is, a narrative detailing the classed body of woman as both hungry and desiring, as both a member of the body politic and a sexual body. These gaps occur sometimes at "the level of the sentence"—textually, as Virginia Woolf argued—and sometimes as the "insurgence of the body" celebrated by Hélène Cixous. This elision of body

63

and text, of history and desire, produces the "thematic structuration . . . the form of content" of radical women's narratives.[1]

To speak of women's revolutionary fiction as a genre requires a series of theoretical moves. First, genre theory, which has become an important literary critical tool for Marxist and feminist theorists, must acknowledge the ways in which it has constituted and has been constituted by gender ideology. Categorizing differences—between genres and between genders—appears to lead back to the simplistic limits of a single identity, because the very process of classification reproduces a dichotomous view of difference. Second, just as a reading of women's literature revises the history and criticism of literary radicalism, so too a reading of women's revolutionary fiction provides another outline of the contours of the radical novel as a genre. Male critics— such as Gold, Cowley, and Hicks—provided schematic renderings of proletarian realism that served to delineate a new genre based in class antagonism. In their readings, sexual difference—the field that narrative maps, according to Teresa de Lauretis—appeared submerged. In order to be legible, however, as I have shown, the narrative of class struggle relied on the metaphors of gender differences. This contradiction—the repression of gender and sexuality by its invocation—ultimately resulted in generic de-formation.

Literary radicalism displays all the elements of what Deleuze and Guattari call "minor literature": "the deterritorialization of language, the connection of the individual to a political immediacy and the collective assemblage of enunciation."[2] Minor literature can never aspire to the universal "mastery" of great works; it remains, according to Michel Ragon, a "secondary zone" of literary production, outside dominant literary historical and generic categories.[3] The secondary status of 1930s literary radicalism within American literary history opens it to a theoretical reading as a genre. The insularity of the genre, like the insularity of contemporary critical theory, is both its drawback and its strength. The "minor" status of literary radicalism provides a case study that allows us to unravel the knots of class and gender within the classifications of literary history and the conventions of the generic analysis.

Women's revolutionary fiction can be read as a genre within a genre, as a "secondary zone" of literary radicalism whose boundaries contain and exceed the narrative of class struggle that animated proletarian realism. It inscribes desire into history through the narratives of the working-class woman and the radical female intellectual. Through this "emphasis added" emerge the contours of a genre different from proletarian fiction, one marked by its own narrative types and subject positions. This chapter looks at what the genres of literary radicalism were *not* about: the irruption of female sexuality into its classed narratives.

Genre as Gender

Traditionally, theories of genre (including feminist ones)—like other classifications of literary history: periodization, canonization, and so forth—have reproduced the pitfalls of biological essentialism by codifying, hence excluding, certain bodies of work. Nevertheless, genre has become one site of materialist-feminist inquiry because it historicizes form and content by reading the outlines of genre conventions in the context of class and gender ideologies. In so doing, materialist-feminist genre theory establishes connections among gender, genre, and class. For the most part, those connections have been described in terms of the relationship of different genres to the two genders. So, for instance, romantic poetry is historicized as peculiarly masculine; whereas domestic fiction is categorized as a feminine genre.

Proletarian fiction, with its roots in naturalism and its connections to the tough-guy, hard-boiled prose of 1930s detective novels, has been construed as a profoundly masculine genre to differentiate it from the historical romances and other women's fiction popular during the Depression. Certainly, as I have argued, the rhetoric of gender used by literary radicals themselves to describe class relations contributed to such a characterization. Moreover, discourses of gender hidden within those of class (and vice versa) have tended to deny the possibility of a female working-class or radical intellectual subject within the genre. Once the working class (or at least the workplace) has emerged as masculine, as it did in late-nineteenth-century fiction, the idea of a working-class woman's narrative lacks "authenticity," a criticism applied to *The Girl*. Even the narrative of a radical woman intellectual like *The Unpossessed* is treated as a "curiosity" within a genre that defines the intellectual as an effeminate male. Yet the same conventions of form and content that coded proletarian realism as a genre—the same ones that historicized the working-class subject by depicting the development of class consciousness through class struggle—enabled Meridel LeSueur and Tess Slesinger to speak about the differences of the female body. Thus, gender not only produces a "difference between" but also a "difference within."[4]

Women's revolutionary fiction must be viewed both as a variation of proletarian literature and as a coherent genre of its own. Genres are at once fluid and static. Their boundaries continually shift and adapt, but once they announce themselves, genres depend on distinct icons and codes. In addition, because generic icons encode ideology, a genre's form and content express ideological traces (what Fredric Jameson has called "sedimented ideologemes") through structure, plot, and characterization.[5] Examining these traces has proven remarkably fruitful for Marxist literary theorists because the traces elucidate the ways in which conventional generic codes can contain counterhegemonic expressions. According to Raymond Williams, genre reveals the "question of determinants" in the "social-material process" of writing because it conveys a history of forms within the variations of its contents.[6] So, for instance, Meridel LeSueur could use the icons and codes of proletarian realism to convey the development of feminist consciousness, even though the conventions of proletarianism defined class, not gender, as the determinant of historical agency.[7]

Like a language, a genre usually emerges over time. One of its salient features is its ability to endure numerous revisions in vocabulary and syntax, if not grammar; thus it oscillates both synchronically and diachronically. It retains a flavor of its origin while incorporating contextual changes. Despite radical revisions, generic codes endure as guides to history and ideology. Genre criticism can open a text to an ideological reading by simultaneously placing it diachronically within its period (disclosing a history of forms that reflects its moment) and synchronically alongside other similar works (extrapolating form from its direct historical determinants). In a sense, the divisions within genres point to the fissures within ideology and history and open a space for theoretical intervention into the (con)text. Perhaps, then, it is not to the conventions of a genre that one must look to understand a novel's ideological traces, but to the places in the individual text where generic classification seems to collapse.[8]

For example, Jameson has argued that "the novel is the end of genre" because of its ability to incorporate so many disparate moments in the history of all preceding codes at one time. The proliferation of ideological traces found in the novel ultimately results in the collapse of all generic differentiations.[9] Jameson's argument is essentially a variation on Mikhail Bakhtin's theory that the novel incorporates the subversive qualities of carnival. Bakhtin's ecstatic call for the "novelization" of everything presumes that novels will ultimately disrupt the rigid speech and forms of the monovocal "epic" by allowing contending voices to speak.[10] However, as Nancy Armstrong has argued, the novel may very well be the site for the display of cultural hegemony; indeed, it may participate in its production.[11]

Ironically, Georg Lukács views the realist novel as the epic of modern society, in which the story of the individual replaces the saga of the gods and so creates new social and psychological meanings through narrative by recasting an earlier genre.[12] Yet, as Jameson has shown, realism represents an extreme disintegration of genre, because the use of narrative point of view and other devices to reproduce the bourgeois subject as a psychological individual results in an endless proliferation of narrative forms. For instance, Armstrong argues that the cultural work of domestic fiction is precisely its ability to recast political concerns into the realm of the personal, thereby restricting both the political and the personal by defining the bourgeois subject as the reader/text of literature. Ultimately, then, a genre of fiction reveals itself in its effort to conceal itself, as it continually remakes the world into more of the same.

Read as a genre, the leftist fiction of the 1930s represents a curious revision of the realist domestic novel. Whereas the domestic novel maps the political through psychological disclosures about individual members of the bourgeois family, the proletarian novel overlays the contours of working-class consciousness and psychology onto the political organizations of culture and the workplace. Committed as it was to a verisimilitude that would faithfully depict the living conditions, working experiences, and psychological tensions of the working class under capitalism, much leftist fiction (even many of the proletarian novels that most fully embraced realism) could not fulfill the dicta of high realism because it presented history rather than psychology as the crucial narrative motor. History shaped and intruded upon the narratives, lending them documentary evidence but undermining their realist conventions. For history is not easily contained within the closed pages of a novel or story, especially ones as insistently closed as "ideological" fiction.

Realist domestic fiction may have sought to evoke the real world, but it did so in highly conventionalized ways, presenting "plausible" situations that illustrated common-sense "maxims."[13] For example, it was important in nineteenth-century Russia to describe how to comport oneself at an opera, as does *Anna Karenina*, but certainly not how to self-induce an abortion, as does *Jake Home* (1943). Although nineteenth-century domestic fiction sought to relocate social and political tensions on the body of the woman, this body was a highly restricted one whose desires were confined to supervising personal relations. Proletarian fiction continued to trace the inscriptions of history on bodies, but those bodies were controlled by hunger and forged by labor. They redirected desire through their (re)productive labor. One way that the genre of proletarian fiction encoded gender, then, can be found by examining the ideological traces of desire left from the realist domestic novel.

Another way of exploring the connection between gender and genre is to look at how the very act of classifying by genre is in itself an engendering act. The "law of genre," Jacques Derrida argues, demands allegiance to a set of codes that differentiate one genre from another. "As soon as genre announces itself, one must respect a norm, one must not cross a line of demarcation, one must not risk impurity, anomaly, or monstrosity." As Derrida repeats in the incantation that begins his article, "genres are not to be mixed"; yet constant revision shifts the boundaries of genre, mixing them up.[14] Although what is different changes, the differences always remain. In the Derridean landscape, genre is inevitably linked to the order of genealogy—the capacity to generate, to engender—and so to the patriarchal order—to the Law of the Father, to masculine authority. The law of genre, then, is also the law of gender: that system which demarks the boundaries of and ascribes meaning to sexual difference.[15] And anything that steps outside of those boundaries risks "impurity"; it becomes bastardized, a "monstrosity"—or, put more politely, "implausible" within the codes of difference of either genre or gender.

As Sandra Gilbert and Susan Gubar note, "the contradictions of genre and gender" are fueled by the image of literary paternity, which conversely implies female literary sterility.[16] The equation of literature with masculinity and authority has resulted in twisted metaphors of gender to describe the literary process throughout history. In effect, Michael Gold's declarations about the virility of proletarian poetics recall Hawthorne's horror at the "damned mob of scribbling women," a theme that, Nina Baym has shown, runs throughout American literary history.[17] Indeed, as many feminist critics have noted, the estranged position occupied by women writers has resulted in textual deformation—sometimes quite literally, as in the image of woman confronting herself within the text as monster, but more often symbolically through narrative or generic reconstruction. For a woman to produce a literary text, to enter the (masculine) terrain of genre, she must step out of her gender and therefore, ironically, out of bounds.

Thus more than a pleasant alliteration is involved in the conjunction of genre and gender. Each is bound within a classificatory system that demands adherence to its codes. "Genre[s] should not be mixed," and neither should genders. Both gender and genre function as ways to ideologically position an individual subject/text in a historical context. Through the establishment of definition and description as means of containment, the boundaries of genre and gender have restricted most women's writings and sexualities in cultural history, defined what literary and sexual practices can be (re)produced, circumscribed who can produce them, and prescribed how they are to be interpreted.

If genre slips inevitably into gender, classification systems are of necessity linked to classes. Like the containment of the varieties of sexual relations through the ideology of gender and the institution of heterosexuality, the discourse of political economy—whether bourgeois or Marxist—has produced two classes out of the myriad possibilities for categorizing social relations. It scarcely seems odd, then, that the language of class, as Joan Scott points out, is an engendered one.[18] Like genre and gender, classification and class appear natural despite being historically constructed. It becomes virtually impossible to speak about genre, gender, classification, or class without invoking each of the other terms simultaneously. Women's revolutionary novels of the 1930s, like those of men, posit the development of class conflict in the form of the rising proletariat or the declining bourgeoisie. However, they employ narrative strategies that reconstruct and historicize the gendered bourgeois subject of nineteenth-century fiction; for example, they narrate the history of the working-class woman, a subject as yet unrecognized within either domestic fiction or proletarian realism. To break the classed and gendered silences that hid the working-class woman within realism, women who wrote revolutionary fiction framed their narratives on uncoded bodies and texts—those that (re)produce through birth *and* labor.

Just as they reinvented the narrative of desire for the proletarian novel, so too did radical women writers re-place history into the traditional romances and domestic novels that depended upon a female heroine. By resisting the two strategic imperatives established within nineteenth-century fiction by the romance and the bildungsroman, Rachel Blau DuPlessis argues, twentieth-century women writers have struggled to recast narrative by "writing beyond the ending." Traditionally, these two gendered plots either position the female hero within a saga that culminates in the joining of a heterosexual couple, or they establish the hero's quest for knowledge and self as a fundamentally masculine tale of mastery. In the classic domestic novel, only two options are open to the female hero: either she can successfully transform herself into a heroine and so marry a proper partner, or she can resist this structure and die. Modernist women novelists have devised a series of narrative strategies to undermine this "ending" through the use of "reparenting, female bonding, including lesbian ties, mother-child dyad, brother-sister pairs, familial transpositions, the multiple individual, and the transpersonal protagonist."[19]

In women's revolutionary writings, the use of the collective protagonist—whose multiple stories coalesce not around "individual quests" or "romantic thralldom" but rather around the development of collective solidarity and militancy—also undermines the realist "ending."[20] The desires elicited in the characters as they march together resemble both the transcendent experience of the quest and the confinement of romance, yet they occur within a new social grouping—one based neither on the individual nor on the couple but instead on a collective. This narrative device re-creates the perception of "totality" for the reader that is, according to Lukács, essential to the project of realist fiction.[21] Through its very elaboration of a fragmentary, partial, and discontinuous narrative, the collective novel exhibits the conditions of "modernity" to surpass "not only the number one—the number that determines unity, of body or of self—but also beyond the number two, which determines difference, antagonism and exchange conceived of as merely the moving together of opposites."[22]

By focusing on the mass movement—a historically constituted social organization—rather than the psychologically generated narrative of the individual or family, the revolutionary novel rejects closure. Neither the romance nor the quest plot can textualize the transformation in subjectivity or sociality that the proletarian revolution seeks. As Domna Stanton points out, "discontinuity and fragmentation constitute particularly fitting means for inscribing the split subject, even for creating the rhetorical impression of spontaneity and truth" so essential to the genre.[23] Thus a classic proletarian novel like *Marching! Marching!* (1935) often ends with a mass chorus of strikers singing the "Internationale" while marching toward a plant gate guarded by police. The narrative loses sight of the individual characters who have participated in the strike because the mass movement replaces the character as narrative focus. The narrative never reaches closure; instead of ending, it links its reader to the future struggle.

The generic code of class solidarity provided women writers one device with which to undermine the restrictions on female characters imposed by dominant narrative forms, but additional strategies were essential if their work was to inscribe a female, class-conscious subjectivity. One of these tactics was reconstructing the narrative of desire to speak of (other) classed female subjects than the middle-class heroine. Women often achieved this by reworking the (male) literary radical's gendering of class. The very markers of gender identity that coded the bourgeois as emasculated became elements by which female characters evoked their own developing class consciousness. For them, sexuality (often of a brutalized and alienated nature) rephrased the brutality and alienation that working-class men experienced at the factory. Finally, by encoding the mass movement as maternal, women writers rephrased both the fraternal relations of the working-class struggle and the monstrous mothers of domesticity. Like all literary radicals, women authors found their material in the sites of alienation outlined by Marxist theory—the workplace and labor—but these included the family, maternity, and sexuality in addition to factory or farm.

The gendering of class that literary radicals employed with such uncritical acceptance was thus turned on its head by women authors, who exposed the remnants of bourgeois domestic narratives underpinning the (male) literary radicals' metaphors of gender. This transformation had its own risks: by asserting a difference of sexuality and of gender, these women displaced their class allegiance in the eyes of their male contemporaries. Furthermore, by insisting on the importance of the domestic sphere to (literary) productive labor, women authors veered perilously close to the ideology of domesticity that animated nineteenth-century fiction. Thus much of their writing consists of de-formations: both the taking apart of form and literal disfigurement. Thematically, some female characters describe themselves as grotesque and beastly. In their deformations, these characters resemble the creature in the quintessential female-authored text of monstrosity, *Frankenstein*.[24] Unrecognizable as fully gendered because they are not fully classed, they remain outsiders—bastards, if you will—unable to identify with the class solidarity that offers intellectuals a sense of refuge from their gender identification. Other deformations are structural, acting to undermine the class consciousness of the texts by rerouting the narrative from class to gender.

These textual deformations occur like singularities within the novels— what DuPlessis, echoing Virginia Woolf, calls "breaks in the sequence"—

that temporarily divert the narrative from its mission of reorganizing consciousness and practice through the collective action of the working class.
They are unreconciled contradictions within the narrative whereby gender
positions become marked off; characters become differentiated by gender
rather than by class, momentarily restructuring the genre's focus. Like most
disruptions of convention within a generic work, they are more or less
invisible—a generic convention working after all to disguise itself and to
subsume difference within itself—but a reading that seeks out the instances
of gender ideology within class ideology makes them glaringly obvious. For
example, Josephine Johnson's highly symbolic proletarian novel, *Jordanstown*
(1937)—which follows a year in the lives of various members of a small
midwestern town, during which unemployed, working-class African Americans and whites attempt to build a Workers' Center—is interrupted by two
contrasting internal monologues. Anna, the African American maid of Mrs.
Phillips, recalls her years of activism, struggle, and pain after her first husband was lynched. On the other hand, Mrs. Phillips's "air-conditioned mind"
worries over her luncheon menu, her tightened budget, and her husband's
moodiness, while at the same time she finds herself sexually attracted to one
of the organizers. Mrs. Phillips is peripheral to the narrative and the collectivity, but her desire works to "bridge the chasm" between herself as a
middle-class woman and the impoverished members of her community.[25]

My point is neither that the 1930s were unique in figuring a classed and
gendered discourse through narrative, nor that women's writings are privileged repositories of the class/gender nexus in narrative, but rather that
women's revolutionary fiction of the 1930s provides unique evidence for
theorizing the ways in which narratives reveal gender to be classed and class
to be gendered. The narratives of history and the narratives of desire have a
long tradition. In the domestic novel, the heroine's desire has the political
effect of taming the excesses of an aristocratic or (occasionally) working-class
male so that he may become a fit partner for her (that is, properly bourgeois)
and a fit employer for his men (that is, properly paternal). But the genre of
1930s revolutionary fiction reverses the relationship between the narratives of
desire and history by giving primacy to class, thus moving class struggle out of
the drawing room and onto the stage of history.

Unfortunately, the metaphors of gender employed by literary radicals re-
place women in the drawing room by defining the proletariat as masculine. To
speak as a woman is to declare oneself bourgeois; to speak as a worker is to

declare oneself masculine. Given this scenario, there is no place for the working-class woman (or the doubly excluded female intellectual) as a subject in proletarian realism. Within the gendered constructions of both class and genre, women's revolutionary fiction can be neither truly "proletarian" nor "realist." Radical women's writings de-form genre to constitute their own genre-within-a-genre—the scar within the scar of literary radicalism—indicating the ways in which a difference between (male and female) texts both masks and reveals the differences within (working-class and bourgeois) genres.

What the Genre Is (Called)

I have chosen to use the term *revolutionary fiction* to name the genre of narratives written by literary radicals during the 1930s. In the late 1960s, recalling the literary movement of the Depression era, Josephine Herbst wrote to David Madden that she thought of these writings as "vehicles for change, engines for transformation," because their writers were struggling with a series of "revolutions" in language, sex, and politics.[26] According to Herbst, the usual term used to describe 1930s writing, *proletarian*, tightened the perimeters of the genre, confining it to a specific content, while *revolutionary* addressed both the politics and aesthetics of a work.

Proletarian literature was the term officially sanctioned by the CPUSA for the new writing of the late 1920s and early 1930s. Corresponding to the political line of the Third Period, only a literature that was overtly by, for, and about workers could be considered appropriate to a revolutionary movement of the working class. Michael Gold elaborated the aesthetic requirements of "proletarian realism" in the *New Masses*. This definition was augmented by the series of critical articles by Granville Hicks on "Revolution and the Novel." In particular, Hicks expanded on one of Gold's prescriptions that proletarian realism should express "revolutionary élan" by differentiating two new forms of the novel—the "complex" and the "collective": "The collective novel not only has no individual hero; some group of persons occupies in it a position analogous to that of the hero in conventional fiction. . . . The complex novel has no individual hero, no one central character, but at the same time the various characters do not compose a collective entity."[27] But Hicks's terms are too narrow because some novels clearly had one or two protagonists and thus followed more conventionally realist forms. By the end of the 1930s, when the CPUSA had entered its Popular Front period, proletarian literature had dropped out of the lexicon of Party criticism; however, other literary radicals not so closely affiliated with the Party maintained a critical interest in the form. Furthermore, because proletarian novels continued to be written after proletarianism had been rejected by the Party, use of the term tends to constrict the genre's range to Party-sanctioned works.

The use of the term *proletarian* reflected an American attempt to follow postrevolutionary Russian efforts to establish a proletarian culture (proletcult). In the Soviet Union, this project had been multiplicitous, incorporating a variety of stylistic and aesthetic precepts from the collection of indigenous popular culture to the creation of collective works of art and other experimental new forms. By the time Stalin had consolidated his power, proletcult had been replaced by a call for socialist realism in art. In 1934 the aesthetic of socialist realism in the Soviet Union was premised on the (premature) claim that socialism had already been achieved and a new literary form was needed to reflect this transformation. Most American Marxist critics of the 1930s never advocated socialist realism as an aesthetic appropriate to their country because the United States was still a capitalist nation. However, some examples of the form can be found among the writings of American literary radicals: Myra Page's 1935 novel, *Moscow Yankee*, about a cynical, unemployed American autoworker who becomes an *udarnik*—a shock worker—in Moscow's Red Star Truck plant, is one.

In the ensuing decades, critics have used other terms to describe the literature of the 1930s. Northrop Frye wrote: "Anatomy . . . eventually begins to merge with the novel, producing various hybrids including the *roman à thèse* and novels in which the characters are symbols of social or other ideas, like the proletarian novels of the thirties of this century."[28] Susan Rubin Suleiman, in fact, relies on Frye when she argues that the *roman à thèse* constitutes its own genre. She interchanges this term with *authoritarian* and *ideological* to describe a genre of fiction that overtly proclaims itself as advancing a message—what Marx and Engels called "tendency" writing.[29] Because the category is structural, however, the content of the message is irrelevant; thus, the terms can be used interchangeably for literature advocating any orthodox political or religious position. Because the literature produced in the United States during the 1930s was written in the more heterodox "general ambience of Marxism," I feel these terms lack a specificity needed for understanding the presumptions about class that produce the formal techniques of American literary radicalism.[30]

Even more diffuse is the term *political fiction*, which has been used to identify literature that deals with government—for example, novels about political figures like *All the King's Men*.[31] This is too limited a meaning for my purposes, but, at the same time, the term is too broad because all literature as works of, in, or about ideology is political in nature. A text may not necessarily express an identifiable political line, but it does express, explicitly or implicitly, specifically selected experiences from a specific point of view. This is what Raymond Williams calls the "alignment" of writing. He differentiates this from "committed writing," which implies a "conscious, active, and open choice."[32] Alignment refers to all writing, but commitment requires self-consciousness. Whereas Marx and Engels differentiated *tendenzpoesie* from literature that implicitly (like Balzac's) or explicitly (like Dickens's) presented a "profound social and historical critique and analysis," Williams argues that committed writing becomes merely tendentious unless it recognizes that "it is literally inconceivable that practice can be separated from situation." Much of the literary debate during the 1930s reflects the dual aspects of a reduced understanding of commitment by focusing on "a variant of formalism (an abstract definition or imposition of a 'socialist' style)" or, more typically, on "a late version of Romanticism," which stressed the writer's allegiance to a cause. Williams argues for a definition of commitment that also includes the social relations in which an individual author produces a text and in which it is reproduced by its readers.[33] Because this level of sophistication was beyond most American Marxist critics of the 1930s, I feel *committed fiction* is also misleading as a designation for the genre.

Walter Rideout has defined one genre within twentieth-century American literary history as the "radical novel." Although this term has a political specificity in that it suggests a fiction of the Left that draws on socialist, anarchist, and various bohemian tendencies, it, too, may not be precise enough to elaborate the peculiar cultural phenomenon of 1930s literary radicalism. In fact, Rideout limits his reading of the novels written during the 1930s to those specifically noted as "proletarian" and thus fails to include such important works of the era as Tess Slesinger's *The Unpossessed* or Lauren Gilfillan's *I Went to Pit College*.

Because the literature of the 1930s exhibited traits of all of the terms discussed, but because no one of them includes the combination of specificity and generality that I feel can adequately incorporate women's fiction into a genre, I am using Herbst's term. Of course it, too, is open to various inter-pretations. Is a novel like Fielding Burke's *Call Home the Heart* (1932) really "revolutionary" just because it advocates class struggle? This novel about Ishma, the white mountain-woman-turned-union-organizer, follows classic patterns of both quest and romance plots inherited from nineteenth-century realism. It ends with the heroine retreating from the kiss of an African American woman into the arms of her estranged and apolitical husband. Likewise, can a novel like Gale Wilhelm's *We Too Are Drifting* (1935), which probes the dynamics of a lesbian triangle but ultimately skirts the issue of class conflict, be considered within this same rubric? Wilhelm's novel hardly fits any of the qualities usually associated with 1930s literary radicalism, yet I believe it owes much to other radical works written in the early 1930s.

As a genre, revolutionary fiction of the 1930s can be read as structurally coherent. As a result, a number of contemporary and subsequent critics have characterized it through typologies outlining plots, styles, themes, and forms. Susan Rubin Suleiman's narratological study of the French *roman à thèse* argues that the generic codes governing the authoritarian or ideological novel conform to the most conventionalized of narratives—the folktale. She dis-cerns two types of plots that follow distinct formal and characterological patterns: the "structure of apprenticeship" and the "structure of confronta-tion." The first stresses the importance of the protagonist's interaction with an older "donor" who guides the young ideologue toward correct conscious-ness. Essentially a bildungsroman, this type of novel ideally replicates within the reader the process of the protagonist's transformation as he progresses through the novel. In the "structure of confrontation" novel, the hero, already identified with the correct ideology, becomes an actor within historical events whose contradictory nature demands a struggle with the oppositional party or line, ending in triumph for the hero's politics.[34]

The crucial contradiction of the genre—its dual demands of ideology and aesthetics—suggests that authoritarian literature should be read neither as flawed doctrine nor as failed literature, but as a model for the contradictory designs of the novel in general: instruction and entertainment. One pull of the *roman à thèse* is toward closure, toward a single meaning or message; but as fiction, this project is undermined within the text. Because many works of authoritarian fiction are based on historical events and yet are fictional con-structs, the forces of history and of fiction push against each other. The fictionality reminds the reader that history, like literature, is constructed—if not always consciously. The historicity, on the other hand, serves to link the text (and the reader) to the extratextual political body. The irony of the genre, then, appears to be its contradictory coding, which oscillates between fiction and experience, text and body. This instability was one of the main impetuses, I suspect, behind the taxonomies devised by 1930s critics, who needed to fix an identity onto a form of writing that confused class, gender, and generic boundaries.

Both the theory and practice of 1930s literary radicalism tended to emphasize how important generic and typological categories were to an understanding of the various forms of its works. For instance, Michael Gold's prescriptions for proletarian realism provided nine tips for successfully producing the new writing:

> Because the workers are skilled machinists, sailors, farmers, and weavers, the proletarian writer must describe their work with technical precision. . . . Proletarian realism deals with the *real conflicts* of men and women who work for a living. . . . Every poem, every novel and drama, must have a social theme . . . as few words as possible. . . . We must write about our own mud puddle . . . swift action, clear form, direct line, cinema in words. . . . Away with drabness . . . away with all lies about human nature. We are scientists . . . no straining or melodrama or other effects.[35]

Granville Hicks, perhaps the *New Masses'* most powerful critic during the period, outlined a typology for the "revolutionary novel" that described the subject matter, characterizations, style, and themes that made up the new genre. His dissection of the genre into four types of novels—collective, complex, dramatic, and biographical—appeared to provide a scientific structure by which to distinguish the new writing from older forms of realism or naturalism.[36] By the decade's end, when numerous obituaries for literary radicalism appeared in leftist and other journals, critics were pointing to the formulaic—that is, generic—qualities of proletarian literature as evidence of its lack of literary merit.[37] Malcolm Cowley declared that "strike novels began to follow a pattern almost as rigid and conventional as that of a Petrarchan sonnet." As he summarized the plot: "The hero was usually a young worker, honest, naive and politically undeveloped. Through intolerable mistreatment, he was driven to take part in a strike. Always the strike was ruthlessly suppressed, and usually its leader was killed. But the young worker, conscious now of the mission that united him to the whole working class, marched on toward new battles."[38]

Many critics at various times during the 1930s attempted to chart the rise and decline of the genre, each producing his or her own version of its appropriate conventions.[39] Though they may have disagreed about the relative values of poetry or fiction or drama to the working-class struggle, most critics agreed that reportage best exemplified the kind of work literary radicals should be doing. Reportage, as a site of genre confusion that slides historical observation into fictional form, tends as well to blur the gendered class distinctions separating the "masculine" proletarian from the "feminine" intellectual. Actually, this slippage recurs throughout the genre of 1930s women's revolutionary fiction, in which the narratives of history and desire trace and retrace their sometimes contiguous, sometimes divergent paths within each text.

Another Typology of (Women's) Revolutionary Fiction

Generally, women's revolutionary novels of the 1930s resemble male-authored works within the genre; many of their plots conform to Gold's nine-point plan for the successful rendering of "proletarian realism." However, the variations that their narratives of desire produced in the genre alter the categories literary radicals developed to catalog their fiction. These categories have served as the basis for practically all subsequent analysis of 1930s revolutionary fiction. For instance, following the typologies developed by contemporary critics, Walter Rideout's *The Radical Novel in the United States* presents four typical proletarian plots. Rideout concurs with Cowley that the conventional proletarian plot involves a strike, but he argues that most often these novels were structured by a collective hero. However, they could also follow the experiences of a single protagonist, thus collapsing into Rideout's second type, which traces the developing class-consciousness of the hero, which often led to his conversion to the Communist Party.

The other two plot types, which stylistically often verge on naturalism, mirror one another. Rideout calls his third type after Edward Dahlberg's 1930 novel, *Bottom Dogs*. It depicts the seamy life of the contemporary lumpenproletariat through a series of episodic vignettes. The fourth type, often an historical saga set just after the Civil War during the rise of monopoly capitalism, exposes the decay of the American middle class through a portrait of a family in decline. Rideout also argues that women's (sexual) equality was now taken for granted, and so the concerns with female sexual liberation that had marked socialist novels early in the century died out in the 1930s. Neither assertion was true. In fact, sexuality provided one of the few backgrounds against which a narrative of class struggle could be outlined by women authors, precisely because the gendering of class depended upon a variety of (hetero)sexual metaphors. Ironically, woman's sexuality, an issue nominally erased by the Left's organizing, was central to its rhetoric. Moreover, women were hardly the sexual equals of men in American society or in the Left.

In many modernist (revolutionary) novels of the period, sexuality functioned as the major narrative motivation; however, because the writers of these works sought to denote their temporality, class conflict also became a minor narrative episode. For instance, in *The Daughter* (1938) by Bessie Breuer, the title character, Katy, has an affair with the young man who is her mother's lover and then leaves her mother and the lover to search out her father, whom she has not seen in many years. Entering his life again forces her into another triangle, because he has remarried. Katy had earlier fled her superficial connections to the Left—dabbling in the League of Women Shoppers, radical theater, and a fishing strike in the small Florida village where she vacations with her mother—by returning to her family. Now, fleeing both sets of incestuous entanglements, she attempts suicide. Despite burning her skin in the hot sun, swimming out too far from shore, and taking too many sleeping pills, she survives. Katy, as a modern woman, cannot succeed at either ending of the romance plot. Finally reunited with her mother, she accepts the older woman's suggestion that they go to Spain because "everybody's going."

Another example of a modernist novel about sexual tensions, *We Too Are Drifting* (1934), traces a triangulated lesbian relationship between a San Francisco sculptor, her patron/lover, and a younger protégée with whom she falls in love. Their affair ends when the young woman decides to marry a wealthy banker's son in order to save her father's failing bank. Although it remains more or less insulated from the economic and political upheavals of the time (its failure to mention the General Strike elicited criticism in an otherwise positive review in the *New Masses*), Wilhelm's novel, like *The Daughter*, situates its conflicts among members of the artistic (and sexual) fringes through references to the predominant historical landscape of economic crisis. In both books, as in classic novels of "romantic thralldom," the narrative of history serves as a highly recessed background for the narrative of desire.

According to the dictates of proletarian realism, however, the narrative of history must supplant the narrative of desire as the focus of the novel shifts from the sexual tensions of families and relationships to the class tensions of the workplace. If, as Cora Kaplan argues, female sexuality is the "synecdotal" reference for female subjectivity in narrative, then the strike functions as the synecdoche of working-class subjectivity and ultimately for the entire political culture of the 1930s.[40] Most women's revolutionary fiction intertwines the two tropes—sex and strikes—by conflating the narratives of desire and history. But the two are differentially valued in the two most prominent types of novels: those of collective proletarian struggle and those of alienated bourgeois decay.[41]

Some women's novels, like Mary Heaton Vorse's Gastonia novel, *Strike!* (1930), clearly use the evolution of the strike as a structuring device for the plot; others, like Beatrice Bisno's *Tomorrow's Bread* (1938), which traces the impoverishment of a Jewish family during the Depression, treat the strike as a secondary historical backdrop. The former type traces the development of class consciousness among a group of workers, and therefore solidarity and struggle are foregrounded by deploying the collective narrative and making the mass movement central to the novel. The latter type traces the decline and decadence of the petite bourgeoisie, and so the strike and the mass movement of working-class solidarity figure only peripherally. Instead of tracking the developing class consciousness of workers in struggle, these novels disclose the history of capitalism through the disintegration of one extended family. Grand in scale, they present a multiplicity of characters, but, like Hicks's complex novels, they do not create the circumstances for their coherence through collectivity. Instead of developing the de-centered maternal collectivity of revolutionary struggle, these novels reveal the fragments of patriarchal capitalist alienation.[42]

Two other plots can be found among those written by women within the genre. One tells the story of growing up poor and female in a midwestern or southern working-class or farming family. Although it may be that no instances of class solidarity occur within the narrative, the young heroine's sensitivity to male brutality opens the possibility for her transformation into a class-conscious woman. The other plot presents a different kind of heroine: she is in her twenties, urbane and educated—a young leftist intellectual whose involvement with the collective movement is aesthetic rather than economic. Because she is located within the (female) literary center of the Left, her experience of (male) working-class solidarity—that is, of history— is as alienated as her poorer sisters' experiences of desire.

In the case where the protagonist is an intellectual, the collective action of the poor and working class—a strike, a demonstration of unemployed workers, or the formation of an agricultural cooperative—reawakens within the protagonist some longing for freedom, usually sexual freedom, from a stifling marriage or a repressive family. Her observation of the fervor and determination of struggling (male) workers, farmers, or unemployed empha- sizes her own vacuity and rekindles earlier desires for personal liberation. The memory of early rebelliousness against the patriarchal family, sparked by a confrontation with the havoc that the Depression (or, in the historical novels, monopoly capitalism) has wreaked on the lives of the poor, the workers, and the lower middle class, kindles her revolutionary fervor. The female intellectual rejects the limitations that middle-class feminine identity enforces on her. For her, the (male) proletarian revolutionary struggle is linked to a (female) rebellion against the confines of gender.

In a similar manner, the young proletarian heroine grows from ignorance and poverty into working-class allegiance because her innate sensitivity makes her receptive to the seed that has been planted through her readings of Marx and others and cultivated in the soil of sexual and class exploitation. As with the middle-class woman, more than exposure to a strike or to Marxist theory is necessary to effect a transformation of consciousness. Her early experiences of sexual brutality, which predate her understanding of class struggle, spark a longing for sexual freedom and ignite anger at the limitations of gender. In Meridel LeSueur's cosmology, women are riper for revolutionary organiza- tion than men because of their capacity to mother and nurture children. Their familial experiences of oppression at the hands of abusive, often alcoholic men enable them to envision the possibility of a future free of exploitation more readily than can their husbands or fathers. In LeSueur's revision of Leninist strategy, women become the receptive masses who follow the leadership of a vanguard (often represented and articulated by a male voice) to a mass meeting or demonstration. Once there, the "revolutionary élan" awakens a longing for a new way of interrelating, experienced as an oceanic merger with the maternal.

The theory of revolution may be articulated by a male voice, but the experience of solidarity is distinctly maternal and feminized. The mass demonstration replaces the nuclear family with a larger formation in which the individual's gender differences are erased. In *The Girl*, LeSueur extends this image to envision a demonstration of women only, who demand milk and iron supplements for pregnant and nursing women and their children. Mothers enable the revolution by embodying change as they swell with child and by creating the first experience of merger for their children, an experience that is later recaptured in the collective solidarity of struggle.

The desire of the female subject for historicity takes two forms in women's revolutionary fiction: the first narrates the growing class consciousness of a politically naive subject, particularly as she develops in her family relationships, her sexuality, and her relation to the maternal; the second tracks the political growth of an already committed subject as she develops through struggle. The former retraces the "structure of apprenticeship" outlined by Suleiman; the latter parallels the "structure of confrontation."[43] In the first type, the family (as metaphor and actuality) plays a central role. The "structure of apprenticeship" depends upon the male protagonist's finding a substitute father—the figure of the donor—who enables the hero to see the fallacy of his biological father's ideology and politics and assists his development of correct consciousness. The family remains a retrogressive force for the protagonist in American women's revolutionary fiction of the 1930s, but not because of the false consciousness of a weak father. Rather, the family, by encoding economic and social strife as gender and generational conflict, both cushions and replicates capitalism for its members.

The petit bourgeois family is often a source of conflict within the political consciousness of a young female protagonist. In *A Time to Remember* (1936) by Leane Zugsmith, for example, the Weinsteins try to keep their daughter Aline from her growing involvement in the department store strike. It is the struggle itself, rather than a charismatic personality, that awakens this heroine's class consciousness, which was previously perceived as extreme sensitivity, rebelliousness against bourgeois conventions, social awkwardness, or sexual alienation.

The development of class consciousness in these books, then, is not a result of the parental influence of an older, wiser ideologue (though the protagonist may be inspired by a dedicated organizer who is her contemporary), but the product of direct participation in the collective struggle of the working class. In the working-class family, male violence reenacts the violence of economic exploitation, but the mother retrieves the conditions for a female working-class consciousness. Thus the transformation of consciousness, which is at the core of the "structure of apprenticeship," comes not through a restaging of the Oedipal drama, as Suleiman suggests, but through a restructuring of patriarchal family-based relationships into maternal collective ones. In this way, these narratives display elements of the "structure of confrontation" because the family itself becomes the site of struggle. Revolutionary transformation depends not only on changing texts through education but also on changing the social organization of bodies in the orderings of workplace and family. It may be unseemly for a woman to lead a picket line (as many parents and husbands remind the women), but it is essential for the development of the novel and its union.

Marriage, the family, and sexuality were important themes in men's revolutionary fiction as well, but there they were used symptomatically to evince either bourgeois malaise or proletarian vitality. For instance, Thomas Bell's proletarian domestic novel, *All Brides Are Beautiful* (1936), looks closely at the relationships among sexuality, gender, and class. The novel follows the first years of marriage between an unemployed tool-and-die maker and his sales-clerk wife, detailing white working-class ethnic life in the South Bronx during the Depression. Its (male) author and protagonist are both sensitive to the nuances of women's speech, the repression of female sexuality, and the importance of domestic labor; however, their masculine voices describe gender differences using the prevailing oppositions of the bourgeoisie as feminine and decadent and the proletariat as masculine and pure. The hero discovers that his wife works for a dealer of pornography and demands that she quit; ultimately he returns to work, only to join his union in a walkout, leaving the couple without income.

It appears that the dichotomous constructions of gender and class dominating literary radicalism outstripped the good intentions of this author, who ends up reinforcing the connections between women, intellectuals, and petit bourgeois decadence. In contrast, women's evocations of female working-class sexuality locate the system of heterosexuality, marriage, and the family as the genesis of female revolt, as shown by Agnes Smedley's elaboration of

Marie Rodgers's political development in *Daughter of Earth*. This antidomestic novel sought to narrate a female working-class bildungsroman out of the fragments of its protagonist's abusive family before shifting its focus to her embrace of the mass movement.

Although the "structure of apprenticeship," as Suleiman defines it, implies a critique of the biological family, in women's revolutionary fiction it is actually condemned. By extension, the institution of capitalist patriarchy is implicated in both gender and class oppression. Because the family is only the first site of exposure to masculine sexual violence for the young female working-class subject (just as it is the first site of feminine merger), it becomes the initial site of struggle. In Tillie Olsen's *Yonnondio* (1974), marital rape, witnessed by the daughter, shapes a fearful picture of sexual relations in general and of the father in particular, especially because his brutality often extends to physical abuse of the daughter and her siblings. However, the mother provides the impetus for her daughter's education as the best means to escape the woman's repressed role in the working-class family drama. Trapped between paternal violence and maternal despair, the young working-class girl lashes out against her parents by rejecting the family. The tight enclosures of the working-class home constrict the daughter, closing in on her—as stifling to her imagination as they are to her body, yet providing a memory out of which to forge class consciousness.

Bohemianism makes the middle-class heroine suspicious of the repressive nature of the bourgeois family. Her education and awareness of the world outside, usually fostered by her mother, further alienate her from her father's control; yet the rigidity enforced by a traditional family circumvents her involvement with the working class. Hers also is a family in fragments, though not necessarily because of economic pressures. The failure of the nuclear family to acknowledge women's sexual or political freedom results in divorce, abortion, estrangement, and suicide even when their relationships with men are supposedly unencumbered by traditional domestic roles. Marked by psychological rather than physical abuse, the bourgeois family (even its bohemian reconstitution) is as incompatible with the protagonist's growing class consciousness as the working-class family was with its daughter's growing sexual consciousness.

Collectivity becomes counterposed to the repressions of the family. The figure of the mother, remembered as a source of inspiration and nurturance, is rediscovered through the revolutionary élan experienced within the movement. The bourgeois female protagonist rarely achieves this ambivalent ideal merger, and her failure as a properly domestic woman precludes maternity. She is at odds with both formations. Despite its maternal imagery, the revolutionary body must be identified with the working class, already constructed as masculine. Thus the female bourgeois protagonist is positioned outside of the collective space. Neither maternal nor masculine because she is neither a mother nor a worker, she becomes a "beast," a "foreigner," a "creature," outside the boundaries of class, gender, and therefore genre.

A few novels mirror the "structure of confrontation" in that they concern the struggle itself, as experienced by characters who are already committed ideologically rather than by those who must be initiated into the Left. When the protagonist is working class or a declassed bourgeoise, the development of class consciousness, leadership ability, and political strategy generally occurs during a strike or in some mass organization. It is the power of history that mobilizes desire (for change) within the working-class female subject. In this sense, such novels differ from Suleiman's "structure," in which the contending ideological positions of the Left are played out in struggle.

When the protagonists emerge from the leftist intellectual circles based in New York, distant from the industrial and agricultural heartlands, another situation develops. Far removed from direct struggle, both physically and psychologically, the fragmented characters do not gain the solidarity (and transformative power) imparted by involvement in struggle. They are in disarray; their narratives often cannot cohere, reflecting the contradiction between the rhetorical collectivity of the movement and the actual alienation of the characters within it. In *The Unpossessed*, increasing separation from themselves and from each other causes the characters individually (and their group collectively) to self-destruct. Rather than leading to a subjectivity constructed through confrontation and struggle, the increasing fragmentation (of character and narrative) signals the impossibility of refashioning identity within the group. These novels, which end in abortion, divorce, attempted suicide, failed psychoanalysis, or disease, pose a dystopian vision of the individual and the possibilities of collectivity and thereby redirect the "structure of confrontation" from its prefigurative vision of change to a repetition of bourgeois familial relations. The different experiences of the collective by the working-class female subject and the female intellectual subject are found within the two predominating plot types: the strike novel of working-class solidarity and the historical novel of middle-class decay.

One might schematize the variations of plot type and subject position just outlined as follows:

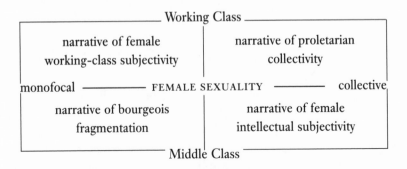

Working Class

| narrative of female working-class subjectivity | narrative of proletarian collectivity |

monofocal ——— FEMALE SEXUALITY ——— collective

| narrative of bourgeois fragmentation | narrative of female intellectual subjectivity |

Middle Class

Roughly, the plots of women's revolutionary novels fall into four oppositional categories. One opposition differentiates the character of a young, uneducated, sensitive working-class girl living in the heartland of American industry or agriculture from another kind of character who is a highly educated, urbane, and middle-class woman. Both in form and content, a manifest difference is apparent in these oppositional groupings. One relies heavily on realism and a monofocal narrative, the other on modernist, discontinuous, multivoiced prose. Yet the latent content is similar: a recognition of the gendered, sexual, politically fragmentary position of the female subject within the class and ideological relations of the family and capitalism and the movements that struggle against them.

Likewise, novels that foreground the development of working-class consciousness can be compared to those novels that delve into the mire of bourgeois family decay. In novels about class solidarity, the environment of the working-class family sets the stage for class consciousness, as does the middle-class family in sagas of bourgeois decay. In both cases, the family and the collective are posed in opposition to the individual. Separate characters emerge from the family and link up with others in the movement created through working-class struggle. Thus the social space of the domestic novel, the family, is replaced by that of the collective as the site where characters are constructed as subjects. Again, the difference in the manifest content masks a similarity in rhetorical and thematic structure. By "de-centering" the text, a collective space is etched out within the bounds of the novel.[44]

Both the fiction of working-class collectivity and the fiction of bourgeois deconstruction attempt to circumvent the construction of the monofocal realist novel formally and rhetorically. Fragmented narratives, which follow a series of protagonists from a variety of points of view, build a collective portrait of "revolutionary élan" in the collective novel. In the novels of deconstruction, alienated characters can only be described through fractured narratives. In either case, individual quests and heterosexual couples have been displaced by fragmented subjectivities or by de-centered collectivities. The fragmented narrative of alienation and the multiple protagonists of class solidarity become a means by which to portray the dismantling of social, economic, and gender hierarchies in ways impossible for the monofocal text. This rhetorical strategy produces gaps through which to glimpse the gender ideology of class, because both the family and sexuality, as much as class, determine sociality for the female subject.

The Singularity of Sexuality

Notwithstanding my four-part typology for reading women's revolutionary fiction as a (sub)genre, enough differences exist—politically, stylistically, thematically, and so forth—to undermine a coherent structure. The differences call into question the validity of grouping all these works together as a genre. But as I have argued, factors other than the "official" politics of either literary radicalism or academic literary history reinforce such a reading. Nina Baym notes that despite the similarity of the "overplot" among the numerous sentimental novels by nineteenth-century American women, the individual texts themselves vary widely.[45] In the case of revolutionary fiction, too, although wide variations divide the texts, key unifying elements link them together.

These "thematic structurations" are produced as much by what is missing from the texts as by what is present. The narrative of class conflict masks its gender presumptions; in effect, gendered class and classed gender are the *non-dit* of the genre. Women's revolutionary fiction raises questions about ideology (particularly gender and class dichotomies) that cannot be answered within the genre, producing gaps and discrepancies among and within the texts. These are primarily located at the site of the female body, which, as I have suggested, signifies plenitude in marked contrast to the hunger-ravaged male working-class body. Within the women's novels, sexuality is called up simultaneously with class consciousness or political activity, each in dialectical relationship to the other. Yet these relationships cannot be fully enunciated and produces fissures within the texts. History can be spoken through the laboring male body of proletarian fiction, just as desire can be spoken through the interiorized female body of domestic fiction, but it is at the intersection of the two narratives that women's revolutionary fiction finds itself. Here, the discourses of female sexuality disrupt the gender oppositions of the proletarian aesthetic and of the domestic ideology, even when sexuality is repressed.

Within women's narratives, sexuality functions as the seedbed of political consciousness. Speaking primarily of the male-authored proletarian novel, Walter Rideout comments that "worker's sexuality is almost always considered in a matter-of-fact way as evidence of healthy vigor." Of course, he is following official pronouncements that gendered the worker as masculine, and so he finds that the "explicit linking of political revolution and sexual freedom rarely appears, as it did in *Daughter of Earth*."[46] When read for the irruptions of female sexuality, however, women's revolutionary novels call into question much of what Rideout reads as "healthy vigor." In a dialectical process, the repression of female sexuality within familial relations precedes an understanding of the oppression of the class system. At the same time, class solidarity necessitates a confrontation with gender ideology and with its repression of female sexuality.

Because the proletariat has been constructed as masculine yet must efface its gender markings to achieve collectivity, female sexuality functions as a means to understand the politics of class consciousness, even as it stands forever in the way of the female subject's complete merger with the working class. This contradiction works its way into the texts in the form of significant "blank pages, gaps, borders, spaces and silence, holes in discourse" within the narrative (which may appear as an awkward moment in an otherwise "rigid" plot, as in *Marching! Marching!*, or fully reconstruct the plot, as in *The Unpossessed*).[47] In either case, the connection of female sexuality to class politics is disruptive of the "virile" grammar of the genre.[48] According to the "political history" of the genre, there is no place for female sexuality; its presence results in de-formations of narrative.

The sexual politics of rape become one channel through which literary radicals could connect narratives of sexuality to class and gender. The occurrence of a rape within narratives that trace the development of working-class solidarity or middle-class decline is a common motif in 1930s literature;

however, the meanings associated with the rape differ widely.[49] For instance, James T. Farrell ends the second volume of his Studs Lonigan trilogy with a rape. Farrell's narrative device is to convey bits of conversation, fragments overheard by a narrator who is one of several drunken men at a New Year's party. The brief rape scene has been anticipated when Weary convinces Irene to leave the dance hall with him and go to the hotel room where his buddies are already drinking. He fantasizes about "brutalized sex" with her. Later, another woman escapes from the bedroom shouting "rape."[50] This scene draws on many cultural fantasies about rape for its meaning: women really want to be raped; they falsely accuse men of rape; they provoke it by lascivious behavior. Irene is raped after she refuses to make love to Weary because she is a virgin, but her resistance has been feeble and ineffectual. He beats her unconscious, rapes her, and then, after she escapes, gets rid of the evidence by soaking the bloody sheets.

The use of the rape within Farrell's novel conforms to the prevailing gendered aesthetic categories that link the bourgeoisie to sexual perversity. Rape encodes the gender polarities of class relations in a neat narrative package. The petit bourgeois male, as an emasculated figure within capitalism, reasserts the power of his body when he actively expresses his violence and anger through sexuality, by beating the resisting female into passive acceptance of her own degradation. Her body metonymically represents the powerless working class prior to its class-conscious development. Studs's subject position as petit bourgeois man is ambiguous: because he—like the working-class woman—possesses neither a fully bourgeois nor proletarian body, his class and gender identities are unclear. The sexual exploitation of the rape becomes a metaphor for his class position.

Locked out of the historic struggle of the proletariat against the bourgeoisie, the petit bourgeois man reenacts the coded behavior of extreme masculinity to dispel his feminized and marginalized position. The final scene in Farrell's third volume, *Judgment Day*, restages this image as Studs's father stands apart from the Communist parade passing through his old neighborhood. Although Paddy Lonigan wants to see this "swarm" of humanity as a "dangerous mob," he cannot help noticing that the mass of people—white and black, Jew and Gentile, worker and student—are "happy." They are moving "forward," while his son lies dying of pneumonia.[51] The metonymic use of the rape in the second volume gives way to the metaphoric use of the mass demonstration in the third. Both are constructed to reveal the disintegration of Studs and his class through figures involving the female body, literally as victim of rape and figuratively as devouring mother. The woman's body is important only for what it reveals about the disintegration of Studs and his class.

The rape that underpins the narrative of *Gathering Storm*, Myra Page's 1932 novel about Gastonia, functions entirely differently. Even though this novel also premises rape as one element of bourgeois male perversity, the narrator's point of view coincides with that of Martha, an African American woman who is a servant for her assailant's family. In this case, rape becomes a constitutive element of (black) female subjectivity within the race, class, and gender relations of the South. By aligning the narrator with the victim, the meaning and function of the rape alter considerably. Martha reads the signs of danger before they appear. Knowing she is vulnerable once she sees her boss's son's car, she tries to hide from view. He and his friend see her even though she escapes into the woods to hide from them. Her first impulse toward self-preservation is subverted when she cries for help. Realizing immediately that she has given herself away, she picks up a branch with which to defend herself. The son's friend, however, has sneaked up behind her and grabs the stick, forcing her down. Sure of their safety, the two rape and murder her. After her death, the narrator shifts point of view to follow the men as they construct an alibi.

Unlike Farrell, Page portrays rape as more than a symbol of class conflict. The rape loses its metonymic and metaphoric qualities as a text about class when it becomes symptomatic of the racial and gender differences inscribed on the body of the working-class black woman. By placing the narrator in tandem with Martha, this scene inverts many of the clichés associated with rape: Martha has already suffered sexual harassment by this boy; he knows she has left for home late and so he plans to rape her; and she fights back. Both Farrell and Page connect rape to the power and violence of class and gender (and race) privilege (or its illusion); however, the mutilation of Martha's body during her rape and murder opens up narrative development, rather than signal its closure. Page ties the politics of rape to white supremacy when Jim, Martha's lover, is lynched for her murder after he attacks the white men to avenge her death. Martha's brother, who has migrated north with the dream of returning to organize an integrated union of mill workers, cannot come back. The African American mill workers' community is dispersed because Martha's family and others are forced out of the company-owned housing by the owner whose son had raped her. Thus the rape scene functions structurally within the narrative to elaborate the political analyses of white chauvinism and male supremacy within the CPUSA. More than merely a symbolic reenactment of bourgeois male degeneracy, rape functions politically as a form of oppression of the working-class (female) body as surely as do low wages (for the male) and, as such, produces its own historical effect, thereby motivating narrative.

Similarly, many novels by women have a scene in which the heroine encounters marital rape (usually, her mother is raped by her father) and vows to avoid sex and marriage. Male sexual power is not exclusively the privilege of privilege. These scenes suggest that female sexuality, as it is constructed within the family under capitalism, is dangerous for women, especially for the young working-class daughter who cannot enter the proletariat as an industrial worker. These marital rapes are overheard in the dark by the young girl. Her position as a passive voyeur (or auditor) marks her as both masochist and sadist—victim and victimizer—because she identifies with both her estranged mother and her violent father. In *Daughter of Earth*, for instance, the daughter's connection to the earth is forged both from an identification with her coalminer father and with her dirt-poor mother. Because sexuality controls the bodies of men and women differently, its textual elaboration creates discontinuities in the genre, punching holes in class solidarity. Sexuality is essential as a metaphor for defining the polarities of the proletarian plot, yet its narrative remains unknowable because it cannot be fully acknowledged as differences among bodies.

The preceding discussion suggests that male writers saw female sexuality—the coding of woman as a desired and desiring body—primarily as a metaphor for class conflict, whereas women built narratives of female class consciousness out of the political relations embedded in sexuality. Sexuality does not just symbolize class virility or malaise as coded within the literary radicals' metaphors of gender; rather, it alters the genre, skewing the narrative of (masculine) proletarian consciousness toward the construction of a differently gendered working class. In effect, the inscription of the female subject through sexuality marks a moment of de-formation within the genre.[52]

In much the same way, the contradictory trope of the maternal—as beast and as nurturer—produces gaps in the conventional narrative of proletarian fraternity. Maternity, as either a positive or negative sign of plenitude, demands a different kind of narrative attention than the hungry (thus deprived) body of the unemployed male worker. This dilemma posed particularly powerful conflicts for the female, (mostly) middle-class authors already closed out by the genre from the labor process by virtue of both class and gender. These authors needed a figure to reshape class and gender relationships so that the body of the working-class woman (or her radical intellectual sister) could appear in narrative. Ironically, they found it in an image of the mother retrieved, though in altered form, from the domestic novel.

The body of the mother appears in a number of contradictory guises in these novels. For example, in many revolutionary novels, the middle-class woman becomes an extension of the state who supervises the lives of the poor through her role as social worker, nurse, or teacher. Often the social worker enters the home of the working-class mother to discover the chaos born of too many children, too much laundry, and not enough food or space. These cramped homes fail to provide a proper domestic environment for the young daughters of the working class, who then become prostitutes to supplement the family income. The working-class mother, mired in dirty rinse water, fails to realize that her inability to mother correctly (that is, like the middle class) has sent her daughter out of the home and onto the streets. It is up to the proper mother-of-the-state, the social worker, to discipline the bodies of both working-class women—the bestial mother and the sexual daughter. Yet her "social work" goes unrecognized as labor because it is an extension of the domestic ideal of the middle-class woman.[53]

Nevertheless, the social worker does perform paid labor; the working-class woman, paradoxically, rarely works outside the home and so appears even more anomalous. Hence the recurrence of birth scenes in women's revolutionary fiction that redefine women's (birthing) labor as productive, even as they describe maternity as horror-filled, a monstrosity. Likewise, the image of the collective as maternal carries within it a subversion of the rhetoric of proletarian fraternity, even as it also represents the masses as an engulfing, devouring monster.[54]

Because sexuality and maternity are the sites of feminine entry into class consciousness yet, at the same time, impede class identification, the narrative structure begins to break down at those locations. For instance, Ishma's search for "the knowledge" that will free her and other working-class women from the tyranny of perpetual pregnancies yet still enable women to engage in heterosexual sex becomes a focal, though unfulfilled, desire of her narrative in *Call Home the Heart* (1932). This long novel uses a narrator and various characters to instruct the reader in the planting and butchering techniques of mountain people and the work and leisure habits of mill hands; whenever contraception is mentioned, however, the text censors itself. Four different times Ishma tries to learn how to control her fertility, but each time the narrator abruptly shifts point of view and the desired "information" is never divulged to the reader.[55]

Significantly, it is the socialist doctor Derry Unthank who provides Ishma's neighbor Genie with "the knowledge" as Ishma listens raptly through the thin walls. Then Genie's husband discusses it with Ishma's lover, Rad. Women's reproductive freedom becomes commodified as "the knowledge," which is translated through the male voice. The discourse of science supersedes all others, yet regarding female sexuality, as opposed to class relations, Dr. Unthank cannot spell out theories of sexual practice as he can the theories of socialist practice. As the repository of "knowledge," he reins in and controls Ishma's body and her narrative. The series of silences about contraception occur exactly at the moments when the female characters begin to ask questions about their sexuality, threatening class solidarity with their men. These silences are emblematic of the gaps within the types of women's revolutionary fiction that most closely follow proletarian realism. They pose a risk to the genre, potentially shifting it from a class conscious (but ungendered, and therefore masculine) polemic into the degraded position of a feminist (but unclassed, and therefore bourgeois) literature. Too much emphasis on the body and its psychosexual elaboration within history raises the possibility of writing "melodrama" or indulging in "art for art's sake." Because that sexual body is a woman's, its narrative defies Gold's prescriptions for proletarian realism.[56]

Despite these divergences, the revolutionary fiction of the 1930s is best read as a genre, best understood as a system of variations on a set of plots and conventions that both mask and reveal ideology as the individual texts revise generic codes. I have argued that, as systems for categorizing literature, both genre and classification are related to the formations of gender and class; each is likewise embedded in the other. In the case of revolutionary literature, a generic approach enables the reader of women's fiction to discover formal, thematic, and structural strategies for narrating the classed female subject. Gender was implicated in this genre (as in all others, according to Derrida) even when it was not meant to be. Because the metaphors of gender prescribed the boundaries of the genre, women's texts necessarily became "anomalous" and stepped out of line as "renegades."[57] Within the genre of 1930s revolutionary fiction, women's voices distorted the outlines of the virile proletarian figure by attempting to narrate a classed female subject. This deformation gave women's revolutionary bodies and texts their "structural formulation" of "dis-ease," of difference.[58]

The latent content of these works located female subjectivity as the site where sexuality, class, gender, and language met, came into conflict, and realigned within the narratives. For example, read in isolation, Tess Slesinger's novel *The Unpossessed* was labeled a "curiosity." Read in the context of other 1930s revolutionary novels by women, however, it appears emblematic, voicing within its narrative all of the crucial disruptions perpetrated by the female body within the genre. A "doctrinal" novel like Clara Weatherwax's *Marching! Marching!* appears even more quirky when read for the markings of gender on the classed bodies of its text.[59] In short, genre analysis can be a method for reading theory in literature, history in ideology, and gender in class or for locating multivalent differences within a historical moment and among bodies and texts.

Literary radicals of the 1930s hailed the revolutionary novel as a genre that would overcome the differences between history and narrative, between deed and word. These novels skirt the edges of genre, moving between factual accounts of reportage and fictional forms of realism and modernism; nonetheless, they are trapped within a historical moment as they attempt to elaborate and transform it. History, formed by the actions of the proletariat, takes on the attributes of masculinity, whereas narrative, written by bourgeois intellectuals, appears feminine. Literary radicals attempted to overcome the gender inscriptions dividing history from narrative and workers from intellectuals by insisting that the writing itself could manifest attributes of masculinity—the (proletarian) text could act as historical agent. By blurring genre distinctions, revolutionary writing in effect blurred gender and class distinctions. The critical prescriptions for revolutionary literature that were elaborated by literary radicals sought to reclaim it from its "minor" status by insisting on a "vigorous" style that would erase all traces of "the 'nice and waterish' diet of emasculated bourgeois writing."[60]

For the (male) literary radicals of the 1930s, sexual differences, read as markings on the body of the (male) worker (and his literary interpreter), provided the signs of class divisions. By deploying various metaphors of gender, literary radicals could evoke the narrative of sexual difference to engender classes, thereby avoiding recognition of the more problematic differences within either genders or classes. The markings of sexuality and labor inscribed both class and gender differences, de-forming body and text; however, they did so differently for workers and intellectuals, for men and women. The differently inscribed body that marked the female working-class subject was one revealed not only through the etchings of labor and hunger, as in the case of working-class men and their children, but also, like that of her middle-class sister, through markings of sexuality and maternity. This difference threatened the homologous relationship between masculinity and the working class encoded in the "grammar" of proletarian literature and fractured generic cohesion by revealing differences within both the working class and women.[61]

The emergence of the mass movement as a new literary protagonist—one that was neither the individual nor the couple—required a different "ending" than that found in nineteenth-century realist fiction because the creation of mass movements marked the beginning of a historical change that could not be contained within this conventional plot (much as the marriage that caps the nineteenth-century plot marked the beginning of a nuclear family, which exceeded the boundaries of romantic thralldom). The movement from "working stiff" to proletarian or from bourgeois intellectual to revolutionary writer implied a shift from a feminized position to masculinity; but the collectivity of the mass movement ultimately erased all gender (also racial, ethnic, age, and even class) differences as it swept its participants into the river of history.

Male literary radicals glossed over this contradiction by appealing to a conventionalized narrative of gender relations to describe their ambiguous class position. According to Jurij Lotman, in all narratives an always male hero passes through an always female topos, sometimes conquering it, sometimes succumbing to it. Teresa de Lauretis argues that Lotman's gendered and spatial model of narrative is a fundamentally sadistic one that structures dominance and subordination into its plot.[62] Certainly the narrative constructed by (male) literary radicals about themselves and their work conforms to Lotman's model. Female literary radicals of the 1930s occupied an even more estranged position: as intellectuals and women, they were marginalized within the Left, yet they were cut off from the traditions of feminism if they wrote about class conflict. In order to begin articulating a classed female subjectivity, women's literary radicalism necessarily reconstructed the gender/class nexus to accommodate both the narrative of history (located in the laboring and hungry body) and the narrative of desire (located in the sexual and maternal body). This dual narrative, built on the marginalized narrative fragments of maternity and sexuality and of labor and hunger, revised (or disrupted) the revolutionary novel. In so doing, it theorized female class-conscious desire of, for, and in history, rupturing the gender polarities of 1930s literary radicalism and its nineteenth-century antecedent, domestic fiction.

The Great Mother

Female Working-Class Subjectivity

3

Female subjectivity, constructed at the intersections of race, gender, sexuality, and class, demands a variety of narratives in order, for instance, to detail the differences between a working-class woman and a committed woman intellectual. Three novels of the 1930s—*Marching! Marching!*, *The Girl*, and *Yonnondio*—represent variations within the generic typologies outlined in Chapter 2.[1] In Clara Weatherwax's *Marching! Marching!*, the narrative of desire remains secondary to the narrative of history. In *The Girl*, Meridel LeSueur recasts the narrative of desire into the narrative of history. Where Weatherwax follows convention and constructs the proletariat as masculine, LeSueur attempts to undercut the gender ideology embedded within those generic conventions by locating female working-class historicity in women's (re)productive bodies rather than in the markings of labor on male bodies. The divergent narrative impulses apparent in *Marching! Marching!* are finally combined into a single narrative that inscribes female desire within history through a re-presentation of the masses as the maternal body. Through this identification of the masses with the maternal, *Marching! Marching!* locates desire metaphorically. *The Girl*, on the other hand, actually fixes the source of class consciousness within the maternal body of the desiring woman. Female subjectivity irrupts into the strike narrative in *Marching! Marching!*, but in *The Girl*, it produces mass action. By contrast, *Yonnondio* unites the masculine narrative of history and the feminine narrative of desire in the working-class nuclear family. In this novel, the female subject is narrated through a maternal language that holds the possibility of historicity even as it more often confines desire.

Looked at together, these three novels begin to outline for us the difficult task of theorizing the mutual embeddedness of class and gender within culture. By revising the proletarian plot to speak of female desire, each develops a means of narrating that elusive configuration: the working-class woman. But that very project demands the reworking of gender metaphors that inscribe class, and thus the resulting narratives become increasingly opaque as metaphors of gender and production generate metaphors of class and reproduction in multivalent ways. *Marching! Marching!* might be read as an archetype of the proletarian novel; for differing reasons, both *The Girl* and *Yonnondio* appear as anomalies. What made *Yonnondio* and *The Girl* unreadable (and kept them unpublished) in the 1930s, whereas today they are part of our emerging feminist canon? What makes *Marching! Marching!* unreadable today, despite its prominence during the 1930s as a prize-winning novel later chosen as a selection by the Book Union? For both their deviations from and their conformity to the genre's codes, all three books merit close textual attention. As much genre theory tells us, textual variations can outstrip generic categories, only to be recuperated within them. My study, then, like the novels themselves and the theories they produce, is fraught with contradictions. Nevertheless, reading women's novels of the 1930s will provide sources for reinventing the gendered history of literary radicalism.[2]

Clara Weatherwax's *Marching! Marching!* comes as close to a "doctrinal" proletarian novel as possible.[3] It has been read as such by both contemporary and subsequent critics because of its status as winner of the 1935 *New Masses* prize for a new novel on a proletarian theme. Despite its apparent conformity, however, it presents a fascinating example of just how disruptive the female subject is of the narrative of proletarian masculinity. This novel constructs the working class overwhelmingly as male and masculine. Replete with clichés about vampirish bosses and virile workers, its basic plot follows predictable patterns for the construction of proletarian collectivity by tracing how the marks of labor and hunger on the bodies of (male) workers transform their (class) consciousness.[4] The intrusion of female characters, however, reroutes the trajectory of the narrative in various ways, because women's bodies encode sexuality and maternity into a secondary narrative irruptive of the narrative of history.

The transformation of those narrative objects of high realism, the workers, into subjects anchors them to their masculinity and reinscribes hierarchies within the narrative. This generic resolution prescribed by male writers and critics during the 1930s proved as fraught with contradictions for the female author as the effacement of the working class in the bourgeois realist novel had been for working-class authors. Alan Calmer noted, in his announcement of the winner of the *New Masses* prize, that although *Marching! Marching!* was submitted under a masculine pseudonym, it was "easy to spot it as the work of a woman writer, for the book possessed a feminine quality."[5] Exactly what constituted that "feminine quality" Calmer fails to disclose.

If femininity irrupts into the masculine plot of *Marching! Marching!*, acting as its unconscious, Meridel LeSueur's *The Girl*, written at the end of the Depression decade, consciously constructs a narrative of working-class female subjectivity by feminizing the proletarian novel. *The Girl* was rejected by publishers in 1939, and it remained unpublished as a novel until the 1970s, although excerpts appeared in various radical journals such as the *Anvil* throughout the decade. LeSueur's interest in the female experience marked much of her fiction and reportage. By asserting the power of the feminine and the maternal, she revised the narrative of proletarian realism to accommodate female history. In *The Girl*, female working-class subjectivity is forged within the structures of male domination. Heterosexuality and maternity alter the body (and so the discourse) of the working-class woman more profoundly than labor or hunger, producing a different story than that told by male proletarian writers and critics; yet the trajectory of the narrative follows a predictable path. For this reason, even as it revises the gender conventions of the genre, LeSueur's novel displays its narrative conventions.

Like *The Girl*, Tillie Olsen's *Yonnondio* was also not published in full until the 1970s; the first section, though, did appear as a short piece of fiction in *Partisan Review*.[6] Olsen's novel presents a variation on the generative text *Daughter of Earth*, wherein female working-class subjectivity is constructed out of the memory of childhood experiences. Gender restrictions, poverty, and sexual vulnerability mark the points of development for the young working-class female subject. Her consciousness is elaborated within a network of social and familial ties that bind individual subjectivity to psychic, social, and economic formations. Thus the novel becomes more than the tale of a young girl's coming of age. Its ever-shifting narrator relocates subjectivity outside of the seemingly unified individual and disperses the subject within the fields of historical forces, social constraints, and familial relationships. *Yonnondio* presents the complications of gender and class that the working-class female subject poses for realism. By locating the narrative within the working-class family, Olsen avoids the objectification of the working class so typical of nineteenth-century realism; by embodying the female voice, she undermines the inscriptions of masculinity on the proletariat that typically constitute its subjectivity. Thus the fragmentary and disruptive elements of the novel mirror its position within the genre of revolutionary fiction, subverting the neat equation that called for the reinscription of the working class in literature through its masculine construction. Multiple oppressions and alienations result in other subject positions, though these fragmentations perhaps explain Olsen's inability to bring the novel to fruition during the 1930s.[7]

To varying degrees, depending on how self-consciously the inscription of female subjectivity controls each narrative, sexual difference disrupts the picture of the proletariat painted by male authors and critics. The collectivity envisioned foregrounds maternal bonds over the fraternal connections of working-class solidarity. In *Marching! Marching!*, for instance, Annie's raised fist mobilizes the masses, first marking them as feminized and only then giving way to a collectivity unmarked by differences. The chronotope of female genealogy, rather than the fraternity of working men's spaces, becomes the source for an elaboration of female proletarian subjectivity.[8] Gender marks the proletarian woman differently, as does labor. This difference revises generic codes in women's proletarian novels and structures collectivity as maternal.

Marching! Marching!:
The Double Alienation of Labor and Desire

Clara Weatherwax's 1935 novel stands as an icon of American proletcult for critics of literary radicalism; as such, it occupies an interesting space in the debates about the 1930s. On the one hand, it is routinely dismissed as a stunning compilation of the worst traits of tendentious literature. On the other, even those who blast the novel feel compelled to address it because its publication marked such a crucial turning point in the aesthetic formulations of the decade.[9] Although clearly influenced by Third Period prescriptions, the novel seems to have been chosen from the more than ninety manuscripts submitted for the *New Masses* prize because it hints at the changes in Party line that would characterize the coming Popular Front era. Weatherwax was undoubtedly chosen as an example of a middle-class author whose work conformed to the doctrine of the Third Period but who could appeal to a wider audience. The New Deal, the bourgeois press, the legal system, and intellectuals are all ridiculed in the novel, mirroring the Party's valorization of militant working-class struggle during the early 1930s. At the same time, the declassed petit bourgeois Granny Whittle realizes, even before Earl Browder's 1936 presidential campaign slogan declared it, that "Communism is Americanism," anticipating the Party's goal of making itself (and its novels) seem safe (208).

Marching! Marching! uses the Aberdeen, Washington, strikes as its subject. According to Walter Rideout, the strikes at Aberdeen and at Gastonia, North Carolina, were used as models for many proletarian novels because they represented textbook examples of 1930s labor struggles. In Aberdeen, for example, according to Robert Cantwell, "class lines [were] firmly drawn," with the company, company unions, AFL unions, rank-and-file industrial unions, and the CPUSA all in heated contention.[10] However, unlike the cotton-mill strikes in North Carolina, which resulted in defeat for the Communist-led unions, the Aberdeen strikers in the lumber and shipping industries successfully organized and installed militant industrial unions. Despite the divisive influences of company towns, racial animosity, and high unemployment, the strikes were successful.[11]

Furthermore, the strike novel provided an excellent plot form for the elaboration of Communist ideology in literature. Rideout argues that the Gastonia strike worked particularly well as a model because it was bloody; it preceded the Depression, foreshadowing the new militancy of workers during the 1930s; and it failed. A doctrine that predicted the imminence of revolution precluded a resolution within the strike novel. The strike may fail, but history is still an open book; conversely, the strike may succeed, but capitalism remains firmly in place. Although the Aberdeen strike was successful, the novels about it end inconclusively or in failure. In such matters, Rideout argues, the logic of the Party's doctrine superseded reality, and from this he infers the power of the Party's cultural dictates over writers. Yet one could also read these negative or unresolved endings, as Alan Calmer did, as an "imaginative re-creation" of lived history into fictional form, indicating both the difficulty of narrating historical "fact" and the fictional quality of political doctrine.[12] As Louis Althusser later asserted, "History is a process without a telos or a subject." A novel ending with the defeat of the strikers might serve to spur others on to greater efforts; such an ending also offers the possibility of undermining the closed narrative of Party doctrine through rhetorical allusions to an undetermined future history.

Despite its formal disruptions, *Marching! Marching!* self-consciously displays itself as an embodiment of Hicks's and Gold's formulas for writing collective, proletarian, revolutionary fiction.[13] It blurs the 1930s critical distinction between propaganda and art. Furthermore, it blurs generic codes by mobilizing modernist narrative techniques within the proletarian realist plot. Ironically, the economistic and positivistic Marxist criticism of 1930s literary radicals led writers to experiment with literary form even as their critics were calling for a transparent realism.[14] The novel's quintessentially masculine discourse of class solidarity is strangely derailed by its "masochistic, invertedly sentimental" narrative of feminine desire. Mary McCarthy declared *Marching! Marching!* to be the "most neurotic novel of 1935," contrasting the "man-size vigorous strides toward the creation of a proletarian hero and a proletarian epic" taken by John Dos Passos, Jack Conroy, and Robert Cantwell to Weatherwax's "pinched, unhealthy, distorted . . . picture of American proletarian life."[15] I believe that *Marching! Marching!*, as both a typical and an aberrant text of women's proletarian fiction, merits a close reading into the ways that femininity trespasses the borders of the genre.

Women's bodies encode sexuality and maternity into a "secondary zone" of narrative.[16] Female sexuality deflects the narrative by recoding the gender markings of the proletariat. If, as Cora Kaplan notes, sexuality functions as the synecdoche of female subjectivity within the novel, then female desire reroutes the trajectory of history's narrative. Because female subjectivity cannot be fully elaborated within the proletarian plot, the irruption of desire contributes to *Marching! Marching!*'s fissured and fragmented form. This discourse of feminine desire often conflicts with the novel's primary plot of masculine labor that follows the development of a lumberworkers' strike through several decisive incidents.

Briefly, the plot is this: Pete, supposedly the "bastard son" of Mr. Bayliss, the mill owner, observes an industrial accident that decapitates Tim, the brother of one of the white union organizers. Pete later discovers he is actually the illegitimate son of a militant union man, long dead, and reveals to his coworkers that he has been hired by Bayliss to spy on Mario, the leader of the Filipino workers known as the "Down-and-Outers"; he then joins the union. Mario is ambushed by goons, and Toivo, an elderly Finnish newspaper deliverer, commits suicide after being fired. The workers strengthen their resolve, finally coming together in a mass movement for a strike. These events are narrated through the interior monologues of (mostly female) characters and by occasional forays into the saloon that serves as an unofficial union hall, where the reader overhears fragments of male workers' speech. The strike itself eludes narration; history exceeds narrative boundaries and produces a form of textual dialogism on the printed page. Instead, the strike is chronicled by juxtaposing two columns of newspaper clippings, handbills, and leaflets: on the left are excerpts from the bourgeois press, the church, and the chamber of commerce; on the right, articles from the workers' press and reproductions of strikers' handbills and leaflets. The strike leadership ends up in the hospital or in jail, and so, in the penultimate chapter, the narrator shifts focus. Discovering two hungry boys roaming the alleys of Aberdeen, the narrator follows them to a spontaneously organized demonstration in protest of the arrests and beatings. At this moment "we" enter the narrative, brought directly among the masses to march and sing collectively with them.

The typographic experimentation briefly distances both narrator and reader from the strike plot, indirectly pointing our attention to the problematic relationship of narrative to history. By providing traces of documentary evidence for the strike, the novel both confirms its facticity and undermines its narrative coherence. The "interruption" of current events into the narrative, like the interruptions in the cycles of capitalism noted by Marx in volume two of *Capital*, produces another break in narrative sequence. The Real, in the form of "documents," is brought into the fiction only to highlight its unreality. Robert Cantwell notes that a "melodramatic" reliance on "communist magicians" to promulgate the correct line comes into conflict with the novel's obsessively "keen eye for minute, atomized detail."[17] These details provide local color as they carefully differentiate among the kinds of work edgermen, trimmers, and doggers do and the diverse populations of Finns, Filipinos, Quinalt Indians, and southern whites who fill these jobs.

Lukács disparages naturalism for producing sensory data in a tableau for the reader.[18] Weatherwax floods the senses by revealing the sights, sounds, tastes, and smells of a harbor town seething with sawmills, papermills, a whaling station, and lumber camps. Aberdeen stinks, and *Marching! Marching!* is truly a smelly book. Its readers enter the grotesque world of the working class as if it were a corpse whose rank odors simultaneously cannot be avoided, impregnating all who enter it, and yet differentiate the readers from the subject. The novel's obsession with smells serves a dual function: as a naturalistic device, it attempts to provoke a gut reaction in its audience; yet signs everywhere remind the reader that this is a world apart. Like the grotesque or mass body described in Bakhtin's reading of carnival, the working class invites transgression because it cannot contain itself within defined boundaries. So, too, *Marching! Marching!* exceeds realist bounds.

Other devices further signal the novel's differences from high realism. Weatherwax employs an idiosyncratic and quirky syntax. She avoids punctuation; writing in a quasi-stream-of-consciousness mode, she elaborates the inner thoughts of her characters through modernist techniques. Virtually every detail of working life within the lumber mill and its surrounding town is described in flat, monotonic prose. The gory details of numerous industrial accidents, like the smelly bedrooms of the workers, signal the proletariat's distance from the reader and the text's distance from high realism. Like a textbook example of the dual ideological errors that Lukács condemns as nonrealist fiction—modernism and naturalism—*Marching! Marching!* moves between the two styles, avoiding high realism in its struggle to present an ongoing historical moment in fiction.

Periodically, the narrative is interrupted by chapters entitled:

NICK'S PLACE

BEER

Cigars   obacco

ick Paleopolis, Prop.

By reproducing the "sign" of the tavern, these chapters position the reader amidst a group of men drinking and discussing the day's work—a common device in Soviet proletarian literature of the late 1920s. As events leading up to the strike unfold, the men rehash the narrative at the bar. The reader is invited to listen but not participate in the talk. Like Granny Whittle, the declassed petit bourgeois, s/he overhears fragments of conversations at the workers' mass meeting and longs to "catch all they know, and piece the bits together like a patchwork quilt" (181). The petit bourgeois desire to cover over rupture is later experienced by Granny Whittle when she listens to a piano concert by an avant-garde musician. His "intervals dont sound right" to her, yet the workers respond to the music like "a battlefield . . . like all us longshoremen marching" (196–97). The collective portrait of this community eludes middle-class ears, which are tuned to harmony, not dissonance—that is, to identify (with) bourgeois ideology, not class struggle. All of these contradictory devices indicate that even the most doctrinal proletarian novel resisted the ideological closure of the realist text. The pulls of narrative closure (of social realism) and utopian promise (of Marxism) are reproduced within the dual inscriptions of labor and desire within the novel. The typographic, stylistic, and narrative experimentation distances the narrator from the subjects of the novel, the characters and their stories, thereby setting up the final confrontation between the masses and the National Guard at the plant gate, in which narrator and reader merge with the strikers, trading the subject and telos of narrative for the open text of history.

The Words of Work/The Work of Words

In language brimming with tough-sounding slang and violent imagery, *Marching! Marching!* recreates the masculine spaces of working-class bars, lumber camps, and union halls. The excessive violence of the workplace dismembers and disfigures the workers, whose labor inscribes their bodies with deformities as the inscriptions of the labor process further de-form the realist narrative. Because the bulk of the novel concerns the events leading up to it, the strike itself is almost anticlimactic. Weatherwax's emphasis on the degradations and horrors of working-class experience does not easily accommodate the inclusion of proletarian struggle. Despite the scenes of devoted hours spent by many characters working for the union and sycophantic tributes to the organizers, little can be found in this novel to explain the transition from oppression to struggle other than the relentless horrors of work.[19]

Marching! Marching! does not just provide the reader with a full panorama of the various jobs involved in logging and sawyer work; details of paper making, strawberry box making, veneer working, clam digging, and dock-working as well as accounts of the Japanese whaling and British coal-mining industries fill out the novel. Each description follows Gold's prescriptions, elaborating the complex process of manufacturing by focusing on isolated jobs performed by individual workers. Unable to read the "signs" of labor's inscriptions, Granny Whittle wonders how she might reproduce the "patchwork quilt" of the workers' collective knowledge as she ponders how one worker "got his ear squashed that way." This man, as every worker knew, "was Harry, the boom man" who worked the log pond, the space around the chute funneling timber to the mill. There sawyers, boommen, edgermen, markers, sorters, and drivers, along with their numerous helpers, turned logs into lumber, consequently running "risks of smashed feet, cuts, falls, sawed fingers, drowning, ruptures, and accidental death" (187).

The mundane repetitiveness of the jobs is recreated in the flat, affectless tone of the description, yet the picture is aestheticized through Granny's vision of the patchwork quilt (a phenomenon that Tillie Olsen criticizes in *Yonnondio*). Work is also made to seem brutal by references to industrial accidents. By midway through the novel, the reader has already been provided with graphic depictions of decapitations, dismemberments, paralysis, and a variety of other industrial accidents, so that mention of the squashed ear recalls other grizzly images and links the laboring body to the grotesque body of the masses.

The hysterical diction (squashed heads, water-filled crania, burst intestines) that accompanies the details of industrial terror contrasts with the matter-of-fact descriptions of labor; it becomes a rhetorical device for focusing on the dehumanization of work. Workers are "people marked by labor" (33). With "each man stamped with signs of his labor," the practiced eye could pick out the various occupations of the patrons of Nick's Place (27). Mario can speak to the Japanese whalers through sand drawings because, as a former whaler himself, he recognizes the "signs" of their work and they speak the universal language of class struggle—"strike" (111). When two clamdiggers compare their "chapped, cracked hands" after viewing an aerial photograph depicting thousands of diggers, they too discover their isolated labor as an "industry" (157). When Steve, a friend of Pete's, comes to the mass meeting to play his new revolutionary music, the workers cannot believe he has been to college. He does not resemble the "pap-suckers" who are "not men enough" to take action but are "fellows in love with mellow words" (32); he "didn't look as if he'd ever seen the inside of a college" (195). Unlike the "labor faker" from the AFL, who is "dressed in what looked like simple working clothes, but they sat on him like a disguise" (200), Steve carries the markers of the proletariat. He beats the keys of his piano as if he were a "woods man" who approaches the piano as a "great machine" (195).

Descriptions of work dominate the narrative, sometimes interrupting the plot as various workers recall jobs they have had or as the narrator strays from one workplace to another. But the workers themselves are effaced, merely human extensions of the labor process. By undermining narrative coherence, Weatherwax rhetorically achieves a sense of the alienation of labor under capitalism theorized by Marx and Engels. The workers' bodies are deterritorialized, only to be reterritorialized within the machines of labor. So too is narrative deterritorialized away from realism, only to be reterritorialized through the incessant Party doctrine that infuses the novel's form.

Like the male workers, whose bodies are inscribed by their labor, the enemies of the proletariat are read through the inscriptions of their class on their bodies. The novel's most clichéd language is reserved for the lumber baron—"old vampire Bayliss sucking the blood of his workers and smoking his lousy cigars"—and the police who function as his "harness bulls" (11, 141). The university professor is a "squarehead," straddling the fence of "objectivity," who is "tangled up in a mass of theories" (227). The reporter lacks "guts" (39). These caricatures of the middle class, like the excesses of language describing industrial workers, further destabilize the realistic effect. It becomes equally difficult to read the clippings from either the bourgeois press, filled with lies that the narrative contradicts, or the workers' press, filled with repetitious clichés found within the narrative.

In *Marching! Marching!*, Nick's Place and the men's talk that circulates there provide a form of resistance to the mill's domination. Among the men who gather there nightly to retell the day's events, a culture of resistance is slowly developed. In these intermediary chapters, Weatherwax is able to express the growing political awareness of the men in the community through the fragmentary phrases each worker contributes. Over the course of the narrative, Charlie, the British worker who most clearly articulates the Party line, debates with an old Wobbly about sabotage, terrorism, and the use of discipline within the working-class movement. He gains supporters, and the anarchic anger of the workers coalesces into a unified position—strike. Sensing the power of the bar as a barometer of class solidarity, the police close down Nick's Place after a fight breaks out at the plant gates of the veneer shop.

Inscriptions of femininity occur at the margins of the narrative because the female characters live on the margins of their class. They rework the remnants of both bourgeois and working-class culture: Granny Whittle makes quilts from scraps of cloth she collects; as paperworkers, Mary and Annie recycle the sawdust from the mill; Rosa, a domestic, remakes other people's beds; Lorrie and the other prostitutes restore the sexual economy peripheral to the factory (but central to the arrangements of capitalism); and Mom sits mutely remembering earlier failed struggles. Their bodies are only partially shaped by their labor; for them, pregnancy and sexuality transform the markings of labor. Their desire is both essential and disruptive to the working class and its narrative; they are the glue that periodically comes unstuck.

These female characters create the ambience for narrative desire, whether romantic, erotic, or maternal. Yet that very narrative formula interrupts the masculine plot of the strike elaborated through the details of workers at their jobs and the key moments of strife. Lorrie's position on the edge of the dual narrative means that she is pivotal but extremely vulnerable. As such she feels safe to reveal what she knows about Mario's attacker only to another silenced woman. The romance between Joe and Mary, like Lorrie's revelation about Mario's attacker, both impedes and supports the strike narrative. Joe and Mary have a perpetually frustrated sexual relationship that is enacted fleetingly over mimeograph machines, before meetings, and during the endless treks from one to the other; their "reproduction" is limited to text. Their conversations are rarely about personal issues; instead, they discuss strategy or political theory together. When they do give way to emotion, their feelings are expressed through anger at the ways workers are exploited. During one intimate moment, after Joe has kissed Mary and they are lying together in the grass, he begins to undress her only to be interrupted by Silly, who waves the bloodied hammer used to attack Mario. The discovery of this evidence deflects the interlude of erotic desire back to the strike narrative.

If the men's speech circulates freely within the masculine spaces of lumber camp, union hall, and saloon, the women's speech inheres within interiors. Women's unspoken desires threaten to disrupt the novel. When Lorrie speaks to Mom, revealing the identity of Mario's attacker, she becomes a "talking machine" (136). Rather than the machine speaking publicly to the workers through its inscription on the body of a worker, Lorrie, the talking machine, speaks only in a contained space—to the mute Mom. Annie longs for Mary's lover, seething with rage at her cruel father and demented brother, but she keeps her thoughts to herself. Granny narrates through an interior monologue. Female characters seem to stand merely as mute symbols of capitalism's double exploitation of the labor power and domestic work of women. Even when women do speak in public, as do the wives of two brutalized workers (one a suicide and the other a victim of company thugs), their speech is modulated through the voices and words of men. At a mass meeting, Toivo's widow Hanna speaks in Finnish through a male translator, and Mario's wife Rosa repeats the words she transcribed from her husband's speech. The image of suffering and silenced women is a familiar one to the readers of fiction, and its effect reminds the rapt Granny Whittle of the "vivid," "warm," "bright" memories of church suppers she attended during her childhood (175–77).

The figure of Mom—mute, crippled, maternal—proves pivotal to the narrative and, as we shall see, to the genre. Sitting quietly in her rocker, a fixture in the community who observes the street scenes below her window, Mom and her incessant rocking become signs of normalcy in an otherwise depraved environment. The rocking both invites the speech of others and becomes a code for the developing underground of militant workers, setting up the later rhythm of marching feet that will close the novel. Through the codes of her rocking, Mom "tells" Mary to move the mimeograph machine to Charlie's houseboat, lulls Lorrie into disclosing her "secret," and alerts the strikers to the cops' impending bust.

Mary, too, is marked differently as a worker by her femininity. Unlike the men, she is not wholly defined through her work. She, too, outlines her job— at one point discussing the speedup—and works valiantly for the union; but as Joe's lover and as her mother's caretaker (and decipherer), she participates in an economy of sexuality and maternity outside of the productive economy of lumbering. Annie, one of Mary's coworkers and also an activist, is responsible for the care of her alcoholic and abusive father and her retarded brother Silly. Depressed and frustrated, she simmers with hostility at the forces that have thwarted her desire. Disgusted by Silly's stench, she lashes out violently at him, as her father does to her. She fantasizes about making love to Joe after Mary is beaten and arrested; however, she heroically sneaks out to Granny, sending her to care for Mom while she visits the jail to find Mary. When she is unsuccessful, she arranges to see Joe in his cell to tell him about Mary. Although her desire for Joe threatens the workers' solidarity, the movement by now has become a larger force and Annie sacrifices her erotic desire for the strike, ultimately becoming its most visible sign.

Lorrie, the prostitute, is in a pivotal position to mediate the two alienations—the secondary economy of women's desire and the primary one of men's labor. Not only is her occupation unorganized (she suggests that Mary come down to the brothel and organize the girls), but she must submit sexually as well as economically to the power of the bourgeoisie. Yet as she remarks, every man eventually comes to her, and because they usually reveal themselves to be incompetent lovers and boastful, corrupt businessmen, Lorrie also possesses power. Because of this, Lorrie holds the key information about Mario's beating. The "strange" talk she pours out to Mom about Bayliss's plot—to get rid of Mario using a disgruntled worker and then stage it as a lover's quarrel between him and another Filipino worker—is the kind of information that both the men and the women, in their separate spheres of alienation, can never fathom (135). The silence and thwarted sexuality that characterize the women's relationship to the masculine space of labor and its discourse of politics disrupts but also propels the strike narrative.

Granny Whittle's internal monologue becomes the second narrator, who voices the thoughts of a class-conscious convert from the bourgeoisie. When she first enters the Worker's Center for the mass meeting called to organize the strike after Toivo's suicide and Mario's beating, Granny's attention wanders over the crowd, picking up pieces of the talk and mixing them with her own thoughts. In this way, the narrator and Granny can clarify the political line of the Party as well as re-create for the reader the transition from observer to participant. When Granny rises with the masses to sing the "Internationale," she too is swept up into this sea of "sound pouring from the many throats" and is surrounded by "a forest of fists raised" (208). The effect of the masses' becoming identified with a natural element, the forest, after they have already "felt like eagles, seeing everything spread out plain" is to overdetermine their inevitable rise to power (204). In this preview of the final conflict that ends the novel, the individual bodies who listen to the speeches (and are observed by Granny) are transformed into a mass body—one that sings rather than speaks or listens and whose power sweeps all along with it. Thus Granny rises and sings "Arise, Ye prisoners . . ." too, even though she does not know the words because she has previously thought this song was the Finnish national anthem.

For Granny, the Party in its Popular Front form represents little more than a reenactment of her girlhood in New England among the American traditions of church suppers and patchwork quilts. Her reading of Party literature includes quotations by Lincoln and Jefferson, and she comes to associate the workers' struggle with the American Revolution. Like the author, whose biographical blurb stresses that she too "stems from pre-Mayflower New England stock" (n.p.), Granny, who could have worn ten bars in the Daughters of the American Revolution, reminds the reader of the patriotic nature of struggle. The character of Granny seems to indicate that this novel of the working class was intended for the petite bourgeoisie of Middle America. The emphasis on descriptions of the labor process—especially on the horrors of industrial accidents—also seems to indicate a desire to educate those who are not working class about the world of work in nonunionized industry.

Thus, pages and pages are filled with exhaustive details about cutting and marking lumber, killing and rendering whales for blubber, milling veneer, and on and on. The incantation of chores required of domestic workers— "cleaning, sweeping, dusting, cooking, all kinds of housework, looking after the children, the dog, cat, birds, anything they got" (194)—suggests a rhetorical device that translates work into words. In Weatherwax's novel, there is no room for anything other than a workplace plagued by the relentless specters of industrial accidents, company thugs, and police brutality. Workers have no personal lives. Their homes are invaded by the foul odors of rotten food, filthy sheets, and untended wounds. They have no language save for the markings of their labor on their faces and bodies and hands; but if those markings of masculinity must be established for them to become a unified class, the proletariat, they must be shed finally among the masses. As the narrator inscribes work through words, the narrative itself becomes a work of words and recreates within the reader the translation between the two inscriptions, preparing for the transformation that collective action and united song will effect upon narrative, character, and reader.

By the penultimate chapter, all of the characters have dropped out of the narrative. The narrator returns to the classic Depression image of hunger by locating two boys scavenging through the garbage outside a posh restaurant and then follows them through the streets to a demonstration in support of their father, who is to be executed for armed robbery. With Joe and Mary in jail, Lorrie silenced, and Annie committed to the mass movement, the narrative of sexual desire is completely erased. In a quick cross-cut, the cops rally the support of the National Guard against the coming mass picket at the mill. Thus the two classes—the hungry strikers and the bosses' beefy "harness bulls"—stand poised for the "final conflict."

The final chapter shifts point of view and narrative voice. A first-person plural narrator—we—takes over the story, bringing the reader among "us," who march toward the mill gates. This intimacy with the workers' space is a different experience from previous scenes in Nick's Place. There, the reader overheard and observed; here, the reader participates and merges with the text. The voices and marching feet of the masses take over the cadence of the narrative as a repetitive incantation using the word "marching" merges into the slogans, chants, and finally an old labor song, "Hold the Fort." This suicidal march into the flashing bayonets of the National Guard rejects closure, insisting on an oceanic vision of merger and solidarity among the nameless, faceless, and unmarked masses. Voices and feet "find a common rhythm . . . and the ranks flow smoothly forward with the force of a river. . . . We hear only the sound of our own feet," marching endlessly (254–55).

Like nature and feminine desire, history becomes a force that cannot be contained in proletarian narrative. The final song of the collective "we" first articulates itself through the feminine voice. Annie's raised fist signals the beginning of the march, fusing the disparate and frightened cadences of the multitudes into one song, which flows with the marching feet into the waves of flashing bayonets shimmering like the sea before the marchers. Like waves beating the shore, the sound of "our feet" is "a steady pound" pressing on toward the machine guns, bayonets, and gas masks catching the sunlight. Thus the masculine discourse of workplace and bar gives way in the end to a female voice that blends into the harmonized chorus—the masses "unmarked" and "mobile."[20]

When the chronotope of collectivity becomes embodied in the figure of the mother, the conditions of maternity—as both universal and particular (everybody is born to a mother, but only some bodies give birth)—refigure and displace those of the proletariat—as a class that becomes conscious of itself in its struggle to eliminate itself. The inscriptions of labor that form male working-class consciousness become subsumed within the maternal space of the masses, as solidarity erases gender, race, age, and, to some extent, class differences. In *Call Home the Heart* (1932), the "comrade" from the North insists that communism is not "a beast waiting in the dark to devour us and our children. It is the great mother calling us to peace and plenty."[21] This transformation of the fraternity of the working class into maternal space reframes the homosocial bondings of the male workers into another erotic configuration—that of the pre-Oedipal relationship.

The maternal space is productive of collectivity; however, it can also appear as horrifying, monstrous, and destructive of identity. As in *To Make My Bread* (1933), birth scenes usually fill their spectators with dread: "On the bed was a woman Kirk did not recognize as his mother. She was a stranger, a sort of beast . . . and Emma's last cries were the same as those of a pig with a knife at its throat."[22] To the male spectator, birth and its labor present a frightening image of strangeness; for the woman, birth—like labor under capitalism for the working class—is the "vampire . . . weighing you down and sucking your spirit" like a grotesque parasite invading the female body.[23]

The maternal space of collectivity, then, like the mother and the mass body, is an ambivalent configuration. Klaus Theweleit's theory of the rise of fascism suggests that, in the eyes of the bourgeois man turned revolutionary, "mothers are queens around the house, workers serving their husbands, whores for daddy. They are the ones whose bodies entice and repulse their children, who know nothing of their husbands' work, and on and on. 'The mother' is never just one person (Freud's error), nor is she ever simply a *person*."[24] She is a crowd, a group, a flood. The crowd envelops the individual, denying the differentiation of bourgeois identity as a "sonorous envelope" for the singing, marching masses.[25] As Walter Benjamin has remarked, the crowd is both menacing and erotic for participants and observers alike, presenting itself as a "spectacle of nature" or appearing as a "hero"; this characterization is not unlike either Weatherwax's heroic representation of the masses or the bourgeois mother of psychoanalytic theory.[26] The masses reproduce a new subject within a new configuration—the collective—by swallowing the individual.[27] But the body of the masses is figured through images of bourgeois maternity.

This formation mirrors the contradiction of capitalism that simultaneously reduces workers to commodities, enabling the universal equivalence of value, even as it differentiates each worker through specialization and through the ideologies of the free market, racism, and sexism. Like the narrative of class conflict, the ambivalence of maternity and its narrative in effect produces difference in order to erase it. The desire to close off or reweave "differences within" fuels Weatherwax's plot, leading inevitably to her ending, in which differences that formerly were accentuated are repossessed within the narrative as a new collective identity (e)merges (from) difference—in other words, the political construction of the "we" of collectivity is figured through the maternal trope.

The differences between narrative and history, labor and desire, and masculinity and femininity explode in collectivity and its textualized form, the collective novel. The descriptive elements necessary to achieve an alternative realism begin to undermine realist conventions as they flatten rather than elaborate character and plot. The final moment of solidarity cannot be narrated, because both the narrative conventions and actual possibilities of the utopian promise of collectivity are uncodable. The erasure of difference between masculine and feminine discourses is glimpsed as a possibility, but its fulfillment is post-narrative, post-revolution, extratextual. The final moment of solidarity escapes narrative closure, even as it marks the text's ending. Inscriptions of labor and desire are erased within the collective; but again, these inscriptions exceed narrative limits. Neither collectivity nor maternity can be adequately represented. If the collective speaks, it differentiates one voice from another, destroying itself as a mass. The mother has yet to speak to us; her narrative has only been spoken by her children. By fulfilling the prescriptions of proletarian realism, Weatherwax opened up more then she intended. In her novel, feminine desire interrupts the discourse of masculine labor, deflecting the narrative away from the strike, just as history resists closure and demands another ending.

The Girl: *Feminizing the Proletarian Novel*

Perhaps no woman writer from the 1930s more consciously narrated the female working-class subject by revising the proletarian plot than did Meridel LeSueur. Her 1939 novel, *The Girl,* gleaned from the life stories of women living together at the Workers' Alliance in St. Paul, was published in pieces throughout the 1930s and 1940s and was finally issued as a whole in 1977. By the time *The Girl* was completed, proletarian fiction had been abandoned and discredited by literary radicals in both Stalinist and Trotskyist camps. LeSueur recalls that one publisher rejected the manuscript for its lack of "authenticity." The book's descriptions of a bank robbery came under criticism for their excesses. LeSueur, however, insists on their truth, asserting that she spent her evenings recording the stories of the women living in the St. Paul warehouse.

During the early 1930s, LeSueur had been criticized by then Party official Whittaker Chambers for defeatism because she presented too bleak a picture of poverty in "Women on the Breadlines." It seems that the stories of female workers could not be read by male literary radicals. Even though, in *The Girl,* LeSueur reanimates the proletarian plot, transposing gender but not generic conventions, her plot transgresses the boundaries; like the mother and the masses, it becomes "monstrous" and "grotesque." This novel, then, is important for a number of reasons. First, it occupies an anomalous position: it was rejected in the 1930s because it broke conventions, only to resurface as a feminist classic in the late 1970s for precisely the same reasons. Second, it presents another version of the embodied feminine proletarian narrative, one in which the female working-class subject is primary to the plot rather than remaining in a "secondary zone." Finally, in this novel the links between the female body and the language of desire, forged through maternity, encode history.[28] By engendering the proletariat as masculine and relegating the feminine narrative to a secondary zone, *Marching! Marching!* was caught up in the dilemmas separating narrative from history and masculinity from femininity, so that the moment of collectivity only fleetingly erased the differences inscribed through labor and desire. *The Girl* finds history within a feminine space unoccupied by the masculine proletariat; in so doing, it appears to escape the dilemma of narrative and history. But it does so by erasing male political consciousness.

The Girl correlates the developing social consciousness of a waitress—the eponymous "girl"—with her sexual awakening and subsequent pregnancy. The novel literalizes the metaphoric embodiment of the masses in the mother by focusing its narrative on the growing pregnant body of its heroine. As the girl expands, both with fetus and with story, the trajectory of the proletarian plot continues—but without the inscriptions of labor on the body that in other works mark the differences among male workers and their differences from female workers. Maternity appears as the universal equivalent for women, connecting them through a female experience that both resists and produces alienation. The mother as link between past and future becomes the metaphor for Communist revolutionary transformation—the birth of the new out of the old.[29]

LeSueur makes female desire for (the memory of) the mother into the narrative of history for working-class women. The experiences of prostitution, male violence, illegal abortion, forced sterilization, childbirth, and heterosexual intercourse become the focal moments that forge consciousness, in much the same way as industrial accidents, speedups, company goons, and sellout unions do for the masculine proletariat in *Marching! Marching!* Where Weatherwax splits the narrative of history and the narrative of desire, the masculine and the feminine, LeSueur merges them through women's stories of maternity and heterosexuality.

The girl's first-person narrative cannot control the text; it lacks authority.

Like the narrator in LeSueur's "Annunciation" who tries to write her thoughts to preserve her memory, the girl's voice narrates female desire as history. She is naive, "a new girl . . . a virgin from the country scared of her own shadow" (2), and her naïveté and anonymity allow the other women around her to enunciate their own desires. The girl remains evanescent; she is the medium through which a variety of voices are heard, learning by increments until she finally synthesizes the stories. Nevertheless, the narrative does not cohere fully. In form, *The Girl* follows the classic proletarian plot, but the primary narrative proceeds out of (feminine) desire rather than (masculine) hunger. Narrative motivation comes from two sources—heterosexuality and maternity. The first half of the novel locates female desire within a heterosexual economy. In the second half, the maternal, as a source for feminine historicity, takes over after the girl's memory of her mother and Amelia's celebration of maternity link the desire for children to history. Unlike the classic proletarian plot, which ends with the (male) working class on the march, *The Girl* figures collectivity by amassing the bodies of women.

Thus the penultimate moment of collective action occurs at a demonstration before the relief office, as hordes of women demand milk and iron supplements for ailing and pregnant women. In the final chorus, the female demonstrators surround the girl as she gives birth to a daughter on a mattress beside her dying friend, Clara. They do not sing labor songs but rather chant in praise of femininity: "A kind of woman's humming was all around" (148). The connections among memory of the mother, militancy, and the birth of another generation is a constant theme throughout the novel, but all the elements come together in this final moment. The chorus of female voices airs "a kind of sound like Ahhhhhhhh of wonder and delight." The girl calls out to her daughter, who "had the tiny face of my mother, 'oh, girl'" as her mother had earlier called her before giving her the breast (148).[30]

The novel begins with an unrelenting portrayal of the alienation experienced by women because of their sexual slavery to men. The women whom the girl meets at the German Village, the restaurant where she works, are drawn to men who alternately abuse them and seek comfort from them. Forced to bear children in poverty or seek dangerous abortions, to endure beatings and rapes, the women are thoroughly subordinated to their men. Belle is linked economically, erotically, and maternally to her husband, Hoinck, with whom she co-owns the bar. Clara survives as a prostitute by dreaming of one day meeting a wealthy man who will fall in love with her. The girl herself is excited by Butch's attention, even though sex with Butch is painful. As an expression of her newly awakened sexuality, the girl streetwalks with Clara despite Butch's insistence that she not. Later she arranges to spend an evening with Butch's boss Ganz, the local bootlegger, in order to earn twenty-five dollars toward the gas station that Butch dreams of owning. When she is raped by Ganz and his sidekick, never receiving her money, Butch is angry at her for her ability to manipulate his boss sexually. After the girl defies Butch's demands that she abort his child, he beats her—her first beating by a man other than her father. Although female heterosexual behavior entails a number of risks for the girl, she derives some power within the economy of sexuality as an agent of her own and others' desire.

Running counter to these tales of female heterosexuality is Amelia's memory of her worker husband's final words, that "he'd better die fighting than be a scab or live like a rat" (54). This memory propels Amelia to organize women through the Workers' Alliance. She relates female historicity to maternity and so provides an alternative to heterosexual desire. "Yes," she says, as she helps Susybelle deliver her kittens, "one thing comes out of another one. . . . The same with society, one gives birth to another that's the way it is. One dies, another is born" (7). The maternal figures in the girl's continuing ties to her mother, whose memory pervades her thoughts until she is finally drawn back to her rural home after her father's death.

The bond with her mother is reenacted in the girl's loyalty to the women with whom she works at the German Village; however, this female solidarity is interrupted when the girl decides to assist in an armed robbery planned by the men—Butch, Hoinck, his brother Ack, and Ganz. The girl is asked to drive the getaway car. The robbery fails, in part because all along Ganz has intended to keep the money for himself. In the end, the men shoot each other, although Butch escapes, wounded. The girl drives Butch south in their stolen car. She listens to his rambling monologue, during which he begins to achieve some consciousness of his position within capitalism. Her silence enables the voice of another to speak, as it does later when she listens to the women's stories.

Butch's final awakening comes when he discovers that the owner of a gas station where they stop is being forced out of business by Standard Oil; the revelation finally destroys his aspirations for success as a small entrepreneur. Butch has already lost his brother in a battle with striking workers that erupted when the two of them tried to scab. The bank robbery was another failed scheme undertaken without any understanding of the larger system in which a small-time operator is bound to lose. Butch comes to realize that those who are better organized—the gangster Ganz, the monopoly Standard Oil, the unionized strikers—will always defeat the lone individual. His final moments indicate his new awareness of the failures of individualism and propel the girl back to St. Paul to join the women. She realizes Butch "was playing the wrong game . . . trying to win" (134). Whereas men like Butch and Amelia's husband achieve their new consciousness on the threshold of death, women experience childbirth as the threshold of transformation.

The rest of the novel follows the girl through gestation. Her pregnancy, memory, and the changing seasons structure the passing of time during the next six months. She returns to the German Village but finds it closed. With Butch, Hoinck, and Ganz dead and Ack in jail, Belle has abandoned the restaurant but not her position as matriarch among the women. With Amelia's help, Belle lives on relief in a warehouse, taking care of Butch's increasingly disoriented mother, the tubercular and syphilitic Clara, and the pregnant girl. During this period, both Clara and the girl are institutionalized. The girl is picked up for vagrancy and slated for sterilization as soon as her child is born. Clara is treated for "anxiety" with electric-shock therapy "to kill the memory" (134). Amelia manages to get the girl out of the maternity home before she goes into labor; Clara is returned to the women's warehouse, weak and confused after her treatments. As a result of these two events, Amelia organizes the women of the Workers' Alliance to mount a protest demanding adequate health care for the sick, pregnant, and nursing women on relief. Within this "community of women," the girl begins to construct a subject position that is both class and gender conscious.

The demonstration takes place while the girl and Clara wait at the warehouse—the one in labor, the other dying. The group of three hundred women protesters eventually returns to the warehouse to witness Clara's death and the birth of the girl's daughter, whom she names Clara. This apocalyptic (and melodramatic) moment of female genealogy culminates in a female utopian collectivity. Clara's death and Clara's birth spark another demonstration to commemorate the dead Clara as a martyr to male dominance and to celebrate the new Clara as "a sister, a mother" (148). The carnivalesque quality of these feminine masses is overemphasized through the connections between pregnancy and death. Bakhtin argues that the carnival revalues the "grotesque body" because the potent symbol of pregnant death, the simultaneity of fertility and mortality, embodies the reversals of class and authority reenacted within the carnival.[31] The masses debased, degraded, and grotesque are always somehow feminized. However, by literalizing the image of the feminine crowd, LeSueur reinvests the image of the masses as feminine with a positive value, challenging the lack of gender analysis in Bakhtin's model (and in the unspoken configuration of the collective novel), but she merely inverts gender asymmetries.[32]

LeSueur's novel textualizes the "sin" for which Lenin chastised Clara Zetkin after observing her discussion with working women.[33] Lenin was angry that the groups of women were more concerned with arguing about sex and personal relationships than with learning about economic theory. Similarly, whenever LeSueur's "community of women" gathers together to share stories and develop strategies, their language links desire, rather than economics, to history.[34] Their stories grow out of a fascination with and horror of male sexuality; they comprise a litany of pregnancies and abortions and a deep memory as both mothers and daughters.

What Lenin saw as a decadent obsession with the sexual, to the exclusion of the political and economic, LeSueur recasts as fundamentally political and economic; desire is structured by an economy of scarcity as much as history is. The women organize around their bodies, which are determined by their female (hetero)sexuality and so are coded as being outside history. In Le-Sueur's view, a woman's heterosexuality contains her desire by routing it through her potential as a mother. Her entry into history is achieved through maternity, the seemingly natural source of women's subjectivity and political strength, "the tree" of life (111, 136). Yet the community of women reacts to men; the women never question men's aborted attempts at historicity until their own desires for each other develop into a historical force. The men die in their lame attempt at bank robbery, leaving the women to reclaim history from their own simultaneously empty and full bodies—diseased and hungry, pregnant and desiring. However, the gender solidarity that the shared maternal body provides women fails to mark the differences among and within them.

Adrienne Rich feels that the compulsory force of heterosexuality blocks feminine desire, but it is precisely the women's bonds to each other and to their mothers and daughters (one point on what Rich calls the "lesbian continuum"), born out of heterosexual intercourse, that connect them to historical forces.[35] LeSueur's view of heterosexuality tends to conflate female agency and historicity within maternity. Woman is little more than a vessel for men's desire; women mother their men. Belle may have had thirteen abortions, but she still has her brutal husband, Hoinck, to mother. The girl cradles her dying lover in her arms as she would a child, knowing his child is within her womb. Butch's mother still sees him in the playground sandbox, although he is a grown man. But these connections between husband and wife, mother and son, are stagnant, ahistorical. The maternal can only become a force of history when it is linked to female desire—when the women mother themselves and each other and create a genealogy of the female working-class subject.

If LeSueur romanticizes maternity and the energizing power of the maternal without questioning the oppressiveness of the institution of motherhood, she nevertheless reminds us that women's labor brings children into the world, producing value and history just like men's labor. Even if they never develop the political consciousness to rebel against those controlling their lives—whether they be husbands, pimps, relief bureaucrats, or the police—mothers resist masculine control. Butch leads the girl to the abortionist's door, but she refuses the abortion. She has already heard enough of Belle's thirteen abortions and of Clara's health problems resulting from her abortions to know that this action may damage her for life. Her strength lies in her ability to bear children—a sense confirmed in part by the government's attempt to sterilize young women like herself. As the heroine in LeSueur's "Sequel to Love" says, "They don't want us to have nothin'. . . . Now they want to sterilize us so we won't have that."[36] Thus, for LeSueur, there is no subject position for the working-class woman without children; female historicity grows out of women's potential to mother.

Furthermore, motherhood provides incentives for women to join with each other to forge a mass movement. Women are linked to the past and future through pregnancy and its encoded memory. In LeSueur's story "Annunciation," the pregnant wife of an unemployed worker spends her afternoons writing "on little slips of paper." Her "expanding flesh bursting" is what "makes a new world," she thinks.[37] Like LeSueur, who wanted to become "a woman who wrote" and who thought "that we as women contained the real and only seed, and were the granary of the people," Clara and the other women who tell their stories inscribe female desire on history (Afterword, n.p.).

Maternity as History

Throughout *The Girl*, the image or the voice of the girl's mother reverberates at crucial moments. The girl's narrative begins as she recalls her mother telling her that the twin cities were "Sodom and Gomorrah" (1). Amelia's appearance stirs the girl because "she looks alot like mama" (3). After her first sexual experience with Butch, the girl is afraid; she calls on her mother incantationally, "Oh mama, what can I do? Oh mama, you told me it would be dangerous. Oh mama, I'm scared. . . . what would you do?" (29). When she returns home after her father's death, the girl hopes her mother can explain about female heterosexual desire. "Maybe she would tell me something. Maybe out of all the words something would come through" (40). The girl learns that, like Belle, her mother shared a deep connection with the man who had routinely beaten her and left her with so many children. "He was like the wrath of God, something strong and good in your papa. He was good to me . . . it's a good thing. A good man is a good thing" (42). Her mother echoes Belle's earlier revelation about her relationship to Hoinck: "Goddamn him, I love him that's why I'm hooked like this all my life, Goddamn him, I love him" (20). The ritual greeting between the girl and her mother, "oh girl," "oh mama," position the two of them within a female genealogy that will be repeated in other relationships between the girl and her friends (35).

The girl's mother reveals to her, "Nobody can tell you anything, girl. You have to live it and sometimes you have to die it and then it's in you and you always know it" (43). This lesson is repeated for the girl by her other mothers throughout the narrative. Like the fetus she carries, the accumulated experiences narrated through the girl become manifestations of history, shaping action and consciousness. "I was different now, with . . . mama telling me everything. I was into mama's life for the first time. . . . Mama had a secret. . . . I knew I had to jump, be in it like mama" (45). Although the mother's narrative of desire impelled the girl to be "different," it was not enough. She, too, needed to "jump," to enact her desire; then consciousness could be embodied.

Simultaneously overvalued and repressed within Western discourse, the maternal presents itself, according to Julia Kristeva, as a site of female subject construction wherein "biology transpierces speech."[38] Maternity becomes the tunnel that burrows through the semiotic to the symbolic as the mother uniquely recognizes self-in-other/other-as-self. The mother's body links desire to history, and therefore its representation within discourse is fundamentally a historical construction. Appropriated by such authoritarian regimes as the church, Stalinist Russia, Nazi Germany, or less sinister ones like Hollywood cinema, motherhood becomes a location for female colonization; as the individual embodiment of historical processes, however, maternity can resist masculine discourse on a local level. This reading of maternity into the masses in *Marching! Marching!* and into history in *The Girl* marks the proletarian plot as fundamentally gendered in ways that go unrecognized within the codes of masculinity. The maternal configurations of the masses and of the female body produce a contradiction within the genre.

After her reunion with her mother, the girl and Butch have sex for the first time. Afterward, he viciously slaps her face and jumps from her bed, reminding her of her "father always in anger, putting on his pants and leaving, yelling obscenities and coming back later, drunk, when he often beat mama, and it didn't sound too different from love-making" (51). With this initiation into heterosexuality, the girl begins her entrance into history. "I felt I became mama" (51–52). Immediately after sex, the girl, bleeding, leaves the hotel room alone in search of "Belle and Amelia and Clara and mama" (53). She knows that the women will understand something about her because it will be transmitted through their own memories. They exchange stories about their first sexual encounters. This becomes the girl's initiation rite into female (class) consciousness. "I would always now know the naked skin of man and woman. . . . I would know fruits" (52). Heterosexuality, no matter how abusive and destructive, presents the key to female desire, which will be elaborated through memory and maternity into female subjectivity. Through the speech of other women, the girl's desire enters history. She begins to achieve a class/gender consciousness that transforms personal desire into a historical process.

Just as the women gathered together after the girl's initiation into heterosexuality, so do they gather after the bank robbery to find comfort in each other as women at the "root of the tree" (111). Women come together to talk and then branch out with the men to whom they are connected because of sex or money, but they always return to each other. They can tell one another the secrets of turning tricks, rape, battery, illegal abortion, and childbirth because the community of women is perceived to be outside history, outside discourse. Women must talk about the private, intimate details of sexual relationships with men because this is the primary data for their development of political consciousness and their entrance into history. History and consciousness are bound up with sexual experience; but it is maternity—the genealogy of mothers and daughters—that ultimately forges female historicity.

The girl's narrative voice changes after the robbery because from then on she is always with women. She is harder, more cynical; she aggressively walks the streets, seeking relief money and avoiding police spies. When she is institutionalized, she makes connections with other women there, sharing information and sneaking a letter out to Amelia, who ultimately gets her released from the hospital. She remembers her mother more and more often and reexperiences through her own lactation a memory of her mother's breast. Because women have the "same enemy after us, the same mother over us," they must reconstruct heterosexual desire into maternal desire in order to develop revolutionary consciousness (134). Amelia tells the girl, "O girl, the breasts of our mothers are deep with this sorrow, always remember that. We can't tell what happens to us in secret even" (142). Lamenting Clara's demise, the girl asks, "Who cares if she had a name even?" (135–36). Later she declares, "Memory is all we got, we got to remember" (142). Amelia answers, "Remember the breasts of your mother" (143). When Amelia links this ecstatic cry to the deaths of Sacco and Vanzetti and the brutality at Centralia, she constructs a "class" in which women's secrets are expressed like milk from the breast but must be given voice through the struggles of working-class men's bodies. The memory of maternity, then, is linked to history and class consciousness for women. The narration of women's forgotten memories ensures the historicity of female desire and, thus, the presence of subjectivity within collectivity.

By constructing a narrative of female desire in which maternal power is processed through heterosexuality, Meridel LeSueur revises the proletarian novel to speak a language of women's memories and women's bodies. She places women's (re)production, rather than men's production, at the center of her narrative of female class consciousness. Yet her evocation of the feminine verges on essentialism because it invokes women's biological capacity to bear children without interrogating the cultural platitudes surrounding motherhood. By suggesting that women's maternity determines female political consciousness, LeSueur resurrects the proletarian metaphors of gender and the ideology of domesticity, but with different emphases. Women's ability to concretize political theory, she wrote later, is "written in the book of the flesh."

Perhaps, then, *The Girl* cannot challenge either the gender or the genre conventions of the proletarian plot, because both conventions presume as rigid a discourse of sexual difference as did the domestic ideology of the nineteenth century. LeSueur's narrative of female desire—coded as heterosexuality and maternity—locates the female subject in history by placing female subjectivity on the same narrative trajectory that constructed the proletariat as masculine. Adrienne Rich has argued that, just as the proletarian plot effaces the feminine, the consequences of LeSueur's content efface lesbianism. *Marching! Marching!*, the "classic" proletarian novel, differentiated between a narrative of history and a narrative of desire by coding one as masculine, the other as feminine. But in Weatherwax's final vision of collectivity, when the two discourses merged, gender differences were erased. In *The Girl*, though, masculinity is associated not with history and class consciousness, but with its opposite: short-sighted, individualistic acts of aggression and personal gain. Nevertheless, history is inscribed through the stories of men's murdered bodies. This narrative of female heterosexual desire historicizes female subjectivity and consciousness through the memory of maternity, but *The Girl* maintains the gender polarities of proletarianism even as it inverts them to feminize revolutionary class consciousness.

Yonnondio: *Unlimn'd They Disappear*

Marching! Marching! and *The Girl* present two variations on the narrative trajectory of the classic proletarian novel. Although both novels were written by middle-class women, each strives to portray the collective solidarity of the working class as it moves from an objective state to being conscious of itself as historical subject.[39] *Yonnondio*, Tillie Olsen's recovered fragment of a novel "from the thirties," provides yet another elaboration of the female working-class subject. By locating her narrative within an already existing struggle, Weatherwax fulfilled the "structure of confrontation." LeSueur used the girl's pregnancy to build on the "structure of apprenticeship," as her protagonist is transformed from passivity into an agent of history.[40] Mazie Holbrook, the young protagonist of *Yonnondio*, provides, in a sense, the prehistory for the female working-class bildungsroman.

The novel traces Mazie's development through three crucial years of childhood, from age six to nine, when she moves out of the circle of family into a larger social sphere. The organization of the family—at once hierarchical and communal—differs from yet mirrors the rigid economic stratification of the social spaces across which the Holbrooks travel. Mazie must learn to negotiate a different series of obstacles as she grows up and out of the family. Still, it is her sex that marks her, both in and out of the family unit. Gender roles and sexual vulnerability prescribe the range of her space as much as poverty and ignorance.

Tillie Olsen, née Lerner, was one of the few women writing during the 1930s who actually was of working-class origin. She has recently devoted her intellectual efforts to explaining the paucity of working-class women authors in order to rectify the "silences" of those writers whose voices have been dispossessed.[41] Describing her own circumstances, Olsen notes that political activism, economic necessity, and family responsibilities overshadowed her deeper love of literature for many years. Nevertheless, Olsen did join the New York John Reed Club and produced three highly praised short pieces during the 1930s. "Thousand Dollar Vagrant" is an autobiographical account of her arrest during the San Francisco General Strike. "The Strike," a quintessential example of engaged reportage, is also about the San Francisco strike; in it, the distance between observer and participant is bridged through dynamic language and imagery. "The Iron Throat" was Olsen's first piece of fiction. Published in the *Partisan Review*, it was compared to Tess Slesinger's *The Unpossessed*.[42] This story was actually the first chapter of the novel-in-progress that ultimately became *Yonnondio*. Although the author claims it to be a fragment (Olsen notes that she reworked, but did not substantially rewrite, drafts almost forty years old), the novel stands as the preeminent example of women's proletarian fiction.

Yonnondio is perhaps the most widely read novel by a woman from the 1930s. Today, its lyricism and feminism contribute to its favorable reception in the emerging feminist literary canon. Like *The Girl*, its fruition as a novel owes much to the contemporary women's movement, which provided it with a new and more receptive audience during the 1970s. Through a penetrating look at the way that *Yonnondio* both conforms to and diverges from prescriptions about proletarian literature, Deborah S. Rosenfelt finds evidence for a tradition of "women's socialist feminist novels."[43] I want to place the novel in the context of its contemporary works by women and to argue that it presents a prehistory for the embodiment of feminine discourse and desire among the proletariat.

The novel situates Mazie within the social space of the family as well as within the geographic spaces of mine, farm, and city (recalling Gold's "mine, mill and farm"), because, as she is a female child, her developing subjectivity will grow out of the relations of dominance structured within her family rather than those of the factory. The sections of the book set in the western mining town depict a young girl's emotional landscape that is as craggy and arid as the slag heaps, culm banks, and mine tipples that surround her. Later sections, set on a bleak Dakota farm and in the squalid slums of Omaha, only draw the landscape of poverty more graphically. These different environments produce distinct languages of the body for Mazie.

The differential between male and female working-class experience is outlined early in Mazie's narrative. The "iron throat," the mining whistle, wakes the members of her family, who help her father prepare for the day's work, inscribing the body of the worker (and his family) on the machinery of the mine. This narrative is interrupted by another narrator, who tells the story of Andy Kvaternick, a thirteen-year-old boy who is starting work that day to support his family after his father has become the victim of a mine disaster. Unlike Andy, Mazie may never have to "breathe and breathe" the coal dust, a prisoner of the "bowels of the earth," but her life too will be circumscribed and deflected from "her questions" by other forces (6–7). In another reversal of the process by which the workers' bodies become inscribed by their labor, the mine itself is embodied in Mazie's narrative. The suffocating bowels and constricting throat of the mine will be personified for Mazie through her close contact with the deformed male body of a miner. In language mirroring the repetitious breathing Andy Kvaternick must do within the confines of the mine's body, she "fainted and fainted" as the "red mass of jelly" of Sheen McEvoy's lips closed in on her with a kiss (16). By molesting Mazie, this deranged miner seeks to avenge the deaths of all miners by giving "a little child, pure of heart" to the "ol' lady" who "only takes men 'cause she ain't got kids. All women want kids" (15). Thus the mine is not only embodied, but engendered as well. The site of labor for men becomes the desiring and devouring female body, whose entrance is the vaginal passage of childbirth and sex—and, inevitably, death. The mine becomes the grotesque body of life-in-death, whose opening reveals itself to be simultaneously an orifice for food and air, excrement, and children.

Throughout the rest of her narrative, Mazie's vision is colored by her early experience of molestation. Never again can she lose herself within a fantasy as she had just before McEvoy assaulted her. Her flights of escape will always butt up against the "mass of jelly" because, as she develops into adolescence, the dangers of sexual exposure become more overt. The sexed body of the working-class girl more thoroughly positions her in a (sexual) economy than does her laboring body. Thus the family and the sexual and gender arrangements structured within it merit the same kind of detailed attention that Weatherwax gave to the various lumbering jobs. If female working-class subjectivity is to be fully "limn'd," a language that can speak about the forces of gender, sexuality, and class must be produced. The complex evocation of Mazie's consciousness through a fractured narrative style locates this construction in the family.

Swollen Bellies and Jelly Faces

The household is an especially tight enclosure for Mazie, who as the oldest female child is responsible for many chores without benefiting from any of the power her mother Anna gains as a parent. Whereas the dangers for working-class men are physical injury or death, the women also suffer as a result of the deformations wrought on the men with whom they live. Mazie and her mother both suffer beatings and verbal abuse from her father, Jim, as the cycle of domination moves from mine boss to worker to wife and child. Those without family, like McEvoy, become unmoored within this system and lash out more or less at random. When Mazie complains to Anna that it is not fair that her brother Will gets to run to the river, while she is forced to stay home in the heat and help Anna with the canning, she is told that boys and girls are different. Her complaint is primarily about her confinement. There is no privacy for her in the household; she has no "place" (177–78). Because of gender, her behavior has been gradually restricted within the family. She has not participated in the family's Fourth of July celebration because "girls don't get firecrackers" (152). In the night, at the very moment of abandonment to sleep and private dreams, she is often haunted by the image of the "jelly face" closing in upon her mouth. The routines of the home suffocate her under a blanket of dirty laundry, stinking mattresses, and the more painful brutality of paternal violence—including the marital rape that precipitates Anna's miscarriage.

The female body confronts the dangers of molestation, rape, battery, pregnancy, and verbal abuse. It controls Anna; it restricts Mazie, who is not allowed to wander around the railroad yard even though Will can. She gives up riding the ice truck after the boys chant a song about seeing her panties under her billowing dress. Her one moment of erotic fantasy ends in disaster. She falls in love with Ginella, playing "sheik" to Ginella's Nazimova. She brings her trinkets, and together they act out lovemaking scenes from the movies, but Mazie is soon replaced by another girl when Ginella renames her "Miss Ugly." The real Miss Ugly, Erina, provides Mazie with the most horrific image of the female body. Erina, who is "beaten for having been born," tyrannizes the children of the dump with her curses, yet she is fascinating to Mazie (182). In her daily sermons, she spells out the connections between her disfigured body, her sinfulness, and her femaleness for Mazie, who listens with "a sick-happy feeling" to Erina's ramblings (173).

Mazie's environment, however impoverished and dangerous, provides at least the possibility for an expansiveness of the body. Although Mazie's earliest wanderings led to her assault by the crazed miner McEvoy, leaving home later provides an escape from the pain of family relations. Mazie first meets Mr. Caldwell after running away from a beating. Lying with her among the corn fields, he tells her about the constellations. After another escape, he gives her some books—what her mother has called the means to "places your body has never been" (138). Words can provide escape. During one of Anna's childbirths, Mazie escapes to the chicken coops where she goes to read, hiding from the screams. Once the family has moved to the city, Mazie's fantasy world allows her to escape back to the farm. In the city, the dump provides a site for the "Frank Lloyd Wrights of the proletariat" to create new worlds (69). There, Ginella constructs a tent modeled on *The Sheik of Araby* and enchants her idolatrous girlfriends with fantasies of beauty. There, Erina preaches a vision of other worlds—hell and heaven—that transcends the oppressiveness of her body's deformities. Finally, Mazie experiences her most complete escape from oppression with her mother after they have wandered for hours in search of dandelion greens. Discovering an abandoned lot overgrown with weeds and trees, they sink into reverie as Anna recounts stories and songs from her childhood. Holding Mazie, Anna provides a glimpse at her own longing for escape.

Mazie has resisted the move from farm to city, resisted also the stench of the slaughterhouse, her painful memories, and her mother's diseased body through a perpetual fantasy of the farm. She creates another environment within the one in which she lives. This transformation of physical space through desire becomes an on-going metaphor for the transformation of social relations under capitalism that the workers' struggle can achieve. Mazie and her mother read changes in the environment as changes in social relations. In the city, Mazie's first recall of the molestation memory occurs while she is on an errand for her sick mother. She grazes against a drunk, who pushes her onto the sidewalk and forces her face onto a wad of spit. The remembered image is fleeting but the two incidents—experience and memory—combine to dispel the dream of the farm forever. Thereafter, Mazie is increasingly haunted by her horrific memory. When her mother becomes delirious during a series of fainting episodes, Mazie's "nausea of fear" at her mother's possible death brings back "the jelly mass pushing against her face" (102–3). When Jim demands that Anna have sexual intercourse with him against her will, Mazie overhears the rape. After her mother collapses, Mazie tries to wake her drunken father, and her "fear remembered such a breath" (108).

Mazie's memories coincide with her parents' loss of consciousness (from fainting and drinking), suggesting again the connections between birth, death, and the productive mass body. For Mazie, the horror of female sexuality is tied to very concrete sensuous memories of the body: a jelly mass, stinking breath, a shuddering laugh, the grotesque body. Smell, touch, and sound conspire to control fantasy and imagination. Anna's illness and her slow recovery pull Mazie out of her fantasy of a return to the grasses of the farm and force her to confront the body of a working-class female: "so much ugliness, the coarse hair, the night bristling, the blood and the drunken breath and the blob of spit, something soft, mushy, pressed against her face, never the farm, don't cry, even baby's crying, get away from me, ya damn girl" (111). Mazie's memories cease from this point on, having been replaced by the more immediate monstrosity of her mother's sexual body and its relationship to her own body.

The relationship between Anna and Mazie, like those between "the girl" and her mother and, to a lesser extent, between Mary and Mom, provides the central dynamic within the novel. This problematic mother-daughter dyad locates the point of sociality and subjectivity for women. Working-class culture is transmitted through the mother—"learn from your mother," Caldwell tells Mazie—for it is she who provides the strength for eventual resistance (52).

Simultaneously, though, the working-class family, with its endless childbirths and its hierarchical structure, limits, constricts, and almost destroys its female members. In *Yonnondio*, this dual legacy passes between Mazie and Anna both thematically and structurally. Like LeSueur, Olsen images mothers as trees. Anna and Mazie experience their moment of complete fusion under the catalpa tree as Anna sings her daughter a love song. Anna's arms hold her children while she performs her other chores—a tree branching out to accommodate the needs of the family, even though she tells Bess, "I can't stand here and be shade for you" (187). Anna risks death from her fecundity, just as the tree, source of shade and locus of memory, risks dying in the drought of a burning summer.

Structurally, the novel begins as Mazie's narrative, although Mazie's voice is interrupted by a narrator who explains, dramatizes, and propagandizes the working-class experience. Once the family has moved to the city, however, Anna's narrative takes over. This transference back and forth between daughter and mother occurs throughout the novel, as one protects the other at crucial moments. Anna nurses Mazie after her assault; Mazie takes over as the "little mother" after Anna's miscarriage; both assist in their "births" (116). The shifting point of view propels Mazie from girlhood into preadolescence as she learns from Anna what "being poor and a mother" mean for the working-class female (120).

Even though she beats her child, Anna also protects Mazie through a fierce maternal power. Maternity is associated with danger, because pregnancy brings a woman close to death. It deforms her into a bloated being whose vague boundaries make her ripe for battery because she is inattentive to her husband and involved in "a goddamned woman's life" (56). Pregnancy is "monstrous," both for the mother and for the female child who must tend her mother's labor (56). Mazie's memories of her assault become associated with Anna's maternity and sexuality. The sight of her mother's huge, pregnant belly brings on a faint sensation of the "jelly face." Mazie is expected to help her mother through childbirth, but her fear of the "face like jelly" and the "swollen bellies" and "blood and pain" of birth bring on uncontrollable nausea (60–61). "She could feel words swollen big within her, words coming out with pain, bloody, all clothed in red" (61). Language is thus embodied. Mazie's swollen words merge with her mother's swollen belly, which in turn blurs with her memory of McEvoy's jelly face when he abducted her in order to return her to the mine's womb.

Pregnancy has dulled Anna and left her vulnerable to beatings and abuse by Jim. She ignores her children, wrapping herself in the protective chrysalis of her distended belly. Yet she never asked for "a goddamned woman's life," and so she tries to protect Mazie from it. During her labor, Anna comforts Mazie and, at the same time that she gives birth to another daughter, Anna helps Mazie give birth to the "words swollen big within her." Thus mother and daughter exchange roles fluidly, as each delivers the other of memory and of child.

Both Mazie and Anna are adept at reading the signs of their environment. Anna knows where to look for the dandelion greens that she intends to prepare as a vegetable for her family. But engrossed in reverie, she is unaware that she and her children have wandered into a better-off neighborhood. Because Mazie realizes that the neat lawns signal risk for them, she protects her mother by steering them to an empty lot. When Anna regains her strength after her illness, she reads the changing winds as a sign that the heat will break. This vision of possibility for the future is accompanied by her baby's first ecstatic assertion of self, as Bess grabs and releases the canning jar lid on the table again and again. "Centuries of human drive work in her. . . . *I achieve, I use my powers; I! I!* . . . Bess's toothless, triumphant crow" transcends the heat and misery (191). Bess's entry into self-conscious delight at her body's power produces another female lineage for Anna and Mazie.

What Joan Samuelson has called the "pattern of survival" among working-class women writers, the mother-daughter bond, does more than provide a thematic mooring in *Yonnondio*.[44] Elaborated linguistically as well, the dual points of view of Mazie and Anna anchor the novel, even as they accommodate a variety of other voices within their narratives. The moment of narrative fusion occurs as Mazie and Anna sit together under the catalpa tree after picking dandelion greens. Anna sings to Mazie, "Shenandoah, I love thy daughter," and "Mazie felt the strange happiness in her mother's body" as she strokes Anna's hair, "a new frail selfness, bliss, healing, transforming. Up from the grasses, from the earth, from the broad tree trunk at their back, latent life streamed and seeded" (145–46). The bodies of mother and daughter fuse as "heartbeat" and "breath" lose their boundaries, only to be called back within "bounds" by the voices of Anna's insistent sons (147).

This fleeting erotic moment of "unfolding, wingedness, boundlessness" unites their two narratives. In the final chapter, a different narrative effect is created as the point of view is fractured among a series of characters—Jim and the workers at the slaughterhouse, Mazie and the girls at the dump, her brother Will and the boys at the railroad yard, Anna at home canning peaches. Through a cross-cutting between each, a montage is achieved among these various scenes; their common struggle is to overcome the oppressiveness of one-hundred-degree-plus weather. As with other novels that construct the female working-class subject, the final moment of utopian possibility is denoted through the female voice. Anna recognizes the change in the air signaling that the heat will "end tomorrow" (191).

Words and Words

Yonnondio's various narrators sensuously indulge in a lyricism of "broken sequences" and repetitions. Language resides within the body, conveying the sights, sounds, and smells of Mazie's world. Lush but dangerous, language risks becoming a tool of the "master artists" who embellish the lives of the poor for the ruling class (29). Nonetheless, language is the means of escape from the harsh boredom and oppressiveness endemic to the working-class family. Books can take a person "places your body has never been" (138). Mazie delights in the powers imparted by language: "I am a knowin' things. I can diaper a baby. I can tell ghost stories. I know words and words" (5). Once Mazie begins school, "the lessons came easy—the crooked white worms of words on the second-grade blackboard magically transformed into words known and said" (48). She recites poems to her younger brothers because "there was something to escape from," and words provide the means (50). Erina repeats the sermons and invectives hurled at her, turning them into personal jeremiads that she in turn hurls back at the world. Ginella changes her identity through elaborate fantasies spun out of the words and pictures in popular magazines and in the movies. She renames herself from Gertrude Skolnick to the exotic Ginella and spends her days repeating verbatim the title cards from the movies she has seen. Reiteration brings the "worms of words" into the body of the female subject, where they begin to write the narrative of the working-class woman.

For men, and for those female members of the working class locked not in the home but in the factory, language is much more abstract. Jim is uncomfortable with "woman's blabbin'" when Anna recounts Mrs. Kvaternick's figuring of the mines as "da bowels of the earth" (3). He sneers, "Say, what does she think she is, a poet?" (2). Mazie bursts with questions she longs to ask Jim, but when she follows him into town, "somehow the question she had meant to have answered could not be clamped into words" (13). Later, when he finds her bruised and wandering the urban streets, "he could speak no more. . . . The things in his mind so vast and formless, so terrible and bitter, cannot be spoken, will never be spoken—till the day the hands will find a way to speak this; hands" (113). Because men's bodies are inscribed through their labor, they require a language of the hands, a language as yet "unlimn'd" within narrative. Women are particularly mysterious to Jim because their labors are so invisible—their work unseen, their bodies terrifying, their language incomprehensible—so that even when he tries "to ask Mrs. Kryckski about Anna [he] could form neither words nor thoughts" (199).

Because the discourse of the workplace is controlled by the foremen, who insult the workers as "women" who "suck titty," and because the language of the hands is yet to be written, another form of communication develops (86). For instance, through a silent code the workers in the slaughterhouse spell each other and slow down the pace of work during the heat wave. The language of hands—the language of the masculine proletariat—cannot yet be spoken. Like the "woman's blabbin'" he dismisses even though it is spoken by a working-class "poet," Jim cannot recognize the power of "words and words" because they remain disembodied for him. So Jim sells the books that Caldwell has given to Mazie before she gets a chance to read them; their only worth to him is the half-dollar they bring. Women can speak, perhaps because "on the women's faces lived the look of listening" (24). The bodies of mothers and daughters removed from the factory encode language; their experiences are constructed by learning to read and to interpret the signs unspoken by their men, inscribed on men's hands.

Jim, like Anna, alternates between a fierce and vicious anger toward his family and a tender solicitude for them. However, unlike Anna's mood swings—which are ultimately grounded in her body—his appear less coherent. Thus the children fear his hostile interludes and do not trust his pleasant ones, knowing these to be short-lived and capricious, dependent on forces external to home. Jim is the medium between the domestic and public spheres; he moves between exploitation on the job and authority within the home, alternately being brutalized at work and then, in turn, brutalizing those who depend upon him. The reader understands these connections through the inscriptions of Jim's work on his body and in the text through the interpolations provided by the inset narrators. Mazie, unaware of the causes of male violence both bodily and textually, simply experiences it as one more natural phenomenon, like the landscape or the weather.

Throughout the novel, natural elements—snowstorms, constellations, heat waves—function as symbols for the social forces contending in capitalist America. Because Mazie's body controls much of the narrative, the natural and social forces that control her life appear equally weighted. She recognizes some distinctions based on class or gender, but she misrecognizes others. Class consciousness does not inhere naturally within the body of the working class. Just as bodies are constructed through language and language embodied, class consciousness must be forged by collectively organizing and by consciously naming that organization. This is the lesson Caldwell has learned, the one Jim Tracy, the worker who quits his job in anger, has failed to learn. Implicitly, as Olsen gives us to understand, it is knowledge that working-class women possess as (re)producers of their families. Because maternity becomes "the jagged crest where biology transpierces speech," interpolating the natural and the social through each other, motherhood, as a force of nature, inserts a wedge into the gendered and classed social hierarchies.[45] But this wedge depends on one's viewing maternity as ahistorical and outside culture. Like *The Girl*, *Yonnondio* constructs an opposition between the public and productive sphere of masculine labor and the private and reproductive sphere of feminine labor that relies on a dubious analogy: male is to female as culture is to nature.[46]

Yet within the working-class family's suffocating abuse, a space for resistance can be found; ultimately the family *is* socially constructed. *Yonnondio* charts the possibility of subcultural forms to challenge hegemonic culture. The Holbrook family is at its most patriarchal when Jim asserts his male dominance, making the family especially dangerous for the women and children. Yet due to the constraints of class, Jim's power is ephemeral; the poverty that claims Anna's health causes Jim to become the nurturing figure within the household. When the family is most troubled, Jim can least afford his masculine position of authority; out of this fluidity, the family becomes a potential site for resistance. By assuming Anna's work, Jim discovers the family as a site of resistance to the corrosiveness of poverty, rather than as yet one more force among many controlling him. Performing the female labor of domestic chores, Jim is reinscribed as maternal; his body replaces Anna's temporarily as he struggles to learn the language of a "goddamned woman's life."

Each of the three novels discussed employs a different strategy to narrate working-class female subjectivity. *Marching! Marching!* develops a secondary female narrative of desire that conflicts with but also complements the primary male narrative of history when, in the final moment, the collective (e)merges metaphorically in the maternal. *The Girl* replaces the narrative of masculine proletarian consciousness by historicizing female desire. Heterosexuality and maternity become (another) history as pregnancy quite literally (re)produces collectivity. *Yonnondio*, by far the most subtle evocation of the female working-class subject, locates the narratives of both history and desire in the working-class family. By following a young girl's misrecognitions of self and others, *Yonnondio* suggests that external forces of oppression and of sensation—that is, of culture and nature—narrate self-history. Nature is not merely a metaphor for the social; the body *is* history. The sounds of the "iron throat" and the smells of the slaughterhouse are the brutal, yet sensuous, effects of industrial capitalism, whereas the "jelly face" is an emblem of male violence. Maternity moves the external forces inside. Mazie connects "da bowels of the earth" to her "stummie" and her mother's "swollen belly." By linking the mine, language, and pregnancy, the working-class woman embodies the historical process.

The family, as site of bodily (re)production and consumption, is where children become classed (as well as gendered) subjects of American society. Telling the history of a working-class female child can provide insights into the interpenetrations of class, gender, and generation that are missing in the "classic" proletarian novel. The polarities—women/men, worker/boss, child/parent, exploited/exploiter—produce hierarchies between sexes, generations, and classes. Yet, because the family appears as producer and as a product of both nature and culture, the oppositions are not fixed. Thus the family becomes a site of potential resistance even as it constricts its members, just as capitalism holds the seeds of socialism even as it oppresses the working class.

Yet, although each novel presents strategies by which female desire counters the masculine narrative of the proletariat encoded through hunger and labor, a number of troubling questions remain. Why is it that maternity becomes the trope by which to narrate class and gender as a combinatory? Is it due to its universality as an image within our culture and language? Or is it the site where class-specific terms, such as labor and production, assume gender-specific meanings as well? Why couldn't Agnes Smedley write a female working-class bildungsroman without invoking a trope (maternity) and a form (the framed narrative) that set class and gender apart from each other and from history? Why is it that Clara Weatherwax can end class, race, and gender differences within narrative only by resorting to the engulfing, maternal mass? Why must Meridel LeSueur invoke a separatist utopia of mothers? Why does Tillie Olsen situate the connection between nature and culture and between biology and politics in the body of the mother?

What these questions suggest to me, from the vantage point of 1990s materialist-feminism, is that, lacking the critical edge of feminist theory or the political challenge of feminist practice, the authors relied on a conventional narrative of feminine desire derived from domestic ideology to deflect the narrative of history away from the purely masculine proletariat. Women literary radicals could draw on the new aesthetic and political culture of proletarianism to inject the narrative of history into women's texts, and thus they stretched the narrative of desire to accommodate new material. But without a corresponding aesthetic and political culture of feminism, they remained stuck in traditional renderings of femininity. Nevertheless, the narratives of class that appeared during the 1930s enabled radical women writers to revise narratives of gender because history and desire could connect in the bodies of the working-class woman.

The relationship between mother and daughter appears crucial to narratives of female working-class subjectivity. A female genealogy allows the daughter's entrance into a historical landscape shaped by landmarks—childbirth, rape, abortion—that differ from men's outline but complete the map of the social terrain of American working-class life. Not only are the landmarks different, but the language used to describe them differs as well. Repetitions, incantations, circumlocutions, and memory structure the maternal text of the female working-class subject. The body of texts and the body in the text reconstruct genre to narrate female subjectivity and, in so doing, provide another (hi)story for literary radicalism to tell.

Grotesque Creatures

The Female Intellectual as Subject

I have been arguing that female writers who sought to construct the female working-class subject within the proletarian narrative reembodied metaphors of gender governing the genre through the trope of maternal collectivity. They resurrected the narrative of desire and made of it a means for women to enter history by removing it from the realm of the purely domestic, personal, and psychological where it had traditionally been located. In these novels, the working-class woman's body is inscribed through the dual constructs of labor and desire; the maternal trope, though, however liberating, still carries traces of the bourgeois motherhood depicted in domestic fiction.

The novels that treat the female intellectual as political subject—Tess Slesinger's *The Unpossessed* (1934), Lauren Gilfillan's *I Went to Pit College* (1934), and Josephine Herbst's *Rope of Gold* (1939)—present even more ambivalent texts of the maternal body. These novels, to some extent, embrace more fully the metaphors of gender that masculinize the proletariat and, by positioning the female intellectual subject as a spectator within the revolutionary struggle, doubly alienate her from history and from politics. In *Rope of Gold*, the words of writer Victoria Chance run parallel to those of the strike leader, Steve Carson; in *I Went to Pit College*, Laurie, the writer from New York, finds her most fruitful source in Johnnie, the coalminer and proletarian writer; but in *The Unpossessed*, Margaret, as a woman intellectual without contacts in the working class, can only read and listen to "sterile" words.

The unique position occupied by the female intellectual, who experiences class privilege but gender subordination, appears to mirror the position of the working-class male, who dominates as a man even as he suffers from class exploitation. Because literary radicals engendered the male intellectual as feminine but refused a place for the radical female intellectual, such a woman inhabited a multiply contradictory space. Thus the contradictions of gender and genre within the revolutionary fiction of the 1930s became thematized in the novels by women writers. For instance, *The Unpossessed* completely disregards the traditional masculine proletariat through its focus on the sexual politics of a group of friends living and working in the community of New York's intellectual Left. By embracing an essentialism of masculinity and femininity, Slesinger's narrative, like LeSueur's in *The Girl*, maps sexual difference. Yet by divorcing her intellectuals from the working-class struggle, Slesinger provides a critique of the proletarian narrative—something that LeSueur, for example, failed to do as effectively. Paradoxically, even as she retains the form of the proletarian novel without its content, Slesinger twists the gender conventions of the genre into a dystopian vision of literary radicalism.

Lauren Gilfillan, by contrast, appears to embrace the demands made on the middle-class female writer by proletarian realism. Like an intrepid ethnologist, Gilfillan sends herself out into the field—in this case, the coalfields of Western Pennsylvania—to document the miners and "their ways of existing." What begins as a history of an object—the collective portrait of striking miners—develops into a narrative of the subject—a personal account of a female intellectual. Her place of entry into the radical movement is achieved through her writing.

As a revision of the domestic novel, Josephine Herbst's *Rope of Gold* weaves complex layers of social history and personal narrative. Structurally and thematically, it matches Steve Carson, the proletarianized farmer-turned-labor activist who is propelled to activism through sacrificing a series of women—his mother, stepmother, half-sisters, and wife, with Victoria Chance, the bohemian-turned-radical-journalist whose commitment is the result of reconciling a series of memories about her mother, sister, and stillborn son. Both characters develop their political experiences through narratives of struggle—Victoria among the collective of sugarcane workers fighting in the Cuban mountains, Steve in the sit-down strike in a Flint auto plant. Both have stories to tell. The female intellectual, like the male proletarian, enters history, but she does so through her desire to connect the language of the personal to the experience of the political.

Each novel contains some reference to itself as a product of its time:

Slesinger dedicates her novel "to my contemporaries"; Gilfillan uses a first-person narrator to "report" on a real strike; and Herbst includes examples of reportage she herself wrote for the *New Masses*. Even as they accept its form and often its content, all three works provide internal critiques of the aesthetics of the proletarian novel, including its engendering of the working class. In a self-consciously reflexive move, Slesinger's novel follows the plan of three radicalized male intellectuals to establish a journal of leftist culture; both Gilfillan and Herbst provide as their main characters writers who are at work on reportage in support of strikers.

These self-referential devices place the novels within the genre of 1930s revolutionary fiction; yet they also reflect upon its prescriptions. The female protagonist of each novel cannot fully participate in the revolutionary activity surrounding her. Both class and gender differences, exacerbated by her position as an intellectual, keep her forever "foreign" and mark her subjectivity as that of the (linguistic) outsider—the spectator. The trope of maternity, which reembodied the working-class woman within narrative and within history, cannot contain the female intellectual and thus fractures her narrative. By calling attention to the inability of language to bridge the distances separating the woman writer from the committed activist, the female intellectual becomes a spectator to history and collectivity. If the markings of labor and desire on the body construct female working-class subjectivity, the failure of language to convey meaning or effect change deconstructs the female intellectual subject.

Unlike the novels discussed in the previous chapter, all three of these books were widely read and, for the most part, favorably reviewed in both the bourgeois and Left presses. Nevertheless, their popularity appeared to be limited by their topicality. Headlines blazing "A College Girl in the Pennsylvania Mines" applauded Gilfillan as an example of the emerging New Deal ethic of social concern among young people.[1] Slesinger's novel became an exposé of the "lost generation and the new morality."[2] However, by the time Herbst's novel appeared, shortly before the 1939 Hitler-Stalin pact, the appeal of revolutionary fiction had so diminished that her publisher, Harcourt, Brace, decided not to issue her saga of the Trexler family as the trilogy Herbst had originally envisioned.[3]

The construction of the radicalized female intellectual as a subject within 1930s women's revolutionary fiction proved difficult. The dilemma that fiction posed within proletarian aesthetics—as a traditionally feminine form with a masculine content—mirrored the dilemma of the radical female intellectual. Thus her position not only corresponded to that of the male proletarian but, more exactly, to that of proletarian fiction. Her novels have become "documents," as Murray Kempton called *The Unpossessed*, of the classed and gendered narratives circulating in American culture during the Depression.[4] These novels cross the vexing divide between politics and fiction over and over, suggesting that when the woman intellectual wrote revolutionary fiction, the legacy of domestic fiction carried over into political reporting and contaminated the spectatorial relationship that divided both classes and genders within each of these narratives.

The Unpossessed: *Sex or Revolution?*

Tess Slesinger's 1934 novel *The Unpossessed* presents both a synthesis and antithesis of the concerns of women's revolutionary fiction. A precursor to *The Company She Keeps*, Mary McCarthy's definitive statement on the differential experienced by women intellectuals between their sexuality and their class and the ways each was represented in the 1930s, *The Unpossessed* has been seen as a "curiosity" since its publication.[5] Alternately reviling and praising the novel for its insights into the position of the leftist intellectual, critics have had difficulty grasping its emphasis on sexuality and language. This seems to be because they have focused their critical attention on the male characters, who are often viewed as thinly disguised members of the Jewish anti-Stalinist Left's *Menorah Journal* group, at the expense of the female characters. Recently, however, the Feminist Press has reprinted the book as part of its series of novels from the 1930s, and Janet Sharistanian has provided an afterword noting that the three female characters exemplify the divisions that Slesinger herself experienced as she moved from being a flapper in the 1920s (her twenties) to a more developed political and creative engagement with the Depression during the 1930s (her thirties). When the work is thus placed in the context of women's domestic and modernist novels, one can see connections that link the fragmented, multiple female characters of *The Unpossessed* to formal patterns developed in a women's literary history.

The constraints on women's experience appear too narrow to permit a narrative that focuses on the education and development of a single character (as in the male bildungsroman). This "implausible" situation necessitates a splitting of character traits among two (or more) female characters in many middle-class women's narratives.[6] Harking back to the dual representation of woman in Western iconography as monster and angel, middle-class women writers themselves often reinscribed this duality. Thus Jane Eyre is doubled by Grace Poole (and Bertha Mason), her dark side brought to light (literally). In *The Awakening*, Edna Pontellier is triangulated with the maternal Madame Ratignolle and the creative Mademoiselle Reisz. Virginia Woolf divided Lily Briscoe and Mrs. Ramsey, suggesting that the twin desires for maternity and creativity were incompatible within one female character.[7]

The Unpossessed can easily be placed within this bourgeois feminist literary history, but it can also be read in the context of 1930s literary radicalism (as the uniformly male critical responses to its publication in 1934 and again in 1966 demonstrate). I believe, however, that the novel needs to be read as a "document," not about 1930s male literary radicals, but of women's regendering of the 1930s revolutionary novel, for Slesinger's novel opens up new spaces for the texts and bodies of classed and gendered intellectuals as subjects of narrative.

The Unpossessed, this "curiosity" that appears to transgress the proper subject matter of proletarian realism, really only reworks its content, not its prescribed form. For instance, although the characters are all either intellectuals or upper-class New Yorkers, the trajectory of the novel follows the typical proletarian narrative structure. Like a collective novel, the narrative simultaneously builds parallel stories about its six main characters through shifting points of view and narrative voices. The novel examines the attempt by three college friends, now in their thirties, to establish a leftist journal of art and culture. Each man is connected to a woman, who forms part of a secondary circle around the men. Also revolving within their orbits are two other groups: the Black Sheep, young students of one of the magazine's founders, Bruno Leonard; and the Middletons, an upper-class family who agree to bankroll the project.

The primary narrative weight is given to Bruno Leonard and the two other men as instigators of the magazine. Structural weight, however, is given to Margaret Flinders, whose voice opens and closes the novel, and to Elizabeth Leonard, who disrupts it from Europe. Interestingly, this structure resembles that of *Marching! Marching!*, in which the men's strikes are subversively undergirded by the "secondary zone" of femininity. Because she is Bruno's cousin, Elizabeth's presence is not motivated by the heterosexual bond of marriage that links Margaret and Norah to the other founders, Miles and Jeffrey. Instead, she brings another kind of link, a quasi-incestuous bond based in the mutual memory of family and ethnicity. These variations reroute the narrative as sexual jealousy begins to invade the group, resulting in disaster. Thus this novel cannot fulfill the utopian promise of the proletarian plot. When the collective disintegrates, the narrative returns to one hetero-sexual couple, Margaret and Miles, focusing on their loss, alienation, and pain after her abortion.

Revolutionary Dystopia

Structurally, the novel follows the proletarian collective form, in which vari-ous individuals from different backgrounds come together for a common goal. All of the voices are brought together in a climactic scene that should have the effect of suturing the disparate elements into a whole. Instead, in a self-conscious negation of the content of proletarian realism, the results here are cacophony and disarray. Rather than producing revolutionary harmony and the mass (maternal) body of the collective, the penultimate chapter results in schism as factions splinter apart.

The moment at which all of the characters enter the same space occurs not at a demonstration or on a picket line, but at a party. The carnivalesque becomes the grotesque because the group gathers inside the home of the wealthy Middletons rather than amassing on the streets. The gala is a society fundraiser for the Hunger Marchers in Washington and for the magazine, and so, in addition to intellectuals who support the journal, New York society is present as well. The hungry bodies of the workers are a distant, abstract concept for the party-goers. Instead, all eyes focus on Emily Fancher, whose husband has just been jailed for embezzlement, as she enters the room. In an ironic twist on the usual portrait of suffering working-class wives (like those in *Marching! Marching!*), Emily becomes a symbol of the "courageous" upper class, doing whatever is required to survive the troubling times of the Depres-sion.

Slesinger's title is, of course, linked intertextually to Dostoyevski's novel about a group of nihilist intellectuals who are drawn into political action as though possessed by the devil. In Dostoyevski's view, any break with the cosmology of Russian spiritualism would lead to disaster, the result of being "possessed" by insurgent, dangerous, and unsettling beliefs. With Slesinger, the failure is in the lack of those beliefs, because for Bruno, any idea immediately nurtures its opposite. Full of constant doubts, Bruno Leonard is as much an heir to Spinoza as he is to Marx. He is the outsider, too well off and too well assimilated to be connected to Jewish working-class culture, yet too Jewish to be accepted within the elite academy. Thought also stifles action in Miles. His neurotic obsession with his Puritan upbringing marks him as forever alienated from the world of the flesh—not just from sexuality, but from nitty-gritty politics as well—and renders him immobilized. Jeffrey envisions himself in a "pivotal" role, making connections between the bourgeoisie, the Party, and the proletariat, but he is so misinformed that his delusions are based on confusing a Trotskyist for a member of the Party.

For a "Marxist intellectual," as Jeffrey calls himself, theory supersedes action. Everything becomes an "idea" (as Bruno refers to the magazine), so that for them sex and even revolution are abstracted; they become the "opiates" of the intelligentsia. Bruno declares: "We have no parents and we can have no off-spring; we have no sex; we are mules—in short we are bastards, foundlings, phonys [*sic*], the unpossessed and unpossessing of the world, the real minority" (327). Lacking a clear class affiliation, these male intellectuals lose their gender markings as well. Their narratives and their bodies, unmarked by either labor or hunger, remain outside of the gender and genre conventions of proletarian realism; in this lies the psychological modernism of the novel. Despite Bruno's declaration, however, the men's narratives remain fixedly Oedipal as they mull over childhood memories instead of analyzing present-day political events; these "Marxist intellectuals" are really the descendants of Freud, not Marx. Literary radicals could always rely on psychoanalytic jargon to slander each other as neurotics or hysterics. By the decade's end, *The Company She Keeps* demonstrated that the leftist intellectual was best read through narratives of psychoanalysis rather than political economy. Both McCarthy and Slesinger supplement their psychological narratives with political readings of the bodies of female characters; but this course is tricky, and each novel inevitably was criticized as lacking a clear (masculine) political analysis—that is, as (feminine) literature.

Slesinger divides the middle class into layers based on sexuality and gender. The forces shaping the various strata are constructed almost entirely from family history. These characters are less affected by the historical changes in social and economic relations wrought by class struggle. Early formative experiences have already molded the behavior of each: Miles's experience of watching Uncle Daniel shoot his dog or Emmett's childhood as the son of a "too beautiful" mother are invoked to "explain" their personalities. Just as the moment of collectivity occurs at a socialite's party rather than a socialist one, so the static battles between womb and world will not lead to a utopian promise of transformation.

Those truly possessed of any kind of belief develop it from within—literally from within their hungry or pregnant guts. Observing that his students, the Black Sheep, may be the first generation of intellectuals to come from the working class, Bruno envies their embodied class consciousness. As Black Sheep leader Firman says: "A magazine's for propaganda. A revolution is for a full belly" (199). When his fiancée, Cornelia, faints from hunger, the issues under discussion as "ideas" become embodied, paralyzing and silencing the verbose men. Only Norah is able to aid Cornelia, recognizing the needs of this "exclusive twentieth century product, half-boy, half-girl born yesterday of movies, radio and matter-of-fact class-consciousness" (117). Cornelia's hungry body is a body without gender; she is the offspring of working-class and popular cultures and so resists the aesthetics and politics of high modernism that still enthrall the men. Similarly, Margaret's pregnant body will connect her to her working-class neighbors and to popular culture and put her at odds with the talk of the male intellectuals.

Because intellectuals appear outside the class configurations of capitalism yet remain locked in its sexual and gender arrangements, sex talk replaces the descriptions of labor that underpin the proletarian novel. But unlike the working-class women's discussions about sex with Clara Zetkin, the words of the Marxist intellectual are self-absorbed and apolitical. Echoing Bruno's description of the men, Margaret Flinders thinks of herself and her female friends as "sterile; we are too horribly girlish for our age, too mannish (with our cigarettes, our jobs, our drying lips) for our sex" (93). Riding "the fast express," Elizabeth lives "like a man." Bruno worries that "barren women meant the men were sterile" (97). But when Margaret discovers she is pregnant, little changes. Norah responds to the news without enthusiasm, informing Margaret that she and Jeffrey have decided against having children as "some sort of protest against something. . . . I forget just what" (305). Margaret ultimately succumbs to Miles's pressure and aborts the child after the fateful party.

By locating her narrative within a circle of leftist intellectuals, Slesinger eliminates class tensions as a narrative motor. Instead, the tensions of heterosexual marriage, gender ideology, and intellectual labor become the determinants of action (or lack thereof). Because these sexual, gender, and linguistic tensions are the stuff of fiction—feminized and perceived as being outside of historical efficacy—the possibilities for change are severely limited and result in a dystopian revision of the proletarian plot. A dual narrative propels other women's revolutionary novels, creating a confluence of class struggles and sexual desires as motors of history. In *The Unpossessed*, the engine has broken down because one axle, economic history in the guise of the masculinized proletariat, appears to have been eliminated. Nevertheless, its pointed absence in many ways remarks on its importance to Slesinger's politics.[8]

Womb versus World

" 'The real class struggle,' Bruno said, 'is the struggle between the sexes; and rebellion begins at home,' " recalls Margaret at one point (23). But Slesinger has locked this struggle to unchanging essentialist poles, a battle between male and female. She has, in effect, absorbed the proletarian metaphors of gender in which male intellectuals become feminized into the female bodies of Norah, Margaret, and Elizabeth. Because biology seems far more static than class, sexual difference appears natural. But class differences are historically constructed. Thus as an intellectual, Margaret has an inferiority complex because "she had stripped and revealed herself not as a woman at all, but as a creature who would not be a woman and could not be a man" (353, 357). She cannot find a location within the gender arrangements of bourgeois culture.

Margaret and Bruno both regard their projects—his magazine and her pregnancy—as means to overcome their paralyses, brought on for him by the contradiction between his ethnicity and his class and for her by the contradiction between her gender and her class. A parallel recurs between the magazine and the baby, between Bruno's idea and Margaret's body. Margaret experiences in her pregnancy the "third entity" that should develop out of a marriage, an intangible presence akin to the aura of the masses at a demonstration—a "mob" (178). Her maternal body would reproduce the carnivalesque freedom of the mass body, cutting across class barriers, and would overcome the paralysis and sterility of her position. Bruno pictures the magazine producing the same effect for him and his friends.

Both Margaret and Bruno seem to understand that collectivity demands more than simple addition. As Bertolt Brecht said, " 'We' and 'You' and 'I' / They are not the same."[9] For each, paralyzing circumstances intervene. Margaret's intractable and neurotic husband fears "drowning" in the fusion she offers as maternal woman (215). Because "the intellectual doesn't function," doesn't "do a God damn thing but talk," Bruno ultimately cannot act (81, 84). His wit, irony, and defensiveness divide him from the working class with which he is presumably allied, while his Jewishness cuts him off from the middle class for which he is the ostensible spokesman. The transformative power of magazine or baby is not enough to overcome the alienation experienced by each character.

Similarly, Jeffrey and Elizabeth share a common connection as radical artists and sexual compulsives. The inevitability and futility of their connection is described by Elizabeth:

> "I know," she said, "you're a lone wolf and I'm 'nice' and everybody else in the world is neurotic and you're the only communist." (. . . *oh Jeffrey, oh stranger, you know me, you know me as though I were naked*); all right Jeffrey, she thought wearily, you don't want me, I don't want you, and in the end we'll have each other. She felt a wan kinship with him, knowing him to be the same thing as herself, a weary Don Juan whose impulses having lost their freshness were the more compelling therefor [*sic*]. (308–9)

The push and pull between bourgeois masculinity and its history and bourgeois femininity and its desires is most clearly delineated in the characters of Miles and Norah. Miles, the scion of a New England Calvinist family, lives entirely in the mind. His contradiction of "womb versus world" is a gendered rephrasing of the mind/body split (215). Bourgeois masculinity enlists the life of the mind to enter history and change the world; but femininity inhabits the body, implying a retreat from history. Miles wonders whether his wage "cut" will secretly please Margaret because it can be viewed as an "emasculation," a "castration," making him "soft" and apolitical like her (22–24). Norah, the nurturing wife of Jeffrey, exemplifies this essence of femininity. She sits silently knitting during most of the group's gatherings, allowing Bruno to rhapsodize about her breasts as she sits on his lap, "as though his talk were child's play, or something purely male" (97). Responding to Mr. Middleton's advances like a "kitten," she also is always ready to accommodate Jeffrey's desire. Because she does live in the body, she is the only one who can react to Cornelia's hunger.

In all of these configurations, Slesinger has recreated a conventionalized narrative dyad, splitting mind and body according to gender oppositions. Among intellectuals, bourgeois gender differences remain firmly intact, even within the appearance of "a new morality." Because these differences form the central dilemma and conflict of the novel, the penultimate scene at the party, in which all the characters converge, does not result in the vision of a possible reorganization of social relations that the more traditional proletarian novels attempt.

Bruno and Elizabeth offer the possibility of escaping the terrible logic of heterosexuality. Their differences as man and woman are erased, to some extent, by their identity as cousins. Rachel Blau DuPlessis suggests that one strategy twentieth-century women writers have employed to derail the romantic plot is to pair siblings rather than couples. This device erases the sexual tension from the male/female encounter, thus undoing the logic of the romantic plot that must end in marriage (if it is comic) or death (if it is tragic). The fusion that Bruno and Elizabeth seek is presexual, lodged in their memories of a childhood companionship in which, because of their age difference, Bruno functioned in a semiparental role. The entry of another male, however, produces the Oedipal drama. Its reenactment on the dock throws Elizabeth into a shrill and defensive posture that continues to separate her from Bruno. Still, they continually interact in a way that is closer than husband and wife. As Emmett realizes, their kinship and ethnic ties are more threatening to his relationship with Bruno than if Bruno had been married to Elizabeth. Emmett becomes another example of Bruno's failure to take a side, to become "possessed." Emmett's sexual attraction to Bruno is perpetually forestalled by Bruno's inability to respond as a body. Emmett becomes the foil between Bruno and Elizabeth and between the magazine and its supporters. The danger of homosexual relations for Bruno, perhaps, is that they exceed the essences of bourgeois masculinity and femininity.

The male intellectual's world of political discourse is sterile, leading to the death of ideas as well as of action. As Bruno says, "My friends and myself are sick men—if we are not already dead" (330). So, too, is the female intellectual's womb as barren as Margaret's, which is literally emptied "for economic freedom . . . for intellectual freedom" (345). Only the Black Sheep, who are working-class students, begin to straddle the divides between intellectuals and workers, between male and female, between Gentile and Jew. After Firman and Cornelia marry, the students all leave the disastrous party together and hitchhike to Washington to join the real hunger marchers. "Personal life" merges with political action as the new husband and wife plan to spend their honeymoon among the unemployed demonstrators. They may jeopardize their status as scholars, but they connect with the movement and with history. Ideas and bodies elide in their group.

For all its dystopian vision, modernist style, and cultural insularity in form and content, *The Unpossessed* follows some of the thematic and rhetorical devices of the proletarian novel quite loyally. Slesinger seems to agree with the distinction between those who do—virile workers (who remain invisible here)—and those who talk—the myopic band of intellectuals whose sterility precludes action. What is to be done? Start a magazine; have a baby. Produce a text or a body that can be read within the conventional narratives of bourgeois culture. Neither solution is adequate to the unconventional narrative of revolutionary history, and so neither comes to fruition. Bruno's "idea" dies amid the drunken bodies at the Middletons' party; Margaret Flinders's baby dies for an idea of "intellectual freedom."

In establishing the parallel narratives of intellectual sterility and sexual hostility, Slesinger also in effect reproduces tropes gleaned from domestic fiction. Margaret's rage at her inability to find a place politically becomes a personal hatred that she vents at Miles. "She must cut out from him what made him a man, as she had let be cut out from her what would have made her a woman. He was no man: he was a dried-up intellectual husk; he was sterile; empty and hollow as she was" (348). In this case, I believe, Slesinger emphasized the political nature of sexual difference in the domestic narrative by pointing to the female intellectual as obliquely positioned in relation to the male economies of desire and meaning.[10] But as a political statement, Slesinger's novel exceeded the boundaries of literary radicalism because it insisted on reading the political meanings inscribed in female bodies and male texts. Thus Sidney Hook could declare to Alan Wald that Slesinger

> never understood a word about the political discussions that raged around her. . . . Her book shows that. There is no coherent presentation

of any political idea in it. . . . Tess could talk about Virginia Woolf, Jane Austen, some of the characters in Dostoyevski—not Ivan Karamazov— but the political isms were something her "obsessed husband and his odd friends" were concerned about. . . . Tess caught the psychological mood of some of Herbert's friends but she was a political innocent until the day of her death.[11]

As Hook's diatribe indicates, the politics of domestic fiction did not figure among the "isms" current during the 1930s; moreover, he reads her render- ings of intellectual "discussions" as providing psychological insight into the workings of her marriage, not as a political evocation of her dilemma as a female intellectual. In Hook's view, Slesinger could place herself in a female literary tradition of domesticity, but she failed to understand the masculine political realm—even in its literary figure of Ivan Karamazov. In short, as a reader of women's texts and an observer of men's moods, Slesinger remained apart from the virile political sophistication that male intellectuals assumed.

The problematic position of the intellectual within American class struc- ture appeared to most reviewers of *The Unpossessed* as a conflict for the male characters. The female intellectual, unrecognizable in the same terms, was read only within the narrative code of "the battle between the sexes." Her presence here and in the other novels I discuss in this chapter, however, stubbornly persists despite her lack of a suitable name. If she is a "creature," it is because her body, unlike the body of the working-class woman or the mass body of the working class, is not narrated through maternity. Neverthe- less, by possessing a womb she is locked out of the intellectual's world of talk and politics. Yet being a female intellectual and the wife of a male intellectual closes off her maternal possibilities.

"Missis Flinders," the final chapter of *The Unpossessed*, delves into the causes and effects of Margaret's abortion. The deliberate act of terminating her pregnancy sets Margaret apart from the working-class mothers of her neighborhood, and her D and C makes her an anomaly among the women in the maternity ward of the hospital. Like Margaret Sanders in *The Company She Keeps*, Margaret Flinders, as an intellectual woman, can possess no genealogy. She can neither look back to a maternal connection nor forward to a maternal collective in the way that LeSueur's girl can. As "intellectuals they were bastards, changelings . . . giving up a baby for economic freedom which meant that two of them would work in offices instead of one of them only, giving up a baby for intellectual freedom which meant that they smoked their cigarettes bitterly . . . intellectuals, as Bruno said, with habits generated from the right and tastes inclined to the left. Afraid to perpetuate themselves" (345). "Class-straddlers," because they are also gender straddlers, cannot generate. Intellectuals are neither productive—their labor, always at one remove from production, reproduces texts—nor reproductive—their desire, unable to develop into the maternal, destroys bodies.

By relocating the proletarian narrative within a group of intellectuals, Slesinger exposes the essentialist and bourgeois aspects of the metaphors of proletarian masculinity even as she reanimates them. Her "unpossessed" are perhaps not so different from Dostoyevski's "possessed." Each are "tight-rope-walking somewhere in the middle," awaiting their inevitable fall pre-cipitated by "one more war, one more depression"—the historical and eco-nomic forces beyond, yet bound to, their nihilistic "personal lives" (345–46).

I Went to Pit College:
The Proletarian Novel as Spiritual Autobiography

Lauren Gilfillan's narrative about the striking miners of Avelonia, Pennsylva-nia, is probably the most thoroughly self-reflexive piece of proletarian writing to emerge from the 1930s. This work, which poses as reportage about the miners, actually records how a young, college-educated woman develops into a committed journalist. The title embraces the workers' ironic commentary on their class and education. They are graduates of "pit college," not the University of Pittsburgh, and Laurie claims to have become one, too. The narrative contains typical descriptions of mining town life during a strike— encompassing weddings, picket lines, relief, funerals, and childbirth. But it does so through the mediating device of Laurie's persona. Never does narra-tive overwhelm narrator. Laurie's vision continually intercedes, marking off the landscape she witnesses as "foreign" (102). The "I" in the title under-mines the collective picture of the miners. The narrator's empathy with the miners is undercut by her commentary, which appeals to a middle-class, urban audience. This stance as outside observer runs counter to her self-presentation as an insider in Avelonia. This contradiction, which runs throughout the narrative, points to radical female intellectuals' ambivalent experience of their class and gender.

From her first entrance into the town, in a taxi from Pittsburgh, Laurie refuses to be honest with anyone about her origins. Although she expects the miners to open themselves to her, she fails to reciprocate. Instead, she dons "other clothes" and an "air of poverty"—what she comes to call her "Avelonia costume"—and "masquerades" as one of the "natives." Even while pretending to have gone native, she is keenly aware of her foreignness in this land of foreigners; the country of coal is as different from New York as a miner is from a writer. So Laurie constantly translates her observations about the miners into literary or aesthetic terms in order both to understand them herself and to make them legible to her bourgeois readers. She correctly assumes that her audience will more readily be able to identify a Brahms rhapsody than the "Internationale" and that the evocation of an Ingres painting will clarify her description of the pit mining.

Laurie's class alienation is manifested through differences in the use of language. The miners' apparel appears to her as "costumes," a masquerade she dons in order to pass as a native; but to the miners and their families, the outfits are simply "clothes" (86). Like a folklorist or an ethnographer, Laurie records in detail the working-class culture she encounters. She reproduces every lyric of every song the striking miners sing and includes clippings from the *Daily Worker*, a miner's "pome," and the complete outline of a "genuine" proletarian story written by her miner friend, Johnnie. Like the anthropologist, Laurie is an intimate outsider, "to be treated with hospitality, to be offered food and lodging, to smile with, to laugh at, to fall in love with—but never to be trusted" (260). Her sense that the faces and words of the miners created a foreign landscape (as did the mine tipples, slag heaps, and coal dust), which necessitated a masquerade in order for her to enter it, exacerbates the subject/object dichotomy at the heart of her pose and her narrative.

As a result, almost everyone becomes an object of Laurie's derision in this novel. The members of the Party who challenge Laurie are ridiculed by her for their arrogance. Johnnie's melodramatic proletarian story is quoted in full and compared negatively to a Horatio Alger story. The relief workers are exposed as drunks and thieves. Shirley, the "wildcat" Communist organizer, is teased about her beauty. And, of course, the cops, preachers, doctors, and judges are all mocked as hypocrites. Only the descriptions of Archie at work in the mine and Leo on trial for his union work present compassionate, nonsatiric portraits of classically heroic working-class men. In the end, when she destroys her notes, salvaging only the lyrics of the workers' songs, Laurie's ambivalence about taking the guise of a writer when she entered Avelonia becomes the source for her novel; both her subjectivity and the workers' collectivity are mediated through these language differentials. The narrative returns to Laurie as a record of "what I have seen and what I have felt about it" (272).

Shaped by the form of the spiritual autobiography, Laurie's story is complete with a petulant hero who is humbled through a series of encounters.[12] These include the descent into the "Slough of Despond" (coal pit) and the rejection of "The City of Destruction" (the trial).[13] In the end, Laurie is abandoned by all others to find herself. She must first wander alone for a few days, without money or companions—hungry, sick, and suspected by all as a spy. In this liminal state, she appears too ragged to be acceptable to the bourgeoisie of the town who attend church, so the doctor refuses to treat her. She is also left without connections in the miner's community when even her friend, Johnnie, who has been forced out of the YCL because of his allegiance to her, realizes that she never meant to stay with him. He, too, was just another specimen to her.

Johnnie's rejection turns Laurie away from her words, which she now sees as "such mockery." Neither the pose of writer nor the pose of miner's daughter has been successful. As she tells Shirley, she needs more education than an A.B. from Smith College in order to learn the whole of the alphabet. Laurie's final act of destroying her notes leaves her with the substance of her memory. Rerouting the narrative away from its protagonist's attempt to capture the miners' "way of existing" because "it's dramatic," *I Went to Pit College* recounts the process of Laurie's own reeducation as she gathers the miners' stories into her own (6, 252). She enters Avelonia paraphrasing Tennyson ("Avelonia—the Isle of the Blest"), only to be corrected by her cab driver: "No, Ma'am, just Avelonia" (3–4). But she leaves quoting a "miner's prayer," a new "ballad" composed by the workers to document their struggle (288).

The Masquerade

Laurie is a single, middle-class woman in a working-class community. The tensions raised by her gender are intimately linked to those raised by her class. On the one hand, she has the "baby face and pert manners" of the well-bred child and thus is able to enter miners' homes with little difficulty (267).

Everyone appears eager to have her share a bed with their daughters and to take her in as one more mouth to be fed. Yet when she enters the relief station after her first night in Avelonia, she "survey[s] the men" while smoking a cigarette (12–13). She acts, in other words, like a man: looking, smoking, talking to strangers. Her behavior challenges the established standards of femininity in the ethnic mining communities, where the distinction between good girl and bad girl is firmly coded in behavior. Laurie's sexuality is an aid to her investigation, however, because the men are attracted to her; in flirting, they allow her access to meetings, to the coal pits, and to information that they otherwise would keep secret. The fascination she exerts over little girls, to whom she is an exotic outsider representing the world of movies and glamour, enables her to slide in and out of their kitchens and bedrooms. But she goes unrecognized by the women who are her contemporaries; only Shirley, the Communist organizer from New York, engages her in conversation.

From their first encounter, Shirley is presented as the opposite of Laurie. Whereas Laurie ambiguously "masquerades," Shirley is bound by Party discipline to act openly. During the children's outing to Pittsburgh to beg money, Laurie sneaks off downtown to get a decent lunch. But Shirley is arrested for assaulting an officer, and her political defiance stands in stark contrast to Laurie's self-interest. Laurie is fascinated by Shirley's beauty and ethnicity. She dubs her "the Jewish Joan of Arc" (42). This sexualized fascination becomes a source of tension when Shirley ultimately becomes jealous of Laurie's friendship with Johnnie. Shirley finally confronts Laurie about her motives and about her pretensions as an artist, lecturing her about the politics of aesthetics. She condemns Laurie's bohemian "attitudes" as being those of "an adventurer who wants excitement" and provides a damning condemnation of Laurie's writing as *both* "art for art's sake" and "melodramatic"—two epithets Michael Gold might have used (268–69). However, Laurie silences Shirley by redefining her militancy as femininity: " 'Shirley,' I said awe in my voice, 'you're gorgeous' " (289). The two women, both different from the Avelonia women, are differentiated from each other by their class and commitment.

"The miners don't approve of girls smoking," Laurie is told again and again after her identity as "the writer from New York" is made public and she decides to smoke openly again. She is reprimanded for transgressing this rule that divides nice girls from bad girls. Not only do the men look at her differently, but Shirley also reproaches her. When Laurie replies that Communists are supposed to treat men and women equally, Shirley says that although it might be acceptable in New York or at college, "it gives the miners the wrong impression" (112).

The Communists are the most rigid adherents of bourgeois morality in Avelonia. When Shorty tells Laurie before their date, "Nobody can figure you out. You ain't a bad girl—hands off is your motto—but you're free an' easy in your ways" (143), it is Cecil, one of the organizers, who explains Laurie's contradictory position to her. At a wedding dance, she realizes she has never spoken to any of the young women in Avelonia. "There stretched an un-bridgeable gulf between me and my wild hair and untrammeled ways, and these miners' daughters with their primness and knowing glances beneath sweeping lashes" (147). According to Cecil, Laurie is a "suspicious charac-ter" who "didn't have no dates, but . . . smoked." And so the miners thought "maybe you was a bad girl" because she "talked to the men all the time" (148). Like Margaret in *The Unpossessed*, Laurie's position as a female intel-lectual—that is, as an embodied speaker—defies categorization in the class/ gender arrangements of proletarian fiction.

Suspicions about Laurie are voiced over and over again in two ways: either she is seen as "a spy," "a Mussolini," the class enemy; or she is perceived as a "bad girl." Both epithets are connected, because the problem Laurie poses to the community is located in the relationships of her class to her gender and of her politics to her sexuality. She appears to have made herself "as nearly as possible in keeping with [her] present environment" (256), but once she meets the young women who are her contemporaries, it is clear that her "wild hair" and "untrammeled ways" are out of keeping with Avelonian femininity. Because she can only recognize the proletariat as masculine, she has come to Avelonia to learn of its "ways"—that is, its labor—through the men. But because she is young, the older women embrace her and the young girls talk to her about their desires.

Paradoxically, Laurie's gender has facilitated her entry into the town. As a woman, she is not taken as seriously as the male journalists who have been there before. Her behavior is so far out of line with the gender ideology predominating the white, ethnic miner's culture, and she is so clearly not a part of the mixed-race culture of the southern miners in Seldom Seen who survive chronic unemployment as moonshiners, that she is beyond recogni-tion. Yet because of her class she is distrusted. Any writer, even one who reports sympathetically on the trial of the Communists accused of murder, is an enemy. The miners' distrust and Laurie's flippant dismissal of the Party arouse suspicion, causing the representatives of the International Labor Defense (ILD) to investigate her papers to find out which side she is on. Jim Snyder, the state organizer for the Party who spends one evening interrogating Laurie, "wanted to know everything—where I came from, how I got here where I was living what I thought of the place, when I was going to leave. . . . He dug into my past life. Nobody has asked me that" (256). Later, he raids Laurie's suitcase, finding "city clothes, monogrammed ivory mirror, powder and lipstick, camera and typewriter and what was most damning of all . . . a letter from my mother . . . enclosing five checks for five dollars each." He displays them all to "the committee of comrades," who "viewed with rage" these personal effects of a middle-class woman (255).

The violation of her property seems the only way to enforce control over Laurie. Although she is untouchable as a woman, she is vulnerable as a middle-class intellectual. Once Snyder has exposed her class position, she is open to a symbolic rape of her possessions—those trappings that mark her class and gender differences. Her silk dresses and ivory mirror only reinforce the anger her writing and her money have already caused. The public exposure of her private and most intimate belongings makes her a complete outcast among the miners. The men and women who had once sat and talked over the day's events with Laurie now shun her. She has been exposed as a spy for political and, to some extent, sexual reasons.

Transformed into a "grotesque figure," Laurie finally becomes unacceptable to everyone in Avelonia. "My face looked like a map of the moon. . . . And my hair! With rising horror, I plucked at a little animal crawling along a waving tendril" (280). Her sexuality alienates her from her female companions, her class differentiates her from the miners, and both differentiate her from the Communists. As a female spectator, she makes a "spectacle" of herself and becomes a "female grotesque."[14] This convergence of spectator and spectacle in the female intellectual is akin to the "masquerade" of masculinity in femininity that feminist film theorists have argued is constructed for women within cinema and within culture.[15] As a gender and class anomaly, she becomes "monstrous," illegible within the narratives either of domesticity or proletarian culture.

Breaking the boundaries of gendered class narratives, Laurie's narrative also transgresses the borders of genre. The device of the first-person narrative validates the authenticity of the experiences described because they have happened to someone who appears to be real: the author of the book. In fact, though, this device tends to distance the reader from the conventions of realism by turning every detail into a vignette involving the narrator. This was precisely Edwin Rolfe's complaint about the book; he found that the "whole effect of *I Went To Pit College* is spoiled, loses dignity and power and sincerity, by the too-insistent intrusion of the author's personality into the direct narrative."[16]

This character calls herself Laurie in a book authored by Lauren Gilfillan. She is a constructed character: Laurie is different from Lauren Gilfillan, who differs from the Harriet Woodbridge Gilfillan who appears as author in the card catalog. The I/eye who observes becomes of primary importance in the picture that emerges of the miners' strike. Every instance of collectivity—working, picketing, rallying—is narrated through Laurie's experience. For instance, Laurie journeys "de profundis" to the coal pit by wearing a miner's "costume," cutting her hair, and disguising her voice. Once there, she is overcome by the smell of coal dust and dynamite within the dank pit. She forces Johnnie's brother to take her out. Ultimately, the "I" of the narrator is both observer and participant and, as such, begins to locate herself as a subject among a collectivity, rather than simply among objects. Female subjectivity is constructed, then, between and within both gender and class. A dual language mediates her various poses; it lays bare the distances between observer and participant, between bourgeoisie and proletariat, between the University of Pittsburgh and Pit College, between female and male. Its very construction points up the separation of gender and class within proletarian aesthetics, with the attendant marginalization of women that this separation produces.

Unlike "the girl," whose subjectivity derived from her capacity to transmit the stories of others so transparently, Laurie always relates the miners' stories from her point of view. Her narrative is a record of what *she* "saw" and what *she* "felt" about it, and as such it foregrounds the first-person singular. Her subjectivity depends upon elements of the bourgeois realist subject. In a way, this is a kunstlerroman, the story of the development of a committed writer. Laurie carries with her the objects that make up her bourgeois femininity—lipstick, powder, and silk dresses—but hides them. She also carries with her objects that allow her to see both herself and others—mirror and camera—and to record their words—her typewriter—though she must also keep these hidden. That they elicit such rage when found suggests that the position of the female intellectual from which she can write her proletarian document is extremely precarious.

Because she both indulges and rejects a series of contradictory privileges based on her class, age, education, gender, and sexuality, Laurie becomes vulnerable to her own lack of candor. Her series of masks keeps her narrative dishonest; however, she admits her dishonesty. This paradox reveals the contradictory premises of reportage: it documents a collective story of struggle through the narrative of an individual. Ironically, Gilfillan's lack of "dignity," her deliberate crossing of gender, class, and genre boundaries, made *I Went to Pit College* a prototype for other pieces of committed reportage.[17] Its self-consciousness as a fictive document points up the anomalies both of reportage and of the radical female intellectual who writes it.

Rope of Gold: *Family/History*

In her memoir of her experiences as a journalist in Spain during its civil war, Josephine Herbst wrote that, although it had been said that the pen was mightier than the sword, "it didn't seem that the typewriter held a ghost of a chance against the new weapons."[18] The failure of language to overcome the horrors of twentieth-century violence became the focal theme of her novel *Rope of Gold*, the final volume of an untitled trilogy charting the demise of an American middle-class family, the Trexlers. The novel begins in the early 1930s with the protagonists, Jonathan and Victoria Chance, visiting Jonathan's conservative father in Michigan. The Chances have just come from a meeting of militant farmers in Chicago, and although elated by the experience, they begin to doubt its efficacy as soon as they try to put their experience of revolutionary élan into words. Noting that "it would take a new language to convey" what was "a difficult thing to explain in a few words" because it "involves more than meets the eye," Jonathan retreats from his family (7–8). This tension between language and experience resonates throughout the novel until, in the last scene involving the Chances, we find Victoria "hammering the typewriter keys . . . as if the guns had already been mounted" (403). Her desire as a radical intellectual is to articulate the psychological and historical forces pushing the waffling middle class into action.

Rope of Gold completes the cycle of the Trexlers, as recounted to Victoria and her sisters in the storm cellars of their Iowa home by their mother, Anne, to entertain them during the long hours of tornado watches. *Pity Is Not Enough* traces the tragic inability of Anne's older brother, Joe Trexler, to amass the fortune he expects will be his in postbellum Georgia. Joe's generosity and his failure to understand the dynamics of capitalist accumulation make him the victim of fluctuations in the economy and politics of Reconstruction. His final attempt at gaining wealth, gold mining in South Dakota, ends disastrously and leaves him mad and penniless.

The Executioner Waits continues the story of the Trexlers, following Anne's younger brother David and his successful ventures into American free enterprise. Where Joe was plagued by sentimental attachments to his past, David can read the future with cool detachment. And although neither man was constrained by morality, David seems better equipped to survive the horrors of accumulation. However, his end is tragic, too, as workers around the world begin to stir in rebellion against the first world war by organizing unions and demanding shorter hours and better pay. David's business crumbles when his workers go on strike. Counterposed to the lives of both brothers is Anne's family of four daughters. Anne Wendel marries a Quaker farmer and moves west with him in search of the capital that will ensure a better life for her daughters; instead, continual failure follows them everywhere. Anne's only legacy to her daughters consists of the accumulated (hi)stories of several generations in the form of her reminiscences and the letters she kept in her attic—letters dating back to William Penn's settlement of Pennsylvania. This legacy of stories serves as the source for *Rope of Gold*.

The final volume of the trilogy follows the Trexlers through Anne's third daughter, Victoria, who has been named for her uncle Joe's alias, Victor. The stories of the past serve as a thread connecting her to Uncle Joe. In each of the three novels, the Trexlers function as an arena in which various forces—social, economic, political, psychological—interact. Herbst described the structure of the trilogy as "a kind of pursuit" by which

> I have followed first the kind of haunting history of my family to its natural decay and end, that history only meaningful because of its wider implications. Then I found I had to begin picking up clues of my own life and some of them went back to observations seen early in life and those in turn carried me along to a point where an automobile worker in Flint, a peasant in Cuba, a soldier in Spain had become more real and moving

than any memory of my buried family, but not obliterating that family or
its meaning either.[19]

Throughout the trilogy, the narrative is previewed by events that appear as
historical inserts in an earlier volume (such as the South Dakota farmers'
boycott in *The Executioner Waits*, which plays an important part in *Rope of Gold*)
and then become elements of the narrative in the subsequent volume. Time
and space begin to collapse as history rushes forward to the present, so that
the final preview in *Rope of Gold* reveals the defeat of the Loyalists in Spain in
1938, although the narrative itself ends in 1936 with the sit-down strikes in
Flint, Michigan.

In a 1939 review of *Rope of Gold*, Philip Rahv complained that "[Herbst's]
nervous and nostalgic style is fundamentally at odds with her objective subject
matter." Rahv felt that the work lacked a coherence, an "organic center of
consciousness," and thus failed as a novel.[20] Rahv is correct in pointing to the
disjunctures within the novel; however, his criticisms indicate that he has
missed the point. *Rope of Gold* is a prime example of the ways that women who
wrote revolutionary fiction fractured their narratives, presenting one that
encoded history and another that encoded desire. The dichotomy Miles
Flinders sensed between "world" and "womb" in *The Unpossessed* is here
sensed by Victoria between "our life," which for Victoria means the political
and creative work she and her husband Jonathan are doing, and "love,"
the small domestic arrangements of their increasingly unhappy marriage.
Whereas Miles and Jonathan cannot see a reconciliation (as Rahv also could
not), Victoria struggles to reconcile the conflicting tensions posed by history
and sexuality—by hunger and love.

Rahv noted in his review that "*Rope of Gold* is the third volume of a series
that has been advertised as a chronicle of the American middle class in
decline." Herbst's project is to portray the spectrum of experiences and
responses from the Depression, as expressed by the fractured layers of the
middle class. Her trilogy, then, seems to complement two other great trilogies
of the 1930s: John Dos Passos's *U.S.A.* and James T. Farrell's *Studs Lonigan*.
Where Farrell sought to dissect one element of the middle class, the petit
bourgeois urban ethnic, Dos Passos painted the entire panorama of types and
classes in America through the eyes of a radicalized intellectual. Herbst's work
falls somewhere in between. In her novel, the layering of time that weaves

history out of past, present, and future is displayed through the fractions of the middle class. This spectrum ranges from the proletarianized farmer Steve Carson to the declassed petit bourgeois family of Victoria's older sister Nancy Radford, through a variety of radicalized intellectuals to the quasi fascism of Jonathan's industrialist brother-in-law Ed Thompson. Herbst's primary focus is on the middle strata, the alienated (male) intellectuals whose bohemian days have given way to a peripheral connection to the "movement." Within that strata, Lester Tolman finds a niche as a speechwriter (and apologist) for Roosevelt's New Deal and Jonathan becomes a Party "front" whose commitment wavers because he no longer either writes or organizes. Only Victoria finds a way to overcome her alienation by connecting her personal suffering, her ability as a journalist, and her commitment to those in the grass-roots struggle.[21]

This layering process is also accomplished spatially as the novel follows its characters from Michigan, South Dakota, New York, and Pennsylvania to Cuba, Spain, and Germany.[22] At times, various characters unknowingly converge on the same location. For instance, Lester Tolman meets Glen Thompson in Havana. Tolman, a radical journalist, is there to report on the impending general strike; Thompson is there to procure munitions for his brother Ed's strike-breaking goons.

This weblike structure serves a number of rhetorical functions. First, it implies that one cannot build a monofocal narrative about history; too many contradictory forces shape it. Second, one cannot assume the individuality of a family, which is constantly being shaped by economics, history, and politics. Third, although individuals feel atomized within American capitalism, appearing to drift along disconnectedly, they are interconnected by class. Finally, as the temporal and spatial logic is dismembered and reconnected, causality is called into question. Reading *Rope of Gold* is like unraveling a thick cord in which the entwined strands produce a knot of historical complexity.

Herbst's title seems to be a paradoxical play on the phrase *rope of sand*, whose sense of incoherence, disjunction, and noncohesiveness is obviated by the substantial power of a weighty metal—the universal equivalent, gold.[23] Money links the characters of the novel as it links the workings of American society. The rope of gold pulls things together into a whole, consolidating the various fractions into a portrait of America. Certainly an on-going concern of each successive generation of Trexlers is money—getting it, spending it, and saving it—and this intergenerational obsession mirrors the mad frenzy of capital accumulation that followed the Civil War and continued until the threads unraveled after the 1929 stock market crash. Rope can be entwined in complex ways to produce webs, linking a system together; but it can also prove illusionary, built out of many individual threads that, once frayed, leave nothing behind.

Words and Deeds

Rope of Gold poses a series of oppositions between word and deed, love and politics, idea and experience. Jonathan eschews his literary career as he becomes increasingly involved in the lives of the farmers who are his neighbors in Pennsylvania. Despite (or because of) his effectiveness at organizing them to demand more relief and to build a cooperative meeting house, he is urged by the Party leadership to become a "front"—that is, to return to the world of middle-class intellectuals who dabble in leftist politics in order to raise money for the cause. Victoria, already resentful that Jonathan joined the Party alone and feeling like a "bride jilted at the church," rails against the Party for so misusing Jonathan's talents (171).

Throughout the novel, Jonathan struggles to reconcile his contempt for his class and education with the advantages he has gained from the resulting ability to use language effectively. Like most literary radicals, he sees virility as residing in the oppressed class of workers and farmers. "The very glibness of it [what he now was saying] chilled his marrow. He had somehow, without his own desire or will, been ripped up from his place among men. . . . [H]e had become that which he abhorred" (328). He feels a death in the falsity of language, hating himself for becoming a "word twister" (329). Shakespeare refers to rhetoric as a "rope-trick" in *Taming of the Shrew*, and Jonathan, too, thinks language is deceitful; like the rope of gold, it produces disastrous effects. "Talk. Would he never break free of it? He thought of Jack London whose faith had flickered and paled the longer he had remained away from the source of his beliefs. Surrounded finally by money and talk, he had killed himself" (398). Jonathan aches to be able to repeat the words of a retreating American soldier fighting in Spain: "A book is only another's lies. I'm one of those fellows that has to look" (407).

If Jonathan is plagued by the contradictory position of his class, which he sees as the "reliance well-intentioned men and women gave to the word rather than the deed," Victoria's conflicts hover between history and desire (239). For Victoria, "doing something with our lives" becomes a way to overcome the contradictions of her class and gender within the movement (285). She needs to see a connection between personal intimacy and political involvement—something that eludes them. She first articulates this clearly to Jonathan when he has arrived in New York from his "front" work. She is reorganizing Tolman's notes about the sugar empire into an article and wants to finish her work before making love to him. As has happened throughout the novel, missed connections impede their marriage. When she is one place, he is always in another; Victoria and Jonathan never meet up despite continually crossing paths. In this case, she has achieved a new relationship to her work and wants Jonathan to understand the importance of historical memory. But Jonathan misunderstands Victoria's reference to "our lives," seeing it as a condemnation of their relationship.

For Victoria, the on-going pain of their marriage coalesces in the stillbirth of their premature son. Throughout the novel, references to her dead baby (and to the deaths of other children) recur, paralyzing Victoria with depression. Just as Margaret Flinders cannot be both an intellectual and a mother, maternity is closed off for Victoria also. However, the image of the dead baby is finally recharted as a metaphor for Victoria's newly born activism. After she visits the sugarcane workers' soviet in Realengo and meets other mothers who have suffered the death of a child, Victoria steps out of her mourning and into history, vowing to "cry no more" (408). Paradoxically, she drops out of the narrative at this point. Ultimately the proletarian aesthetic, which cannot support the presence of a female body that has not become a maternal body, precludes the possibility of an embodied intellectual and a nonmaternal female.

As we have seen in *The Unpossessed*, the male intellectual is plagued by an ambivalent relationship with ideas, which always appear opposed to action. In *Rope of Gold*, much of the thematic discussion of the failure of ideology— one's "faith" in ideas—occurs through the character of Lester Tolman, a college friend of Jonathan's who has spent several years in Germany dreaming of writing a novel. He has been forced to return to America after Hitler's rise to power. Essentially apolitical, Tolman has witnessed enough history—he retells the story of the burning of the Reichstag until it becomes an incantation—to know that he can be iconoclastic yet safe by pursuing a career as a radical journalist in the United States. "He had seen meetings that were something, blocks in Dresden packed with thousands upon thousands waving the red flag and then, also, he had seen houses mutely and submissively draped with the swastika. . . . He thought of this now walking slowly, and in fairness trying to understand what lay back of his lack of faith" (221).

Tolman, like Jonathan, suffers from a sense of desperation created by a discordance between the class upbringing of his youth and the rebelliousness that characterized his decision to become a writer. The events of history unfolding around them have forced each man into a confrontation with the rebellions of the belly, rather than those of the heart or mind that characterize their own bohemianism. Tolman observes and records, leaving Victoria to sort through his notes and draw conclusions. When Victoria insists that Tolman discover what Batista plans to do to the strikers in Cuba so that she can get word to her informants, Tolman says it is pointless. History overwhelms him. "As he had never believed in anything, he shifted from despising those who had faith and in feeling chagrin at an emotion he had not experienced. It was not religious faith he envied but that deeper surer thing, such as led Galileo to his death muttering, *the earth does move*" (324).

The failures of language and faith that plague Jonathan and Tolman are most ferociously expressed by the preacher at the farmer Tub Johnson's funeral. Unable to complete his sermon, finding the words of the Bible stale and incapable of holding meaning, the preacher is literally brought to silence. "The words would not come. He stumbled in his speech." This moment of silence is emblematic of the paralyzed (male) intellectuals faced with the forces of economic ruin and fascist violence. Steve Carson, who "understood the preacher's trouble . . . and understood what he meant," can translate this failure because of his commitment as a labor activist (380). Jonathan, by contrast, socializes with those who "don't talk politics," instead preferring to have him read the final pages of *The Dead* because "it's so poetical, so beautiful" (394).

The Memory of the Mother

Within the Trexler trilogy, memory serves as the repository of family history, keeping alive those lost family members through stories, memorabilia, and letters. Victoria was raised on her mother's stories, and her own memory of her mother fuels her vision of history. The connection between a lost past and an unfulfilled present recurs through the juxtaposition of her memories with her grief over the stillbirth of her child. These memories seem to impede Victoria, keeping her tied to a bourgeois vision of maternal suffering that precludes her commitment to revolutionary change. Yet both Jonathan and Steve Carson draw on the memories of their dead mothers as sustenance for their activism. It is finally the picture of the Cuban women, whose maternal suffering impels them to fight, that prompts Victoria's vision of her family as she rides through the mountains of Realengo. This world, cut off from "autos and big guns and doctors and schools," presents a kind of mythic vision of the collective (370). She rides a donkey, "laughing to herself, everything saturated with delight. . . . Tomorrow or the next day the world down below would have to be faced. But up here fear seemed childish" (371). Her sense of comfort evokes the stories of her mother's family that permeated her early life:

> All the lives of all the people she had ever known joggled and pressed as if they were beams of light and she would not have been surprised to see riding by her side a strange company of faces she had never seen, her grandfather with his straight tall figure and deepset eyes, the optimistic handsome Uncle Joe, and even Uncle David Trexler. . . . Rosamond would be somewhere and Jonathan just behind her, and the boy who took her dress off back of the schoolhouse saying, "Say you love me." (371–72)

For Victoria, the carnivalesque vision of postrevolutionary society connects with the sensuous memories of her mother's stories and her own first sexual encounter. The pleasures of the collective recall the early pleasures hiding in memory—the "sonorous envelope" of her mother's voice.[24] When she is confronted with the reality of violence after returning from the world of memory to the world "down there," she is once again trapped by the paralysis of language that has marked her other political engagements. Earlier in the novel, after Victoria has returned to New York to work, she shares an apartment with a friend and is appalled to find that seemingly all of New York is dabbling in radical politics. The "paper revolutionaries" who argue "Marx, fifth hand," spend endless hours talking of communism but cannot act (165). Victoria feels superior to them: she is married to an organizer and is having an affair with an exiled member of the German Communist Party. Yet she is unable to confront them, paralyzed by the sense that "words were as useless as broken crockery" (203). Now, alone in her hotel room in Havana, with the streets erupting in violence below her window, she is stymied by the inability of words to reach across the chasm between herself and Jonathan, between her feelings and her politics:

> She pulled a sheet of paper toward her and, as a sharp explosion sounded in a nearby street, wrote rapidly, "Jonathan, speak to me, just once more, forgive anything I've said wrong. Just speak to me once more, I don't care what you say. You are so far away, I can't find you." The words looked bloated and deformed with her tears. If there were something she could send him to remind him so he would speak again. She thought of the time Jonathan had told her of the travelling man in North Dakota and his strange love token of curling hair. She reached for the scissors and pulling up her skirts cut quickly. (363)

Jonathan's silence provokes Victoria to make a spectacle of herself—albeit a literary spectacle, as her disclosure is confined to the privacy of a letter. Spectacle accompanies the carnival but, as Mary Russo has pointed out, because the carnival depends on gender (and class) stratification, its meaning is never completely liberating for women within patriarchal relations (or for the poor within feudal or capitalist relations). Women remain outside the excesses of the carnival because they are vulnerable to those very excesses.[25]

If Victoria's obsessive memories of her estranged husband silence her on politics, leaving her unable to complete her article on the Cuban sugar strike, she is also unable to find words for her sexual alienation from him. Thus she resorts to her mother's device of concretizing memory through objects and sends him a lock of her pubic hair in a letter. She has enabled him to keep a piece of herself. Her mother, "who had never thrown string away . . . had died with an attic full of letters hanging from the rafter like beheaded corpses as if the written words of the dead somehow pledged the family to immortality" (169). Victoria reenacts the process of storing history. Jonathan, though, busy with politics and feeling guilty for abandoning Victoria, carries the unopened letter in his pocket "as if he had concealed the ashes of her body," thereby consigning Victoria to the attic of family history from which she has always drawn her narrative (398). The dance Victoria choreographs between enacting her desire and acting in history revolves around her maternal memories, memories that continually re-place her within (family) history.

This connection between failed communication and the obsessive quality of memory and mementos differentiates the female intellectual from the male proletarian. At the same time, however, Herbst identifies the female intellectual with the male worker by pairing Victoria and Steve Carson throughout the novel. They first encounter one another at the Chicago convention of farmers to which Jonathan alludes in the novel's first pages, and they meet again when Victoria accompanies Lester Tolman on his cross-country trip to investigate the sugar industry. Moreover, each has had a childhood encounter with death. Steve's mother and sisters all died in a tornado that he alone survived. His stepmother tells him, "You weren't spared from the cyclone that time for no purpose" (156). Victoria survives a scarlet fever epidemic. After she has recovered her mother tells her, "You were meant to live for something" (315). Both Victoria and Steve have been marked by their mothers for some historical purpose.

After returning from Havana to Miami, Victoria receives a final letter from Jonathan. A storm is rising as she returns to her room, and she remembers "crouching in the cyclone cellar as they did long ago" (403). Determined to send her notes on Cuba to Tolman, she sits "hammering the typewriter keys . . . as if this might be the last deed she would ever do, as if the guns had already been mounted and were training upon that very room" (403). As if answering Victoria, Steve sits in a Michigan auto plant surrounded by the militia:

> He thought of himself in the cyclone cellar and his mother's cold hand growing colder, then his father's voice with its indignation against the wrongs in the world. He had escaped death from the cyclone but now if he should die, he at least knew why. He searched in his pocket for a bit of paper to write a word to Lorraine . . . and it seemed to him he had never loved her so much as now, lying on this cold stone floor with all the men around him. . . . This is my job, he thought. (428)

Victoria's determination to "cry no more since there were those who had shed blood, not tears" overcomes her loneliness by connecting her pain to a worldwide revolutionary struggle. Her desire for historicity, glimpsed through the windows of a bus en route north, literally drives her out of the narrative. "She sat bolt upright and watched the bus run into daylight. The road and fields were solid ground and the objects of the earth like sleepy animals were rising to their knees" (406). Throughout the novel, Victoria's struggle to come to terms with her sexuality, the burdens of memory, her marriage, and her desire to be part of history has turned the motors of the narrative. When she finds reconciliation in the solid ground and objects surrounding her—the narrative of masculine struggle and history simply overriding the narrative of feminine memory and desire—her story is over. The novel, however, ends with Steve's reverie (and his plan to write his "big newsreel") inside the auto plant in Flint. In a quintessential vision of pro-letarian fraternity, Steve and his coworkers sleep together amid the machines as they wait for a confrontation with the militia outside.

Although the proletariat remains mostly invisible in *Rope of Gold*, as it was in *The Unpossessed*, Herbst like Slesinger seems to conform quite closely to two of the conventions of proletarian realism: the working class is marked by labor as masculine and (male) intellectuals are feminized as effete, ineffectual, and self-involved. Whereas Slesinger's female intellectuals are consumed by their inability to reconcile class and gender contradictions, Herbst reconciles the dilemma of the female intellectual subject by linking Victoria to the male worker and by maintaining the maternal within the narrative. But male intellectuals, who at worst embrace fascism and at best become resigned to liberal politics or routinized Party hack work, are surely "the dead."

Decentering the Sexual Center

More than metaphorically gendering the proletariat as masculine, Herbst describes Steve Carson as the heroic proletarian through a traditional bil-dungsroman. Leaving behind his wife and child, Steve moves from the repressive world of family and farm into the oppressive world of the factory, but also into the potentially liberating realm of the struggle; by so doing, he exchanges the clutches of psychodrama for the open arena of history. Early on, Steve's stepmother has "sacrificed" her three daughters to him, believing him to be special because he was spared by the tornado that killed his mother and siblings. Carson becomes the model revolutionary at the expense of a series of female characters: his mother, stepmother, sisters, and wife. But their idealized memory returns to him during his moment of struggle.

The melodramas of female sacrifice and loss and of maternal memory have been played through Victoria's narrative as well. The reconciliation of Vic-toria's memories of her grandmother, mother, and sisters with the lives of the Cuban peasant women re-members Victoria's severed family history. She has no husband, no child, but these connections to her past reinvest her present struggle. The novel closes with Carson's final action of class solidarity, but by connecting Victoria to Steve and both of them to maternal memories, Herbst reconnects the fraternal community of the auto plant to the trope of maternal collectivity glimpsed by Victoria in her vision of the earth rising up, which follows her encounter with the mothers of Cuba and the mother of memory.

Ostensibly, the construction of the Herbst trilogy echoes that of Dos Passos's *U.S.A.*, and yet a number of disjunctive elements undermine the latter's effect. Herbst's quirky chapter headings, dual narratives, turgid repetitiveness, and odd characters—some stereotypes, others remarkably complex—all tend toward a disequilibrium that recasts the revolutionary novel. If, as Donald Pizer has argued, Dos Passos was constructing a masculine identity using the camera's eye sections as the "sexual center" of *U.S.A.*, then Herbst seems to be decentering sexuality, identity, and narrative.[26]

In her biography of Herbst, Elinor Langer wonders rhetorically about the discrepancy between Herbst's actual lover, a woman, and Victoria's fictional lover, Kurt Becher, both of whom occupy a similar position between the real and fictive married couples—Herbst and Herrmann, Victoria and Jonathan. The desire not to offend the extremely homophobic leadership of the Communist Party must have played a part in Herbst's decision to make Victoria's lover a man. Herbst was aware of Michael Gold's indictment of Thornton Wilder as a "pansy," and, as Elsa Dixler speculates, it is unlikely, at a time when motherhood was being saluted by the Party as woman's highest goal, that those associated with the Party would expose their homosexuality.[27] Because Herbst never joined the Party but remained a loyal follower and supporter, she may have been inclined to adhere even more strictly to the line than if she were a member in good standing. Charges of bourgeois bohemianism were raised whenever it was politically useful, so the appearance of correct politics and behavior would be especially important for a fellow traveling woman intellectual who had been living a bohemian life for some years.

Furthermore, Kurt Becher, who is a marginal figure within the novel, affects both Jonathan and Victoria more powerfully as a symbol than as a character. To Jonathan, Becher represents the kind of revolutionary that he himself can never become. Becher is a man whose faith and commitment are complete. He is not plagued by the self-doubts and ambivalence toward the

Party that so trouble Jonathan. Thus Jonathan decides that Victoria has chosen Becher over him because Becher has given himself totally to the movement while Jonathan has faltered. For Victoria, Becher becomes a means for understanding how the forces of history collide within individuals. As a refugee from Hitler's Germany, Becher is a man whose life is determined by the imperatives of power. His relationship with Victoria, which begins when he asks her to give him English lessons, quickly develops, and each speaks to the other of past secrets. Victoria tells Becher about her sister's suicide, finally breaking a silence that had been absorbed into her life; in turn, he tells her of the German resistance. Her stories tell of hidden desire, his of underground history.

Ultimately Becher enables Victoria to shift her position from observer to participant in the Cuban struggle. While she is visiting the headquarters of the opposition newspaper, trying to set up an interview with the leaders of the sugarcane workers' soviet, she glances at an article in the paper about Becher's arrest in Brazil. After showing the editor a letter Becher had written her, Victoria is ushered into the hidden world of the workers' collective in Realengo. Becher's writing, his signature, have become Victoria's ticket out of her claustrophobic family—her dependence on Jonathan and her depression over the death of the child—and into the openness of history—the possibilities of collectivity in the international workers' movement.

Becher's presence, as symbol for Jonathan or as signature for Victoria, places him in correspondence to "the woman in the text."[28] He is hidden within the discourses of the others and is felt as a presence primarily in his absence. Hidden from view, he is repressed in the text, like lesbianism or collectivity in our own culture. Perhaps Herbst's transformation of her female lover and her lesbianism into this elusive male revolutionary and his commitment speaks for the hidden history within the text itself: the history of the Trexler women, whose narrative presence has often taken the form of telling the histories of their men and the hidden stories of women's desires to each other. Within the class and gender configurations of 1930s revolutionary fiction, one is always situated in relation to the male worker. His excessive virility marks both the working-class woman and the intellectual man as insufficiently gendered—she as the masculine female, he as the effeminate male. But like lesbianism, the female intellectual exceeds the limits of even these classed gender differences and remains unspoken. That the lesbian in the text has become masculinized along with the proletariat suggests how difficult it was for the female intellectual to narrate herself within the genre.

In her foreword to *The Company She Keeps*, Mary McCarthy distinguishes between the three elements of her heroine: "intimate 'she,' the affectionate, diminutive 'you,' the thin, abstract, autobiographical 'I.'" The combinatory she/you/I would seem to be conclusive, charting the multivalence of personality in various pronouns. Yet those singular pronouns still miss the connections between self and others—we and they—that determine the place of the subject in history. And so McCarthy concludes that "the home address of the self . . . is not to be found in the book."[29] History stretches out beyond the text, undermining narrative closure, just as collectivity disperses unified identity.

The articulation of a female subjectivity within the revolutionary novel requires a dual narrative of "love and hunger." These two narratives encode the relationships of gender and class by historicizing desire and by embodying collectivity in the mother. For the female working-class subject, sexual alienation, encoded in/through a brutalized vision of heterosexuality and/or a celebration of maternity, is the mechanism for entry into history. The movement of the working class is embodied in the utopian promise of maternal merger that transforms the hierarchies of difference into a new social organization of the collectivity. Conflating the polarities between love and hunger, the female body (particularly the maternal body) embraces these differing narratives simultaneously.

For the female intellectual, sexuality and maternity are also fundamental to the elaboration of subjectivity, but they are subsumed by linguistic alienation. Because the body of the female intellectual cannot always be reclaimed in a maternal collectivity, her primary narrative entry into history is accomplished by speaking or writing from the spectatorial position of outsider. The working-class (male) body of proletarian realism is fundamentally a hungry body, marked by its labor and its lack. This body is refigured within the working-class female into a maternal trope of collectivity; the female intellectual, however, remains outside of this narrative because her body remains both unmarked by labor and unscarred by maternity. Hers is not a body that (re)produces with either hands or womb. Instead, she possesses and is possessed by eyes and ears to see and hear and a mouth to speak; she is a spectator, both speculator and spectacle of history.

For Tess Slesinger, who polarizes gender differences within a framework of the eternal battle of the sexes, words mark the male intellectual's point of entry into the world. Babies mark a woman's entry into history; however, the female intellectual, poised between wombs and words, is denied even the confining access provided by maternity. A dichotomized world is a sterile world in which neither words nor babies can add up to historical change. *The Unpossessed* narrows the utopian promise of the collective; it turns the proletarian novel on its head by creating a narrative populated by those "swamp people"—intellectuals who sink into the mire at precisely the moment of historical upheaval.[30]

I Went to Pit College suggests one way to overcome this intellectual stasis. Because the "I" is positioned within a movement for historical change—a mining town in the midst of a strike—the development of the female intellectual subject is refracted through the characters surrounding it, who are sometimes seen as "we," at other times as "they," and occasionally as "you." Nevertheless, Laurie's writing separates her from the people of Avelonia, because history becomes refracted through the "I" and "she" of her desire. Just as Laurie's class and gender mark her as foreign, her words reveal a secret (desire for historicity) and become the sexual emblem of her self after they are scrutinized and finally exposed to the community. This symbolic disclosure of sexual and class differences precipitates Laurie's recognition of herself as an actor in her narrative and thus as a subject in history. Once exposed, she no longer needs her "sketches" because her narrative has turned its lens on the differential between her privilege as an intellectual woman and the privation of the coalminers and their families. She concludes her narrative with the words of an unknown worker torn from the *Daily Worker*. She holds the "fragments" of "the new, a miner's prayer," as the memento of a future, just as her narrative holds the fragments of Avelonia, but also of herself, and displays them for her middle-class audience.

In *Rope of Gold*, the fragments of narrative are spread across time and space. Herbst reveals the multiple layers of the middle class in an attempt to locate the radical female intellectual within the class and gender formations of twentieth-century America. Again language is the medium that both forges and destroys connections between individual subjects and historical movements. The failure of language to transform social relations paralyzes the male intellectuals, much as Bruno and Miles are stymied in *The Unpossessed*; however, language takes on a dynamic quality when it can express a vision of "life as history," as it does for Victoria. By connecting one person's private language to another's and recording a moment of history, a letter links thought to action and becomes a means by which to historicize desire. In the service of activism, the letter coalesces sexuality and history, concretizing desire and language through commitment. Otherwise it becomes a "corpse," the "ashes" of the dead language of memory and desire hung suspended like the fragments of a mutilated body.

In all three novels discussed here, the dual narratives cannot contain the I/you/she; pieces fall away, separate, and get lost. The impossibility of reconciling the dual narrative results in the disastrous party that propels the Flinders into their own orbit. Margaret's abortion forecloses the possibility of a future for her by destroying her illusion of the maternal body. Laurie and Victoria recognize that only their effacement within their personal narratives can enable their entry into history. They embrace the utopian promise of collectivity, hoping to lose themselves within it, even though their entry actually will be gained through writing, which demands differentiating themselves from the collective body. Nevertheless, when the female intellectual enters history to report on it, her writings disclose more than a personal accounting of her desires; her words textualize (rather than embody) the collective. Like the female working-class subject's sexual alienation, the female intellectual's linguistic alienation impedes yet ultimately produces the bridge between her self-consciousness and her political activism.

Epilogue

Bread and Roses Too:
Notes toward a Materialist-Feminist Literary History

As I finished this book, I juggled two conflicting images. The final months of the 1980s are etched into our collective memories by the power of the masses of people in Eastern Europe and the Soviet Union who moved to reshape the past forty years of their histories. The last vestiges of 1930s Stalinism unraveled daily as poets and workers marched together to demand their freedom. In a less visibly dramatic change, American women were once again forced to submit their bodies to the control of state authorities in the wake of the Supreme Court's Webster decision and the Bush administration's "war on drugs." Abortions can no longer be easily obtained by young, poor, and minority women throughout the United States; pregnant women in Florida, South Carolina, and Idaho are being jailed for distributing controlled substances to their "unborn children" because they have been found abusing crack or alcohol.

I do not think these two images are unrelated. It is my hope that the arguments in this book have shown how repressive ideologies that govern the bodies and texts of all citizens take on peculiarly obscene characteristics when applied to the bodies of working-class women. At the same time, the power of a mass movement is so profound that one of its members can literally stop tanks in their tracks.[1] State control of a woman's body and the people's power to dismantle a state are linked paradoxically in the image of the mother. Although the mother cannot exist as an individual when the state determines that her womb is a factory for producing babies, she is invoked by the masses in their call to oust invaders and return to the "mother tongue."[2] This contradiction—that the body of the mother has no place in history, but the maternal metaphor is everywhere—has been one of the ideas theorized in women's revolutionary fiction. In fact, we might begin developing a material-ist-feminist literary history of American women's writings by examining the various ways in which the working woman (as woman, worker, and sometimes mother) remains unscripted.

Articulating the contradictory interrelationship of productive and re-productive labor for African American women became the impetus for So-journer Truth's question to the 1851 Women's Rights Convention: "Ain't I a woman?" She demanded that they recognize her status as an African Ameri-can woman and a mother despite her having been a slave who had worked for forty years in the fields. By setting the power of her physical presence ("look at my arm") in opposition to the cult of domesticity ("that man say women need to be helped"), Truth cut to the heart of the race, class, and gender ideologies underpinning nineteenth-century American society. Her rhetorical question became an assertion of her difference—one that could not be contained within conventional narratives about either women and mothers or workers and slaves. One might begin a (literary) history of the working woman's body with Truth's pointed question.[3]

By the mid-nineteenth century, the ideological erasure of the body of the (black or white) working woman was almost complete. Sojourner Truth, Harriet Wilson, and Harriet Jacobs had revealed the conditions of their lives and labors as slaves and servants in the fields and households of America, yet slavery was perceived primarily to exploit the productive labor of African American males and the reproductive labor of females.[4] Additionally despite Lucy Larcom's and Sarah Bagley's descriptions in *The Lowell Offering* of their lives and work in the mills, factory work was understood to be primarily the occupation of white men.[5]

Because this study has looked at the class/gender nexus primarily as it affected white women (as writers and workers), race appears outside their dissections of classed female subjectivity. Its very absence, however, points to its unspoken presence in American literary and political history. With the exception of southern white women authors like Myra Page and Fielding Burke, few of the authors I have discussed tackled racism in their works. I am afraid my study has reproduced their silences and omissions, and so I will leave aside what would amount to superficial discussions of the ways race reshapes these two matrices of subjectivity in this brief outline for a literary history of white women's political fiction (or a political history of white women's literature).

Rebecca Harding Davis's *Life in the Iron Mills: Or, the Korl Woman* (1861) has attained new status within the American literary canon since it was reissued in 1972 by Feminist Press. In her afterword to the reprint edition, Tillie Olsen claims that Davis's novella is the first piece of fiction about what she referred to in *Yonnondio* as the "grotesques" of the working class written "in absolute identification" with the working class.[6] The novella frames the story of the Korl Woman within another narrative in which a presumably female writer reanimates her own alienation through imaginative projection onto the sculpture of the Korl Woman, which she finds in her basement. According to Olsen, the artistic puddler Hugh Wolfe substitutes for Davis's suppressed self. Within the sexual economy of the mill, Hugh is feminized (his nickname is "Molly") because he refuses to participate fully in the masculine rivalries of the other workers; but his devoted cousin Deb is bestialized (she is likened to a "spaniel" sniveling underfoot). In Olsen's reading of Davis, we see a presentiment of the parallels that middle-class women drew within proletarian fiction between the working-class male and the middle-class woman.

Not only is the author struggling with the representation of the dual constrictions of class and gender in the mid-nineteenth century, however, but she is also staging the drama of narrative itself. Differences and their representations in this framed narrative place the narrator in an ambiguous position. On the one hand, she lives in the Wolfe house, possesses the Korl Woman, and looks out the window on the same sights and smells as Hugh: "There is a secret underlying sympathy between that story and this day with its impure fog and thwarted sunshine" (14). On the other, she can only repeat "fragments of an old story," which has as yet remained "dumb . . . I dare not put this secret into words. . . . I dare make my meaning no clearer, but will only tell my story" (13–14). Meaning is impure, like the fog and thwarted sunshine; Hugh's (and more so Deb's) story is an unspoken secret, barely imaginable except within the frame of the narrator's own (middle-class) story.

Increasingly, as the narrator drops her direct first-person address for third-person narration, the tensions of reading and interpretation, as class- and gender-bound processes, become exacerbated. Appearing to possess "no story of a soul filled with groping passionate love," Deb remains unread by the middle-class "amateur psychologists" to whom the narrator addresses her story (21, 12). Under the weight of "her thwarted woman's form, her colorless life, her waking stupor that smothered pain and hunger—even more fit to be a type of her class," crippled Deb cannot possibly be viewed as the object of romantic desire, as the heroine of romance (21). There was "nothing worth reading in this wet, faded thing . . . no story"; no one had ever "taken the trouble to read its faint signs" (20–21). Because she is lame, Hugh "sicken[s] with disgust at her deformity" (23). Even the (female) narrator can "only give you the outside outlines of a night, a crisis in the life of one man" (23). His "depth" is left for the readers to fill in when the narrator invites the reader to "look" at Hugh (25); but Deb remains "stupidly invisible" (26).

Moreover, once the middle-class men enter the foundry and examine the Korl Woman, the politics of reading the markings of working-class femininity are aestheticized.[7] The inevitability of their class- and gender-bound reading is revealed by the art object itself. "The meaning" of the figure escapes the three observers, one of whom responds to Hugh's explanation that "she be hungry" by suggesting that there is "no sign of starvation to the body. It is strong—terribly strong. It has the mad, half-despairing gesture of drowning" (33). Like Deb, the Korl Woman is illegible within the frame of bourgeois ideologies of femininity and art. Hugh's position as artist, however, becomes readable for the narrator through her insistence that he possesses "a great blind intellect . . . a loving poet's heart" beneath the coarse exterior forged of "grossness and crime, and hard grinding labor" (25). In other words, Hugh's position, though obscured, can nevertheless be interpreted; like his sculpture, he possesses surface and depth in the differential between the body's hunger and the hunger of desire, at least for the sympathetic middle-class audience the narrator has constructed.

The plot depends for its impact on the different moral systems expressed by Deb (who takes to heart the words of Mr. Mitchell that workers also have rights by stealing his wallet) and Mr. Mitchell (who then deplores the depravity of the working class, condemning Hugh as a common thief). Similarly, the story depends on the identification of narrator and Hugh.[8] Their identity is underscored by the device of framing, of setting up a distance between story and plot—a distance that both confirms difference and erases its significance as the Korl Woman's story is enfolded into Hugh's and Hugh's story is enclosed (through the trace he left, the sculpture) in the narrator's. Framing establishes beginnings and endings, marking off the unruly complexities that intervene. The frame contains the narrative, in a sense undermining its system of difference as it makes the circuit from narrator to Korl Woman to Hugh to Deb and back to narrator. The framing device suggests simultaneously that there are at least two stories and that there is only ever one story—that of the innately creative artist cramped and suffering within the confines of socially imposed restrictions. This story, however, becomes the story of the (male) working class, subsumed and wrapped in the frames of (female) bourgeois perception. Because neither plot nor story can find a language to tell the "secret" of class and gender as representations of each other and of themselves, the position of Deb and, to an extent, the image of the Korl Woman remain excluded from either the (gendered) frame or the (classed) narrative.

The problem of finding a narrative form capable of addressing the complexity of class and gender as mutually sustaining representations poses questions of interpretation: Who tells what tale? of whom? to whom? When the middle-class woman tries to tell the story of a working-class man, both figures slip inexorably into each other. Although this merging would seem to undermine the distinctions between class and gender differences, those differences actually appear rigidly locked in a homologous relationship that makes middle-class women and working-class men more or less interchangeable within the sexual economy of narrative and leaves the working-class woman shrouded in undisclosed "secrets."

This reading of Davis, which I have borrowed and extended from Tillie Olsen, repeats many of the arguments I have made throughout this book. The body of the working-class woman cannot produce a conventional narrative, and the female intellectual finds (a voice for) herself in the expressions of the male worker. These positions suggest that the narratives constructed by female literary radicals retained many cultural assumptions inherited from mid-nineteenth-century ideology. As such, women's revolutionary novels of the 1930s were not able to address Sojourner Truth's question.

Alice Jardine distinguishes between a fiction that thematizes women's disruption of social order and one that "practices . . . gynesis" (or "the putting into discourse of woman" or the feminine) by problematizing narrative and thus theorizes itself.[9] Clearly, women's revolutionary novels of the 1930s do not confront the issues of "modernity" in quite the same ways that Jardine intends. In fact, steeped in realist conventions of narrative and politics, 1930s revolutionary literature usually is thought of as anything but modern. Yet, as I have been arguing, women's revolutionary fiction provides the material for a theory and a history of the gendered rhetoric of class as it appeared among the leftist intellectuals of the 1930s. This gendered and classed (literary) history and theory may contain at least some crucial points of linkage between contemporary political and theoretical feminisms and the politics that animated earlier renderings of class and gender in narrative, as in Davis's novella. In short, these works are all about "modernity."

Women's revolutionary novels from the 1930s are situated in an extremely marginalized space within dominant American literary history. As Deborah S. Rosenfelt argues, the fragmentary traditions of both women's writings and radical writings formed the background for, but could not contain, these works.[10] Virginia Woolf argued that women writers, historically cut off from the public sphere, traditionally "magnify" the internal, and their novels become "the dumping-ground for the personal emotions."[11] Thus the private writings of letters and journals have formed the basis for a history of women's literary practice. But the aesthetics of 1930s literary radicalism stressed the importance of external social forces in shaping a literary work. This shift of emphasis denied a feminine literary tradition to the 1930s woman writer and separated her from her bourgeois female literary precursors. In one sense, this freed women writers from a tradition of muted, personal literature and allowed them to move out of the parlor and into the world in their prose and poetry. Yet these women were not really equipped to write about the "mines, mills, and farms" that were the basis of Michael Gold's proletarian realism; they never worked as miners, machinists, or farmers, just as earlier generations of women lacked training in Greek and Latin. These gaps in nineteenth-century middle-class women's education "deformed and twisted" their narratives because, as Woolf says of Charlotte Brontë, middle-class women were "angry."[12]

Anger also fueled the writers of the 1930s, who saw the Depression and fascism destroy millions of lives. Yet only certain kinds of anger were appropriate, a condition that explains Walt Carmon's complaint that *Daughter of Earth* was "marred" as a proletarian novel because it gave voice to Smedley's anger as a woman. In this sense, women's revolutionary novels of the 1930s broke with one facet of women's literary tradition as they conformed to another. In addition, they remained within yet stepped outside the bounds of the radical literary tradition, which for the most part ignored women's writings as apolitical. What distinguishes women's revolutionary fiction of the

1930s from other political fiction by women is its allegiance to a political movement concerned primarily with class struggle. Thus, in these novels, the aesthetics of proletarianism are historically specific. Yet the elaboration of female subjectivity within a social field marked by gender and sexual differences links women's revolutionary fiction to women's novels as diverse as *Jane Eyre* and *Les Guérillères*.

I see more in common between Josephine Herbst's trilogy and Marge Piercy's *Vida* or Alice Walker's *Meridian* than I see between the trilogy and Katherine Anne Porter's *Pale Horse, Pale Rider*, though Herbst's and Porter's books were written at the same time, by two women who maintained a friendship. Both *Vida* and *Meridian* develop female subjectivity within movements for social change: the antiwar and civil rights movements of the 1960s. Ironically, each maintains certain narrative conventions first elaborated in the 1930s. The bodies of Jewish female intellectuals like Vida Asch and Lynne Rabinowitz can pursue their desires—for sex, for history. *Meridian's* body becomes the site of maternal merger with the (southern black) masses.

In *Meridian*, where the name of the woman is literally the place all others pass through, the connection between Lynne, the northern white civil rights worker, and Meridian, her southern black coworker, turns on their triangulated sexual relationship with Truman Held, which in turn depends on Lynne's never-to-be-spoken-of rape by another black civil rights worker, Tommy Olds. Racial, class, and sexual differences within the movement are linked in multiplicitous ways within and through the class and racial differences marking the (sexual) bodies of Meridian and Lynne. To cite another example, in Nadine Gordimer's *Burger's Daughter*, the traditional determinants of Rosa's subjectivity—her family—are overdetermined by her parents' involvement in the antiapartheid struggle in South Africa. Nevertheless, female sexuality is crucial to the elaboration of the female subject within the political space of the novel. Despite living underground or being imprisoned, both Vida Asch and Rosa Burger narrate themselves (and are narrated) as much through their sexual encounters and fantasies as through their political developments.

In all of the above cases, the struggles against class, race, and colonialist oppressions often do not register sexual and gender differences as political categories. However, Monique Wittig's materialist-feminist novel of utopia, *Les Guérillères*, seeks to overthrow the domination of realist narrative and androcentric language as much as the sexist social relations they encode.

Interestingly, this feminist revolutionary novel recalls 1930s revolutionary fiction in its closing gesture. In *Marching! Marching!*, Clara Weatherwax transformed the omniscient third-person narrator into another voice, whose inclusive "we" engaged the reader in the revolutionary élan of the maternal collectivity. Wittig also changes pronouns in the final section of *Les Guérillères*. No longer does the narrator speak of "the women" (*elles*); she too changes voice, shifting to include the reader in the collective moment of solidarity through the inclusive "we."

Wittig's visionary novel about the struggles to eliminate sexual and gender differences reinvents the maternal collectivity that dissolved the class-based conflicts motivating women's revolutionary novels of the 1930s. The author's attempt to eliminate the markings of gender does not produce an undifferentiated identical unity. Instead, her vision remarks upon and celebrates the differences within and among "the women" as much as it seeks to unite them. Her closing gesture, then, pushes the limits of 1930s renderings of the maternal mass into a postmodern, de-centered collectivity:

> Moved by a common impulse, we all stood to seek gropingly the even flow, the exultant unity of the Internationale. . . . The great song filled the hall, burst through doors and windows and rose to the calm sky. The war is over, the war is over, said a young working woman next to me. Her face shone and when it was finished and we remained there in a kind of embarrassed silence, a woman at the end of the hall cried, Comrades, let us remember the women who died for liberty. . . . And then we intoned the Funeral March, a slow, melancholy and yet triumphant air.[13]

Wittig's deconstructive novel revisits the maternal collectivity imagined during the 1930s. Perhaps there are links between the ways women writers of that day combined the narratives of history and desire, opening generic spaces to contradiction, and postmodern deconstructive feminism.

Jacques Derrida "would like to believe in the multiplicity of sexually marked voices . . . would like to believe in the masses, this indeterminable number of blended voices, this mobile of non-identified sexual marks whose choreography can carry, divide, multiply the body of each 'individual,' whether he be classified as 'man' or 'woman.'" To produce such a choreography, Julia Kristeva demands that "we listen to the music" of collectivity. Because "only the re-invention of the collective and the associative can concretely achieve the 'decentering' of the individual subject . . . ; only a new and original form of collective social life can overcome the isolation and monadic autonomy of the older bourgeois subjects," Fredric Jameson believes that the methods of Marxism produce the practice of utopian decentered collectivity. Postmodern feminist theorists suggest that feminism shares with deconstruction this utopian desire to eliminate the hierarchies implicit within dualisms and, in so doing, demands new narrative forms.[14]

Ironically, even those forms have their precursors in the narratives that women literary radicals constructed for the class-conscious female subject. Because women's revolutionary novels of the 1930s were participating in a literary conversation that spoke primarily of class relations, their inscriptions of female desire create a possibility for theorizing the multiplicity of differences—racial, class, gender, ethnic, sexual—in a more complex way than simply repeating a litany of Otherness. Subjectivity is packed within a matrix of differences, each elaborated, inhibited, and articulated from the others. Recently American feminist critical theorists have stumbled up against the multiple walls of these differences, aware of their existence but not yet fully equipped to surmount them because they do not lie sequentially or hierarchically, but are related in multivalent, unsystematic ways.

The young female mill workers' strike in Lawrence, Massachusetts, united women who did not speak the same language. Though they stood silently at times, their banners demanding "bread and roses too" declared that the dual narratives of history and desire have a political history. I hope that my study has provided some entry into the web of this alternative political history— which speaks in many tongues at once about the multiplicity of our labors and desires, which is written differently in the many books of our flesh, and which can never be contained within any one identity.

Rita Felski argues that we must go "beyond feminist aesthetics" by acknowledging the ways in which feminism produces a(nother) public sphere.[15] The contemporary feminist novels she surveys grew out of and helped build the second wave of feminism, and they exhibit both the powers and the pitfalls of our movement—for example, they politicize privacy yet universalize women. In this and other ways, white, middle-class women's feminist literature is foreshadowed by white women's revolutionary literature of the Depression decade.

During the 1930s, radical women authors developed their writings from the worldwide struggles against capitalism and fascism; their work tried to speak of and to subjects traditionally left out of literature. Women's revolutionary fiction rephrased the rhetoric that encoded the proletariat as masculine by putting female sexuality and maternity into working-class narratives; in this way, they helped produce a(nother) class-conscious private sphere, thereby revising the genre of the revolutionary novel. By foregrounding class conflict, they also sent women's traditional narratives into the public sphere. The novels I have been discussing are full of faults; however, following those literary fault lines has provided us with material for theorizing ourselves as laboring and desiring subjects who are positioned in and by a myriad of conflicting forces. Thus, women's revolutionary novels of the 1930s stand as emblems for many of the concerns of postmodern materialist-feminist critical theory.

Notes

Preface

1. This study is limited to the novels by white women literary radicals. Although I was able to identify a number of African American women writers on the Left, for example Marita Bonner and Margaret Walker, none had completed a novel during the 1930s. These writers—along with the many other contributors to *Crisis* and *Opportunity*—deserve fuller study for the ways in which their writings produce a complex rendering of the race/class/gender nexus. Of course, Zora Neale Hurston, Jessie Redmon Fauset, and Nella Larsen wrote significant African American women's novels during the 1930s, but none of these writers demonstrated an active involvement with the Left.

2. Snitow, Stansell, and Thompson, eds., *Powers of Desire*.

3. Elaine Showalter, "Introduction: The Feminist Critical Revolution," in Showalter, ed., *The New Feminist Criticism*, p. 10.

Prologue

1. Using James Agee and Walker Evans's *Let Us Now Praise Famous Men* as the paradigm, William Stott's *Documentary Expression and Thirties America* has provided the most comprehensive analysis of reportage and the documentary tradition among 1930s artists. Taking its cue from the reportage of the 1930s, Studs Terkel's *Hard Times* reiterates the importance of going directly to the source of experience to capture the history of the people. Oral history has become one of the primary forms of 1930s historiography. For instance, William Alexander's *Film on the Left* and Russell Campbell's *Cinema Strikes Back* rely on the oral histories of members of the documentary film collectives active during the 1930s for their analyses of films, and Robbie Lieberman's *"My Song Is My Weapon"* uses interviews with people who were active in the People's Songs organization.

2. LeSueur, "Women on the Breadlines."

3. LeSueur, "The Derned Crick's Rose," p. 38.

4. Westin, *Making Do*, p. ix.

5. Armstrong, "Literature as Women's History," pp. 351–57.

6. See below, Chapter 2, for an explanation of the term *revolutionary*. Charlotte

Nekola and Paula Rabinowitz's anthology, *Writing Red*, provides examples of the range of black and white women's writings during the 1930s.

7. Quoted in Madden, ed., *Proletarian Writers of the Thirties*, p. xxi. This is how Herbst described Daniel Aaron's book (*Writers on the Left*), but the same observation is also true of James B. Gilbert's study of *Partisan Review* (*Writers and Partisans*), David Peck's dissertation on the *New Masses* ("Development of an American Marxist Literary Criticism"), Arthur Casciato's dissertation on the League of American Writers ("Citizen Writers"), and Eric Homberger's analysis of the John Reed clubs (*American Writers and Radical Politics*), all of which are primarily institutional studies fixated on the vicissitudes of the leadership and their relationships to the Communist Party.

8. I am referring to Aaron, *Writers on the Left*; Gilbert, *Writers and Partisans*; Wald, *Revolutionary Imagination* and *New York Intellectuals*; and Rideout, *Radical Novel in the United States*. Kessler-Harris and Lauter, introduction to *Call Home the Heart*; Rosenfelt, "From the Thirties" and "Getting into the Game"; and Nekola and Rabinowitz, eds., *Writing Red*, all provide alternative points from which to begin this reconsideration.

9. Even a more recent, "revisionist" history of modern feminism like Cott, *Grounding of Modern Feminism*, implicitly reproduces earlier arguments by limiting its scope to the first three decades of the twentieth century.

10. Inman, *In Women's Defense*, pp. 94–95.

11. Hutchins, *Women Who Work*, p. 159.

12. Inman, *In Women's Defense*, p. 136.

13. See Chafe, *American Woman*, pp. 112–32, for a discussion of the conflicts and splits among feminists over the ERA; and Scharf, " 'Forgotten Woman,' " for details about New Deal women's attitudes toward feminism. In her autobiography, Margaret Sanger describes her efforts to secure women's access to birth control as a continual struggle between the needs and desires of middle-class women and those of the working class (*Margaret Sanger*; see esp. chap. 16, "Hear Me for My Cause," pp. 192–209).

14. See Armstrong, *Desire and Domestic Fiction*, for a full analysis of privacy as a political construct.

15. I am choosing to discuss Gilbert and Gubar's work here, not because they are solely to blame for ignoring works by women that fail to conform to a certain essentialist version of men's and women's histories, but because their work presents a powerful argument for reading women's literature apart from men's.

16. Rosenfelt, "Getting into the Game."

17. Judith Newton and Deborah S. Rosenfelt, "Toward a Materialist-Feminist Criticism," in Newton and Rosenfelt, eds., *Feminist Criticism and Social Change*, pp. xx–xxxix. For many years, Lillian Robinson has argued that feminist criticism has been woefully lacking in a class analysis (*Sex, Class, and Culture*). Many Third World and minority feminist theorists have pointed to the Eurocentrism of much feminist criticism. See, for example, Walker, "One Child of One's Own," and Spivak, *In Other Worlds*.

18. See de Lauretis, *Technologies of Gender*, pp. 3–7, for an elaboration of the ways in which gender is a representation.

19. Kristeva, "Stabat Mater," p. 118.

20. Rabine, *Reading the Romantic Heroine*, p. 5.

21. Scott, *Gender and the Politics of History*, p. 40.

22. See Nancy Armstrong's analysis of how the boundaries separating the genres of literature and history are produced by and reproduce gender and generational boundaries ("Literature as Women's History," pp. 349–51).

23. Jameson, *Political Unconscious*, pp. 28–29; White, *Metahistory*, p. 7.

24. De Lauretis, *Alice Doesn't*, p. 121.

25. De Lauretis puts it this way: "Feminism has produced, at least for feminists, a political-personal consciousness of gender as an ideological construct which defines the social subject; in thus en-gendering the subject, and in en-gendering the subject as political, feminism understands the female subject as one that, unlike Althusser's or Jameson's or Eco's, is not either 'in ideology' or outside ideology (e.g., in science), but rather is at once inside and outside the ideology of gender, or, as I have used the terms, is at once woman and women" (*Technologies of Gender*, p. 114).

26. Althusser, "Ideology and Ideological State Apparatuses," in *Lenin and Philosophy*, p. 170.

27. Scott, "On Language, Gender, and Working-Class History," pp. 7, 40. For instance, in *Reconstructing Womanhood*, Hazel Carby has effectively argued that womanhood as it was constructed in nineteenth-century American culture was as much a racially inscribed category as it was one that circumscribed gender and sexuality. The "cult of true womanhood" denied yet paradoxically depended upon the image of the sexually voracious black slave in order for its ideological power as a re-presentation of gender and racial differences to be effective. Furthermore, as Hortense Spillers demonstrates in "Mama's Baby, Papa's Maybe," even when gender differences appear to be thoroughly repressed—as, for instance, in the narratives of slave traders—the absence still calls attention to the gendered embodiments of racial difference that were enforced by slavery.

28. Page references to Smedley, *Daughter of Earth*, and McCarthy, *The Company She Keeps*, will appear parenthetically in the text. Within months of *Daughter's* publication, the stock market crashed and ushered in the Depression; *Company's* release as a book (portions of it had appeared in various journals in 1939) came shortly after the beginning of the economic recovery created by the United States's entry into World War II. Whereas Smedley's politics caused her to celebrate the Communist struggle in China in the pages of *New Masses*, McCarthy, theater critic for the journal of the anti-Stalinist Left, *Partisan Review*, spoke out in support of Trotsky and the Fourth International.

29. For one view of the relationship between documentary and fiction, see Foley, *Telling the Truth*.

30. DuPlessis, *Writing Beyond the Ending*, pp. 2–7.

31. Wright, "Between Laughter and Tears," pp. 22, 25.

32. Carmon, "Away from Harlem."

33. Deborah Rosenfelt discusses the dilemmas faced by working-class women writers like Smedley and Olsen in "Divided Against Herself." As Rosenfelt's title suggests, the three terms—working class, woman, writer—are themselves incommensurable. This disjunction is visually displayed in the title of Lillian Robinson's essay "Working/Woman/Writing" in *Sex, Class, and Culture*. Using Macherey's *A*

Theory of Literary Production, Candida Lacey suggests in "Engendering Conflict" that the silences in Smedley's texts, like the *non-dit* of any text, point to gaps in ideology—in this case the gaps in proletarianism produced by sexuality and gender.

34. See Armstrong, *Desire and Domestic Fiction*, pp. 224–50, on Freud's Dora as a modern(ist) domestic narrative. Virtually all reviews of *The Company She Keeps* focus on the impact of the final section, in which the "pieces" of Margaret's narrative are fitted together. Whether the novel appears to be "a clinical study" of "the relationship between extremist narcissism and Trotskyism," as Helen Clare Nelson claimed ("A Clinical Study," p. 26), or whether it possesses "the still unusual quality of having been lived," as Malcolm Cowley declared ("Bad Company," p. 737), it is this one moment of psychological disclosure that makes the text legible.

35. See Silverman, *Acoustic Mirror*, for an analysis of the relationship of the disembodied cinematic voice to the construction of power, desire, and gendered subjectivity.

36. For the significance of the term "pansy" to discussions of literary radicalism, see my discussion of Michael Gold on Thornton Wilder in Chapter 1 below.

37. One recent example comes to mind: the marketing campaign by R. J. Reynolds for their new cigarette, Dakota, which is aimed at the "virile woman" who has a high school diploma, works in a factory or small office, and likes to spend time with her boyfriend at drag races or tractor pulls.

Chapter 1

1. The term "infection" is Grace Paley's (remarks made in public reading at the University of Minnesota, Oct. 20, 1988).

2. See Alan Wald, "Introduction: Political Amnesia," on the ramifications of the "politics of memory" for the study of the American Left (*New York Intellectuals*, pp. 3–24).

3. Rahv, "Proletarian Literature." In *Of Woman Born*, Adrienne Rich distinguishes between motherhood as an institution and as an experience. In many ways, the history of American communism can be expressed the same way, as a series of disjunctures between the day-to-day experiences of Communists and the official doctrine of communism.

4. For their penetrating analyses of literary radicalism, I am indebted to Aaron (*Writers on the Left*), Rideout (*Radical Novel in the United States*), Gilbert (*Writers and Partisans*), Pells (*Radical Visions and American Dreams*), and Wald (*Revolutionary Imagination*), each of which offers a unique perspective on the diverse individuals in this group and the institutions and texts they produced, though all proceed from Rahv's contention. My work could not have been undertaken without the earlier scholarship of these critics. Both what they do and do not say about literary radicalism informs my study.

5. See Papke, "Analysis of Selected American Marxist Criticism," for a compatible though slightly different analysis.

6. In addition to major publications like the *Daily Worker, New Masses,* and *Partisan Review,* for which the "head boys" wrote, one should look to the less well-known literary journals of the Left for the writings of women and minorities. In my search for examples of women's literary radicalism, I surveyed the following journals: *The Anvil;*

Black and White; Blast: A Magazine of Proletarian Short Stories; Clipper: A Western Review; Contempo: A Review of Ideas and Personalities; Crisis; Dynamo; Hub: A Quarterly Magazine; The Left: A Quarterly Review of Radical and Experimental Art; Left Front; Left Review; The Magazine: A Literary Journal; Modern Quarterly/Monthly; New Force: A Proletarian Magazine of Art, Literature, and Current Events; New International; Opportunity; Party Organizer; Signatures: Works in Progress; The Unemployed; Vanguard: Journal of Anarcho-Communism; The Windsor Quarterly; Woman Today; Working Woman.

7. Pells, *Radical Visions and American Dreams*, p. 404.

8. Gold's novel implicitly contained a gendered elaboration of his theories about "proletarian realism" that to some extent contradicted the explicit claims he made in his critical remarks for the *New Republic* and *New Masses*. His mama, whose "female realism" made her into a "workhorse" with "proletarian instincts," contrasts sharply with his papa, whose "male dreams" stemmed from his skill as a "storyteller" and love of the theater as well as from his belief in the American version of the tale of the Golden Bear (*Jews without Money*, pp. 81, 157, 214, 84). In Gold's novel, proletarian realism is clearly tied to femininity—both his mother and his aunt organize strikes—but his criticism implies that it is through masculine workers that Marxist intellectuals can find their proper literary stance. Gold's regendering of (masculine) workers and (feminine) artists in his criticism was perhaps a refusal of the novel's gender implications.

9. Gold, "Go Left, Young Writers!" p. 3.

10. Gold, "Wilder," p. 266.

11. Jack Conroy, in "Author's Field Day," p. 28.

12. For instance, Alan Wald's archival work on Ella Winter and Elinor Langer's on Josephine Herbst revealed the extent of their lesbian relationships, which were closeted in their public writings.

13. See Schwartz, *Marxism and Culture*, for a discussion of the divergences between CPUSA and Comintern cultural programs.

14. In the United States, the primary vehicles for the development of proletarian culture were the John Reed clubs, whose functions were to sponsor readings, lectures, debates, and discussions and to publish a journal. Named for the poet, journalist, and revolutionary, the John Reed clubs were conceived as a training ground for young, gifted writers from the working class but were actually composed of committed intellectuals from the middle class.

15. Of course, one could argue that the hard-boiled detectives prowling through the pages of Dashiell Hammett novels were the literary precursors of the virile proletarians. See Madden, ed., *Tough Guy Writers of the Thirties*.

16. Lillian Robinson provides a moving reading of one of the anonymous stories ("Working/Woman/Writing," in *Sex, Class, and Culture*, pp. 223–53). In so doing, she condemns the ideology underpinning the conventions that determine a work's literariness, conventions that have left these texts illegible.

17. Hart, ed., *American Writer's Congress*. Waldo Frank ("Values of a Revolutionary Writer," pp. 71–77) and Moishe Nadir ("The Writer in a Minority Language," pp. 153–56) exemplify just two of the types of speeches collected in this fascinating volume, whose diversity belies the insistence of Max Eastman that literary radicals were "artists in uniform." Interestingly, despite the range of topics addressed only one woman, Meridel LeSueur, was asked to speak by the organizers—and only as a

representative of the Midwest. On the other hand, three speeches were devoted to "Negro Writers," whereas Nadir's speech ostensibly addressed Yiddish authors.

18. Ibid., pp. 60–62.

19. Schachner, "Revolutionary Literature in the United States Today," pp. 27–28.

20. Lumpkin, "Southern Woman Bares Tricks of Higher-Ups to Shunt Lynch Blame." See also interview with Myra Page by Jonathan Bloom, Westchester Co., N.Y., 1982, in Oral History of the American Left, Tamiment Collection, New York University library. In this interview, Page expressed a similar analogy to explain her political affiliation: When her brother told her she could not be a doctor like their father because she was a girl, she gained insight into racism for the first time. The same analogy also formed the basis for Tillie Olsen's critical recovery of Rebecca Harding Davis's *Life in the Iron Mills* (see epilogue, below).

21. A Group of Workers and Jane Benton, "Stockyard Stella"; Barton, "Our Reader's Forum."

22. Mitchison, "We're Writing a Book." With the forging of the Popular Front in Europe to fight fascism, Communists made peace with their socialist and Social Democratic enemies. This policy had as its cultural counterpart the establishment of large organizations of progressive writers and artists to disseminate antifascist ideology. Mitchison's pleasure at the mutual purpose she and her worker-authors shared reflected the increased ease with which intellectuals could align themselves with the Left once proletarianism had been officially abandoned.

23. Two speeches at the 1935 American Writers' Congress discussed the political and economic difficulties publishers were facing. Henry Hart and Alexander Trachtenberg stated that most proletarian novels were issued in runs of less than 2,000 volumes and were often poor sellers. See Hart, "Contemporary Publishing and the Revolutionary Writer," and Trachtenberg, "Publishing Revolutionary Literature," in Hart, ed., *American Writers' Congress*, pp. 161, 162.

24. Adamic, "What the Proletariat Reads," p. 217.

25. Rahv and Phelps, "Recent Problems of Revolutionary Literature," p. 372.

26. Farrell, *Note on Literary Criticism*, p. 46.

27. For instance, V. F. Calverton discovered a rekindled faith in the masses that had been dormant among intellectuals since Whitman, because "colleges were producing more and more intellectuals" who, like the workers, faced massive unemployment, thus precipitating a crisis of confidence in liberal humanism ("Leftward Ho!," pp. 27–28).

28. Gold, "Notes of the Month," p. 5.

29. Wright, *American Hunger*, p. 105.

30. Lawrence, "Who Slew Proletcult?"

31. Papke, "Analysis of Selected American Marxist Criticism," pp. 53–69. Lukács's work did appear in translation in *International Literature*, but it is never mentioned by American literary radicals in their analyses.

32. Maynard Solomon finds the roots of Zhdanovism in "the insistence by revolutionary movements on the creation of a body of exemplary myths in art; the rejection of complex and advanced styles in art; the censorship of the arts and their subjection to repressive modes of patronage" (Solomon, "General Introduction: Zhdanovism," in *Marxism and Art*, pp. 235–37). In the Soviet Union, Zhdanov declared the birth of "socialist realism" at the 1934 Writers' Congress. Taking his cue from Stalin's

pronouncement that writers were "engineers of the soul," he outlined the formulas necessary for achieving this new writing: the artist must create "a truthful, historically concrete representation of reality in its revolutionary development. Moreover, he must contribute to the ideological transformation and the education of workers in the spirit of Socialism" (quoted in Arvon, *Marxist Esthetics*, p. 86).

33. See Gilbert and Gubar, *No Man's Land*, for an extended discussion of the gender tensions encoded in modernism that World War I produced for male writers.

34. "In Reply to Authors."

35. Gilfillan and Herbst, in "Author's Field Day," pp. 29–30.

36. Cited in Rideout, *Radical Novel in the United States*, p. 311n.

37. Herbst, "Yesterday's Road," p. 103.

38. Solow, "Minutiae of Left-Wing Literary History."

39. Eddy, "Ballad of a Slightly Addled Cultural Worker."

40. For example, Katherine Anne Porter wrote to *Partisan Review*: "I am not convinced that everyone who has a quarrel with the *New Masses* is per se a Trotskyist or indeed anti-Soviet. . . . I am pretty sick of name-calling. . . . Let me tell you frankly, I am not a Trotskyist, but I am not a Stalinist, either" ("Correspondence," p. 62).

41. Kenneth Burke, "Revolutionary Symbolism in America," in Hart, ed., *American Writers' Congress*, pp. 87–93.

42. Both Herbst and LeSueur insisted that they remained relatively unconnected to Party dogma and bureaucracy because of their distance from New York and because of their sex. Herbst once wrote David Madden about the "claustrophobia of New York City" (see Madden, introduction to *Proletarian Writers of the Thirties*, p. xxii), and Meridel LeSueur talked to Elaine Hedges of her relative freedom from artistic constraints because she was a midwestern woman (*Ripening*, pp. 14–15).

43. For instance, Mary Heaton Vorse had earlier written stories for *The Masses* that portrayed the working-class woman. She wrote the first novel about Gastonia and thereafter reviewed other proletarian narratives by Lauren Gilfillan, Josephine Herbst, and Grace Lumpkin for the *New Republic* and the *New Masses*.

44. Scott, foreword to *A Calendar of Sin*, n.p.

45. Hicks, "Writers in the Thirties," p. 84.

46. Swados, introduction to *The American Writer and the Great Depression*, p. xi; North, introduction to *New Masses: An Anthology*, p. 23; Conroy, introduction to *Writers in Revolt*, pp. ix, xi; Lewis, "Down the Skidway," p. 120 (emphasis in original); Wright, *American Hunger*, p. 63.

47. Conroy, introduction to *Writers in Revolt*, p. x; Herbst, quoted in Madden, introduction to *Proletarian Writers of the Thirties*, p. xix; Hicks, "Writers in the Thirties," p. 78; Gilbert, *Writers and Partisans*, p. 48.

48. Rabine, *Reading the Romantic Heroine*, p. 5.

49. In this, these writings resemble such memoirs of women revolutionaries as Emma Goldman's *Living My Life* or Vera Figner's in Engel and Rosenthal, eds., *Five Sisters*. A more contemporary fictional rendering can be found in Zane, the heroine of Alix Shulman's *Burning Questions*. As a youthful rebel, Zane leaves Indiana for Greenwich Village to make her mark on History, but the year is 1958, and the historical possibilities she pursues have not yet coalesced; instead, she pursues Desire.

50. Herbst, "Yesterday's Road," pp. 84–85.

51. Gornick, *Romance of American Communism*, pp. 100–101. In a recent letter to

The Nation, Dorothy Ray Healey challenges Vivian Gornick's reconstruction of her story as a "fiction," explaining that "I would never use the words 'fruit pickers' . . . or the rest of her inflated prose" (*The Nation*, Feb. 4, 1991, p. 140).

52. Dennis, *Autobiography of an American Communist*, p. 71.

53. Smedley, quoted in MacKinnon and MacKinnon, *Agnes Smedley*, p. 145.

54. Mitford, *Hons and Rebels*, pp. 55, 63; idem, *A Fine Old Conflict*, p. 15.

55. According to Virginia Woolf, "towards the end of the eighteenth century a change came about which, if I were rewriting history, I should . . . think of greater importance than the Crusades or the Wars of the Roses. The middle-class woman began to write" (*A Room of One's Own*, p. 68).

56. In *American Hunger*, Wright describes how he spent much of his life cultivating his feelings (pp. 13–21).

57. Deleuze and Guattari go on to say:

> Precisely because the flows of capital are decoded and deterritorialized flows; precisely because the subjective essence of production is revealed in capitalism; precisely because the limit becomes internal to capitalism, which continually reproduces it, and also continually occupies it as an internalized and displaced limit; precisely for these reasons, the identity in nature must appear for itself between social production and desiring-production. . . . This is because the decoded and deterritorialized forms of capitalism are not recaptured or co-opted, but directly apprehended in a codeless axiomatic that consigns them to the universe of subjective representation. (*Anti-Oedipus*, p. 337)

58. Rosenfelt, "From the Thirties"; Taggard, "Life of the Mind."

59. "When political involvement takes priority, though the need and love for writing go on. Every freedom movement has, and has had, its roll of writers participating at the price of their writing" (Olsen, *Silences*, p. 143).

60. Taggard, "Life of the Mind."

61. Moishe Nadir, "The Writer in a Minority Language," in Hart, ed., *American Writers' Congress*, p. 154.

62. Warshow, "The Legacy of the 30's," p. 38.

63. See Ross, *No Respect*, chaps. 1 and 2, for a fuller discussion of the anti-Stalinist intellectual as crusader against popular culture.

64. Lasch, *New Radicalism in America*, p. 256; Kristeva, "New Type of Intellectual," pp. 296–97.

65. See Gramsci, "The Intellectuals"; Foucault, "Truth and Power"; and Williams, "Alignment and Commitment," in *Marxism and Literature*, pp. 199–205.

66. North, "College Men and Men," p. 14.

67. Kenneth Burke, "Revolutionary Symbolism in America," in Hart, ed., *American Writers' Congress*, pp. 87–93.

68. Kristeva, "New Type of Intellectual," pp. 296–97.

69. See also Lasch, "Woman as Alien," in *New Radicalism in America*, pp. 38–68.

70. Gold, "Go Left, Young Writers!," p. 4.

71. Foucault put it this way: "The ['left'] intellectual is thus taken as the clear, individual figure of a universality whose obscure, collective form is embodied in the proletariat" ("Truth and Power," p. 126).

72. Hart, introduction to *American Writers' Congress*, p. 9.

73. "The woman question" was the Party's shorthand for any issues relating to sexuality, feminism, women, or the family. See Marx et al., *The Woman Question*.

74. "Work among Women," p. 27.

75. Girls' Commission of the YCL, "Appealing to the American Girl."

76. "What Can a Woman Do?"

77. Golden, "A 'Capitalist' Speaks."

78. Lapsley, "Scaffolding."

79. Millet, "Last Night," p. 17. The "fifteen-year-old working-class girl" (as Millet now describes herself when she wrote the poem) seems more clear-headed about what the revolution could do for her than the fourteen-year-old Mikey does when he encounters the soap-box orator at the end of *Jews without Money*. His poem is both politically and stylistically sentimental; Millet's is much less so.

80. Vorse, *Labor's New Millions*, p. 86.

81. Millet, "Drawn into Life."

82. Page, "Women Heroes of Socialist Construction."

83. Lens, "Flashes and Close-Ups."

84. Logan, "Tennessee Women's Auxiliary."

85. Taggard, "At Last the Women Are Moving," in *Calling Western Union*, p. 6.

86. Page, "Revolution Made a Person out of Me." Typically, articles about women workers painted a direr picture than those about men, as can be seen from the following titles: "Not Sunny for Girl Slaves in 'Sunny' Florida"; "Women Slave in Steel Mill"; or the more extreme "Capitalism Kills Women."

87. Bodenheim, "Revolutionary Girl."

88. Lewis, "Man from Moscow."

89. See Nekola and Rabinowitz, eds., *Writing Red*; Kessler-Harris and Lauter, introduction to *Call Home the Heart*; Dixler, "The Woman Question"; Coiner, " 'Pessimism of the Mind' "; Lacey, "Engendering Conflict."

90. Margaret, "Our Readers' Forum."

91. Leknorf, "Our Readers' Forum."

92. Chambers, "Editorial Note."

93. Gilfillan, *I Went to Pit College*, pp. 260, 280 (foreigner, grotesque figure); Burke, *Call Home the Heart*, pp. 373, 384 (dragon, beast); Slesinger, *The Unpossessed*, p. 357 (creature); see also Johnson, *Jordanstown*, pp. 99–100.

94. Ann Weedon chastises the editors of the *New Masses* for "the predominance of women in the ranks [of communism] and a man in every position of any consequence.... When I mention these facts to Communists they react in one of three ways. They point with pride to some lone woman who holds a third-rate post.... Or they sneer, and say with fine sophistication, 'What! Still a suffragette?' ... The third reply is a lengthy recitation of the whole attitude of Communism toward women, plus a retreat to Moscow for concrete examples" ("Correspondence").

95. Gilfillan, "Why Women Really Might as Well Be Communists as Not."

96. Winter, "What Fascism Means to Mothers."

97. Taggard, "At Last the Women Are Moving," in *Calling Western Union*, p. 5.

98. McHenry, "The Nation's Finest."

99. McHenry, "Mothers Join Fight."

100. McHenry, "Women Mass in Capital."

101. Girls' Commission of the YCL, "Appealing to the American Girl."

102. McHenry, "Catholic Mother Hears the Truth."

103. Susman, "The Thirties."

104. Two notable exceptions are Taggard, "Romanticism and Communism," and LeSueur, "Fetish of Being Outside," both published in the *New Masses*.

105. One of the themes of much new scholarship on the CPUSA argues that rank-and-file members and organizers in the field deviated significantly from the prescribed strategies and doctrine of the Central Committee. See, for example, Isserman, *Which Side Were You On?*; Naison, *Communists in Harlem*; and the film *Seeing Red*, produced, directed, and edited by Julia Reichert and James Klein, 1983. Rae Bernstein, an organizer for the needle trade's union in Connecticut during the 1930s, described being brought up on charges by Party officials because she refused to surrender to the Party a portion of the monies collected at a New York rally in support of the striking women she was leading (telephone conversation with Bernstein, Aug. 2, 1985).

Chapter 2

1. Miller, "Emphasis Added," p. 37.

2. Deleuze and Guattari, *Kafka*, p. 18.

3. Ragon, *Histoire de la Littérature Prolétarienne*, p. 2.

4. Johnson, *Critical Difference*, p. 55.

5. Jameson, *Political Unconscious*, pp. 99, 141, 145.

6. Williams, *Marxism and Literature*, pp. 180–85.

7. In film theory, classic Hollywood genres such as Westerns have been read as vehicles that provide writers and directors with opportunities to introduce heterodox ideas into mainstream entertainment. For example, films from the 1950s, including *High Noon*, *Shane*, and *The Gunfighter*, relied on classic icons—guns, horses, ten-gallon hats—to display ideological tensions within American culture over McCarthyism and the cold war.

8. Macherey, *Theory of Literary Production*, argues for a reading of the *non-dit* in narrative in order to discern the ideological implications of a text. His method does not, however, suggest that there is a hidden meaning lurking beneath the surface of narrative; but rather that the work of narrative is to say as much as possible. Therefore, what is left out becomes significant. Macherey's theories of narrative inform my study of genre.

9. Jameson, *Political Unconscious*, p. 151.

10. According to Bakhtin, "The novel appears to be a creature from an alien species . . . a genre that is both critical and self-critical . . . in all its openendedness" ("Epic and Novel," in *The Dialogic Imagination*, pp. 4, 10, 11).

11. In *Desire and Domestic Fiction*, Armstrong argues that one function of the novel has been to create a middle-class cultural hegemony by establishing a common sensibility among the disparate members of the emerging English bourgeoisie.

12. "The novel is the epic of an age in which the extensive totality of life is no longer directly given" (Lukács, *Theory of the Novel*, p. 56).

13. Jacobus, "Question of Language."

14. Derrida, "Law of Genre," pp. 202–3.

15. Johnson, "Gender Theory and the Yale School," p. 102.

16. Gilbert and Gubar, *Madwoman in the Attic*, p. 63.

17. Baym, "Melodramas of Beset Manhood."

18. See Scott, *Gender and the Politics of History*, pp. 53–93.

19. DuPlessis, *Writing Beyond the Ending*, p. 35.

20. Ibid., p. 2.

21. "The central category and criterion of realist literature is the type. . . . In it all the humanly and socially essential determinants are present . . . rendering concrete the peaks and limits of men and epochs" (Lukács, *Studies in European Realism*, p. 6).

22. Suleiman, "(Re)Writing the Body," p. 24.

23. Stanton, "Autogynography," p. 13.

24. Many feminist critics are fascinated by Mary Shelley's *Frankenstein* as a narrative that encodes maternity as monstrosity. See, for example, Gilbert and Gubar, *Madwoman in the Attic*, pp. 213–47; Moers, *Literary Women*, pp. 137–51; Jacobus, "Is There a Woman in This Text?" pp. 117–41.

25. Johnson, *Jordanstown*, p. 99.

26. Madden, ed., *Proletarian Writers of the Thirties*, p. xix.

27. Hicks, "Revolution and the Novel: Complex and Collective Novels," pp. 23, 25.

28. Frye, *Anatomy of Criticism*, p. 312.

29. Suleiman, "Some Problems of (the) Genre: Definitions and Method," in *Authoritarian Fictions*, pp. 3–17.

30. Chester Eisinger argues that the political culture of America during the 1930s produced an "ambience" rather than fundamental economic or social transformations ("Character and Self in Fiction on the Left," in Madden, ed., *Proletarian Writers of the Thirties*, p. 158).

31. Blotner declares that this work addresses "the overt, institutionalized politics of the officeholder, the candidate, the party official" (*Modern American Political Novel*, p. 8).

32. Williams, *Marxism and Literature*, p. 199.

33. Ibid., pp. 201–5.

34. Suleiman, *Authoritarian Fictions*, chaps. 2 and 3.

35. Gold, "Notes of the Month," p. 4.

36. Hicks, "Revolution and the Novel."

37. Two notable examples are Cowley, "Farewell to the 1930's," and Rahv, "Proletarian Literature."

38. Cowley, "Farewell to the 1930's," p. 42.

39. In addition to the works cited above, see Arvin, "Letter on Proletarian Literature"; Calmer, "The Proletarian Short Story"; Taggard, "Romanticism and Communism."

40. Kaplan, "Pandora's Box," p. 165.

41. Clearly, these two types mirror two of Rideout's.

42. Novels that are structured around a strike or mass demonstration include Brody, *Nobody Starves*; Burke, *Call Home the Heart* and *A Stone Came Rolling*; Davidson, *South of Joplin*; Gilfillan, *I Went to Pit College*; Herbst, *The Executioner Waits*; Johnson, *Jordanstown*; LeSueur, *The Girl*; Linn, *Flea Circus*; Lumpkin, *To Make My Bread*; McKenney, *Industrial Valley* and *Jake Home*; Page, *Gathering Storm*; Spadoni, *Not All Rivers*; Vorse, *Strike!*; Weatherwax, *Marching! Marching!*; Zugsmith, *A Time to Remember*. Those that include a strike or mass demonstration, but not as a central device of the plot, are Bisno, *Tomorrow's Bread*; Breuer, *The Daughter*; Cassady, *This Magic Dust*;

Gellhorn, *The Trouble I've Seen*; Herbst, *Rope of Gold*; Russell, *Lake Front*; Scott, *A Calendar of Sin*.

43. In France, argues Suleiman, the structure of confrontation is a more prevalent narrative among the *romans à thèse* of the Left, like *Man's Hope*, whereas novels that follow the structure of apprenticeship are usually politically right wing and stress the need for proper patriarchal relationships between youths and elders and between men and women; Soviet socialist-realist novels of the 1930s, however, often conformed to this structure as well, indicating the rigidity that increasingly marked Soviet literature under Zhdanov.

44. Jameson, *Political Unconscious*, p. 125.

45. Baym, *Woman's Fiction*, p. 12.

46. Rideout, *Radical Novel in the United States*, p. 153.

47. Gauthier, "Is There Such a Thing as Women's Writing?," p. 164.

48. See Gilbert and Gubar, "Sexual Linguistics," p. 532, for an analysis of the ways that various literary movements have constructed "male linguistic fantasies."

49. Novels by women in which a rape occurs include Burke, *Call Home the Heart*; Davidman, *Anya*; Gellhorn, *The Trouble I've Seen*; LeSueur, *The Girl*; Olsen, *Yonnondio*; Page, *Gathering Storm*; Scott, *A Calendar of Sin*; Smedley, *Daughter of Earth*.

50. Farrell, *Young Manhood of Studs Lonigan*, p. 397.

51. Farrell, *Judgment Day*, pp. 355–61.

52. Ultimately, the confusions generated by the sexual metaphors in proletarian novels led one reader of the *New Masses* to complain that the novels all "centered around smutty vulgar sex stories" and "disgusted" him (West, "Our Readers' Forum," p. 22).

53. The novels in which social workers appear are Burke, *Call Home the Heart*; Gellhorn, *The Trouble I've Seen*; Johnson, *Jordanstown*; LeSueur, *The Girl*; Linn, *Flea Circus*; Olsen, *Yonnondio*; Slade, *The Triumph of Willie Pond* and *Sterile Sun*; Spadoni, *Not All Rivers*. Marita Bonner's story "The Whipping" suggests that this scenario has deadly results for the African American working-class mother (*Frye Street and Environs*, pp. 185–95).

54. The novels in which the themes of birth and maternity become central are Bisno, *Tomorrow's Bread*; Burke, *Call Home the Heart*; Herbst, *Rope of Gold*; LeSueur, *The Girl*; Lumpkin, *To Make My Bread*; Page, *Daughter of the Hills*. Slesinger's *The Unpossessed* culminates in an abortion rather than a birth and so inverts the scenario.

55. Interestingly, the pages of *Working Woman* were full of pleas by poor women for "the knowledge" and "information" on contraception. The magazine offered advice columns by physicians about how to obtain birth control devices and how to avoid pregnancy. Their medical credentials were used to rebuke folk methods such as the "safe period." In addition, the editors exhorted readers to organize for passage of the Worker's Unemployment Insurance Bill, H.R. 7598, which included legislation allowing women access to contraception. See, for example, Rhinehart, "Another Baby?," p. 13; Davies, "How About That 'Safe Period'?," p. 12; Hutchins, "Birth Control," pp. 13–14; and Lone, "What Women Should Know," p. 15.

56. Gilfillan, *I Went to Pit College*, p. 269, rephrases Gold's indictments against "straining or melodrama or other effects" (in *Notes of the Month*, p. 4).

57. Derrida, "Law of Genre," p. 202; Gold, *Hollow Men*, p. 58.

58. Jehlen, "Archimedes and the Paradox of Feminist Criticism," p. 582; Gilbert and Gubar, *Madwoman in the Attic*, p. 57.

59. Jon Suggs calls *Marching! Marching!* a doctrinal proletarian novel ("Influence of Marxist Aesthetics on American Fiction"). As will be obvious, I disagree with his reading.

60. Rahv, "Open Letter to Young Writers."

61. For a dissection of the grammar of race and gender within discourses of slavery, see Spillers, "Mama's Baby, Papa's Maybe."

62. De Lauretis, *Alice Doesn't*, p. 116.

Chapter 3

1. Page references to Weatherwax, *Marching! Marching!*, LeSueur, *The Girl*, and Olsen, *Yonnondio*, will appear parenthetically in the text.

2. Joseph Urgo argues that Robert Shaffer ("Women and the Communist Party U.S.A.") and Elsa Jane Dixler ("The Woman Question") fail to consult a third source for constructing the history of women's radicalism in culture and politics during the 1930s. Not only should we consult the women's pages of the various leftist journals and the few works of theory by Marxist-feminists like Inman and Hutchins, but we should also read the fiction women wrote as well. He begins this revision by reviewing the four women's novels about the Gastonia strike ("Proletarian Literature and Feminism").

3. Suggs, "Influence of Marxist Aesthetics on American Fiction," p. 98.

4. In contrast, many other proletarian novels by women more explicitly address female characters and female spaces. Zugsmith's *A Time to Remember* chronicles the Ohrbach's strike and thereby examines the world of the female shopper and female salesclerk, linking women and commodities in a number of complex ways. Linn's *Flea Circus* and Slade's two novels, *Sterile Sun* and *The Triumph of Willie Pond*, focus on the social welfare system and the unemployed families it serves; all three look at women in poverty and the female social workers who arbitrate between them and the bourgeois state. The four Gastonia novels by women—Vorse's *Strike!*, Lumpkin's *To Make My Bread*, Page's *Gathering Storm*, and Burke's *Call Home the Heart*—center on the martyrdom of Ella May Wiggins as a central plot device, thus elaborating female working-class heroism. Finally, as I have indicated, both Olsen's *Yonnondio* and LeSueur's *The Girl* violate the norms of the genre so strongly that they were not published during the 1930s.

5. Calmer, "Reader's Report."

6. Olsen [Lerner], "The Iron Throat"; the story was later republished in Hicks et al., eds., *Proletarian Literature in the United States*, pp. 103–9.

7. This also explains why Olsen can read Rebecca Harding Davis's *Life in the Iron Mill* as the first fiction by an American woman about class. It seems, in shape, theme, and form, to anticipate her own writings.

8. Bakhtin, *Dialogic Imagination*, p. 84, describes the chronotope of a novel as its time/space coordinates.

9. Both Rideout, *Radical Novel in the United States*, and Suggs, "Influence of Marxist Aesthetics on American Fiction," treat *Marching! Marching!* as a pristine example of dogma-cum-literature. Dixler believes that the gender of the author further reveals

some of the contradictions for women that heterosexuality created within the Communist movement. She finds the relationship of Joe and Mary paradigmatic of "movement lovers," noting the frustrations that seem to make any satisfying relationship unlikely. Dixler suggests that this dissatisfaction between the protagonists—that is, their inability to consummate a sexual relationship—was Weatherwax's (and, by extension, other women's) way of criticizing the Party for its failure to address women's issues or engage women as anything other than working men's wives ("The Woman Question," esp. pp. 110–11).

10. Cantwell, "A Town and Its Novels," p. 51.

11. Two other novels about the Aberdeen lumber strikes are Cantwell, *The Land of Plenty*, and Colman, *Lumber*.

12. Calmer, "The Proletarian Short Story," p. 17.

13. See Hicks, "Revolution and the Novel," and Gold, "Notes of the Month," for their outlines prescribing how to produce good proletarian fiction.

14. Barbara Foley made this point in her paper "*New Masses* Critics and Bourgeois Ideology," delivered at the Midwest Modern Language Association meeting, St. Louis, Nov. 1988.

15. McCarthy, "Saint Francesca of the Pacific Northwest."

16. Ragon, *Histoire de la Littérature Prolétarienne*, p. 2.

17. Cantwell, "A Town and Its Novels."

18. Lukács, "Narrate or Describe?," in *Writer and Critic*, p. 116.

19. By contrast, Grace Lumpkin, Myra Page, and Fielding Burke focus their novels about Gastonia on the preindustrial mountain setting from which many of the mill workers emerged. Although life was hard and poverty extreme for these mountain people, certain residual values of pride, struggle, and solidarity were developed through kin networks, trading practices, and home industry. These resources carried over, strengthening the efforts of those who become active in organizing the industrial workplace.

20. Derrida and MacDonald, "Choreographies," p. 52.

21. Burke, *Call Home the Heart*, p. 290.

22. Lumpkin, *To Make My Bread*, p. 13.

23. Page, *Gathering Storm*, p. 101.

24. Theweleit, *Male Fantasies*, 1:367.

25. See Silverman, *Acoustic Mirror*, pp. 72–79, on the maternal sonorous envelope as a trope for that which is simultaneously entrapping and soothing.

26. Benjamin, *Charles Baudelaire*, pp. 45–66.

27. See Le Bon, *The Crowd*, pp. 20, 33, for various references to the feminine character of the crowd and its threat to masculine autonomy. See also Huyssen, "Mass Culture as Woman: Modernism's Other," in *After the Great Divide*, pp. 44–62, for a historical account of the various discourses through which the masses became feminized.

28. "The Cooboo," a story by the Australian woman writer and Communist Party member Katharine Prichard, also brings maternity into the workplace. The heroine of this story herds cattle with her nursing infant strapped across her breast.

29. This image is, of course, also the image of the grotesque body of carnival, the death-in-life represented for Bakhtin by the masses.

30. According to Constance Coiner, who examined the 1939 manuscript, this

cultural feminist ending was added when LeSueur edited the manuscript for publication in the 1970s. In the original manuscript, the baby was male and there were fewer references to male and female polarizations. Nevertheless, the novel remained substantially the same. See Coiner, " 'Pessimism of the Mind,' " p. 150.

31. Bakhtin, *Rabelais and His World*, pp. 303–67.

32. See Russo, "Female Grotesques," for a discussion of Bakhtin's (and theory's) failure to encode gender in their analyses.

33. Zetkin, "From My Memorandum Book," in *My Recollections of Lenin*, p. 58.

34. I am using the phrase "community of women" differently from Marx and Engels in the *Communist Manifesto*, where it refers to prostitution; yet there are reverberations and connections between my use and theirs that I want to emphasize through the quotation marks.

35. Rich, "Compulsory Heterosexuality and Lesbian Existence," p. 87.

36. LeSueur, "Sequel to Love," pp. 3–4.

37. LeSueur, "Annunciation," in *Salute to Spring*, pp. 54–72.

38. Kristeva, "Stabat Mater," p. 113.

39. See Lukács, *History and Class Consciousness*, for a thorough reading of the process by which the working class, an unconscious formation produced by capitalism, becomes the proletariat, a self-conscious formation to produce socialism.

40. Suleiman, *Authoritarian Fictions*, pp. 101, 63.

41. Olsen, *Silences*.

42. See Rosenfelt, "From the Thirties," p. 385.

43. See Rosenfelt, "Divided Against Herself," for an insightful analysis of the political, sexual, and aesthetic contradictions operating for women writers associated with the Left during the 1930s. *Yonnondio* clearly recalls *Daughter of Earth* and, as a novel of childhood, *Call It Sleep*. Burkom and Williams, "De-Riddling Tillie Olsen's Writings," a biobibliographic study, also provides a larger contextual frame for reading Olsen's works. Samuelson, "Patterns of Survival," looks at the ways in which the connections between mothers and daughters form an empowering motif within women's proletarian novels.

44. Samuelson, "Patterns of Survival."

45. Kristeva, "Stabat Mater," p. 112.

46. Sherry Ortner, "Is Female to Male as Nature Is to Culture?," in Rosaldo and Lamphere, eds., *Women, Culture, and Society*, pp. 67–88.

Chapter 4

1. Gale, "College Girl in the Pennsylvania Mines."

2. Nuhn, "Lost Generation and the New Morality."

3. Langer, *Josephine Herbst*, p. 240.

4. Kempton, *Part of Our Time*, p. 122.

5. In her review of *The Company She Keeps*, Edith H. Walton notes that McCarthy comes close to Slesinger in "reflecting the exact talk and temper of certain circles in New York" (*New York Times Book Review*, May 24, 1942, p. 7). On *The Unpossessed* as a "curiosity," see Frederick J. Hoffman, "Aesthetics of the Proletarian Novel," in Madden, *Proletarian Writers of the Thirties*, p. 192.

6. Miller, "Emphasis Added," p. 37. Carolyn Heilbrun makes a similar, though less nuanced, point in her chapter entitled "Women Writers and Female Characters: The Failure of Imagination," in *Reinventing Womanhood*, pp. 71–92. The most elaborate argument for reading the split personalities of female characters as indicative of psychological division within female authors is made in Gilbert and Gubar, *Madwoman in the Attic*.

7. In her afterword to the novel, Janet Sharistanian notes that Slesinger was reading Woolf and Katherine Mansfield while writing *The Unpossessed*.

8. Both Lionel Trilling ("Young in the Thirties," p. 49) and Alan Wald (*New York Intellectuals*, p. 72) consider it significant that Slesinger drifted into the CPUSA orbit in Hollywood. Both imply that her novel was both a political and personal repudiation of the anti-Stalinism of her former husband, Herbert Solow.

9. Brecht, "The Exception and the Rule," p. 56.

10. Slesinger was the screenwriter for Dorothy Arzner's film *Dance, Girl, Dance* (1940), which stresses the relationships among desire, meaning, and specularity through the diverging and converging careers of two dancers—Tiger Lily White, the sexually alluring burlesque dancer played by Lucille Ball, and Judy O'Brien, the aspiring ballet dancer played by Maureen O'Hara.

11. Wald, *New York Intellectuals*, p. 40.

12. See Bercovitch, *Puritan Origins of the American Self*, for an analysis of the influence of Puritan spiritual autobiographies on American narrative.

13. Bunyan, *Pilgrim's Progress*. As a spiritual autobiography, Gilfillan's novel draws parallels between Bunyan's depictions of the "Slough of Despond" and "City of Destruction" and Laurie's physical surroundings and their effects on her.

14. Russo, "Female Grotesques," p. 213.

15. See, for example, Doane, "Film and the Masquerade," and de Lauretis, *Alice Doesn't*.

16. Rolfe, "College Girl Writes about Western Pennsylvania Miners."

17. Ibid. Rolfe expresses dismay at Gilfillan's loss of dignity. This sentiment is echoed by Mary Heaton Vorse, who cannot understand why Laurie gets thrown out of Avelonia ("Lauren Gilfillan's Education"). Other book-length examples of women's fictional reportage include Davidson, *South of Joplin*; Gellhorn, *The Trouble I've Seen*; and McKenney, *Industrial Valley*. Margaret Bourke-White's photo-essay *You Have Seen Their Faces* (written with Erskine Caldwell) came under attack by James Agee for its melodramatic effects.

18. Herbst, "Starched Blue Sky of Spain," p. 78.

19. Quoted in Millett, *Contemporary American Authors*, p. 389.

20. Rahv, "Variety of Fiction."

21. Herbst's first published piece of reportage was entitled "Feet in the Grass Roots," and it was among the people that she felt most comfortable politically.

22. For a discussion of the Trexler trilogy that focuses on the interweaving of various strands, see Kempthorne, "Josephine Herbst," pp. 110–11.

23. The phrase "rope of sand" can be found among the synonyms for incoherence in *Roget's Thesaurus*.

24. Silverman, *Acoustic Mirror*, p. 72.

25. Russo, "Female Grotesques." See also Bakhtin, *Dialogic Imagination*, p. 84.

26. Pizer, "Camera Eye in *U.S.A.*"

27. Langer, *Josephine Herbst*, p. 179; Dixler, "The Woman Question."

28. See Jacobus, "Is There a Woman in This Text?," for a full discussion of the absent presence of the (body of) woman in discourse and narrative.

29. McCarthy, *The Company She Keeps*, p. x.

30. This is Herbst's description of intellectuals in "Author's Field Day," p. 30.

Epilogue

1. Of course, I am referring to the image of the young Chinese man who bravely stood before the approaching tanks outside Tiananmen Square. Unfortunately, the forces of Stalinist repression remain alive and well in China, despite the peaceful demonstrations of millions.

2. See Martin, *Woman in the Body*, for detailed discussions of the factory metaphor. The Florida woman was jailed because she had smoked crack while she was pregnant; her body thus became a cocaine-producing factory, and she a pusher distributing it to her fetus. Also see Fanon, *Black Skin, White Masks*, for a discussion of the political meanings involved when oppressed people speak another's language.

3. Truth, "Ain't I a Woman?"

4. Wilson, *Our Nig*, and Jacobs, *Incidents in the Life of a Slave Girl*, both reveal the interconnections between the systems of productive and reproductive labor dominating the African American woman's body. See Spillers, "Mama's Baby, Papa's Maybe," and Morrison, *Beloved*, for elaborations of the ways in which race and gender are mutually sustained ideologies that nevertheless cannot be articulated.

5. Eisler, ed., *Lowell Offering*. See Schofield, ed., *Sealskin and Shoody*, for late-nineteenth- and early twentieth-century sources of other institutionally produced working women's fiction. In "Gender and the Work of Words," Nancy Armstrong and Leonard Tennenhouse discuss how the woman worker's body resisted analytical categories in midcentury Britain.

6. Olsen, *Yonnondio*, p. 30; Olsen, "Afterword: A Biographical Interpretation," p. 69. Page references to Davis's work will appear parenthetically in the text.

7. Walter Benjamin calls fascism the aestheticizing of politics ("Work of Art," p. 242).

8. Victor Shklovsky distinguished between story (*fabula*) and plot (*sjuzet*), which, according to Tony Bennett, roughly corresponds to the "temporal-causal sequence of narrated events which comprise the raw materials of the work, and the way in which these raw materials are formally manipulated" (Bennett, *Formalism and Marxism*, p. 19).

9. Jardine, *Gynesis*, p. 236.

10. See Rosenfelt, "From the Thirties" and "Getting into the Game."

11. Woolf, "Women and Fiction," in *Women and Writing*, p. 51.

12. Woolf argues that these disturbances ultimately "deformed and twisted" *Jane Eyre*; when Jane is interrupted by the "low, slow, ha ha" of Grace Poole's laugh as she stands on the rooftop indulging her reverie of freedom, Charlotte Brontë let her own anger disrupt her artistic vision (*A Room of One's Own*, p. 72). However, noting Woolf's omission, Cora Kaplan argues that Jane Eyre's soliloquy links the expression of female

desire to the rebellion brewing amid the "millions," the "masses" of "human beings" against their thwarted lives ("Pandora's Box," p. 170).

13. Wittig, *Les Guérillères*, p. 144.

14. Derrida and MacDonald, "Choreographies," pp. 75–76; Kristeva, "Stabat Mater," p. 118; Jameson, *Political Unconscious*, p. 125. The literature on the relationship between feminism and postmodernism represents a growth industry among feminist theorists. For an early and still compelling discussion of the interconnections between the two movements, see Meese, *Crossing the Double-Cross*, pp. 69–88.

15. Felski, *Beyond Feminist Aesthetics*, esp. p. 154.

Bibliography

Women's Revolutionary Novels: A Partial List

Bisno, Beatrice. *Tomorrow's Bread*. Philadelphia: Jewish Publication Society of America, 1938.

Breuer, Bessie. *The Daughter*. New York: Simon and Schuster, 1938.

Brody, Catharine. *Cash Item*. New York: Longmans, Green and Co., 1933.

———. *Nobody Starves*. London: Longmans, Green and Co., 1932.

Burke, Fielding [Olive Tilford Dargan]. *Call Home the Heart*. London: Longmans, Green and Co., 1932.

———. *A Stone Came Rolling*. New York: Longmans, Green and Co., 1935.

Cassady, Constance. *This Magic Dust*. Indianapolis: Bobbs-Merrill, 1937.

Davidman, Joy. *Anya*. New York: Macmillan, 1940.

Davidson, Lallah. *South of Joplin*. New York: W. W. Norton, 1939.

Eastman, Elizabeth. *Sun on Their Shoulders*. New York: William Morrow, 1934.

Gellhorn, Martha. *The Trouble I've Seen*. New York: William Morrow, 1936.

Gilfillan, Harriet Woodbridge [Lauren Gilfillan]. *I Went to Pit College*. New York: Literary Guild, 1934.

Herbst, Josephine. *The Executioner Waits*. New York: Harcourt, Brace and Co., 1934.

———. *Pity Is Not Enough*. New York: Harcourt, Brace and Co., 1933.

———. *Rope of Gold*. New York: Harcourt, Brace and Co., 1939.

Johnson, Josephine. *Jordanstown*. New York: Simon and Schuster, 1937.

———. *Now in November*. New York: Simon and Schuster, 1934.

LeSueur, Meridel. *The Girl*. Cambridge, Mass.: West End Press, 1978.

Linn, Bettina. *Flea Circus*. New York: Harrison Smith and Robert Haas, 1936.

Lumpkin, Grace. *To Make My Bread*. New York: Macaulay, 1932.

———. *A Sign for Cain*. New York: Lee Furman, 1935.

McCarthy, Mary. *The Company She Keeps*. New York: Harcourt, Brace and Co., 1942.

McKenney, Ruth. *Industrial Valley*. 1939. Reprint. New York: Greenwood Press, 1968.

———. *Jake Home*. New York: Harcourt, Brace and Co., 1943.

Olsen, Tillie. *Yonnondio: From the Thirties*. New York: Delacorte Press/Seymour Lawrence, 1974.

Page, Myra [Dorothy]. *Daughter of the Hills.* 1950. Reprint. New York: Feminist Press, 1986.
———. *Gathering Storm: A Story of the Black Belt.* London: Martin Lawrence, 1932.
———. *Moscow Yankee.* New York: G. P. Putnam's Sons, 1935.
Russell, Ruth. *Lake Front.* Chicago: Thomas Rockwell, 1931.
Sandoz, Mari. *Capital City.* Boston: Little, Brown, 1939.
Scott, Evelyn. *A Calendar of Sin.* 2 vols. New York: Jonathan Cape and Harrison Smith, 1931.
Slade, Caroline. *Sterile Sun.* New York: Vanguard Press, 1937.
———. *The Triumph of Willie Pond.* New York: Vanguard Press, 1940.
Slesinger, Tess. *The Unpossessed.* New York: Simon and Schuster, 1934.
Smedley, Agnes. *Daughter of Earth.* 1929. Reprint. Old Westbury, N.Y: Feminist Press, 1973.
Spadoni, Adriana. *Not All Rivers.* 1937. Reprint. New York: AMS Press, 1976.
Suckow, Ruth. *The Folks.* New York: Literary Guild, 1934.
Thomas, Dorothy. *The Home Place.* New York: Knopf, 1936.
Vorse, Mary Heaton. *Strike!* New York: Liveright, 1930.
Weatherwax, Clara. *Marching! Marching!* New York: John Day Co., 1935.
Wilhelm, Gale. *We Too Are Drifting.* 1935. Reprint. New York: Triangle Books, 1938.
Zugsmith, Leane. *Never Enough.* New York: Liveright, 1932.
———. *The Summer Soldier.* New York: Random House, 1939.
———. *A Time to Remember.* New York: Random House, 1936.

Secondary Sources

Aaron, Daniel. *Writers on the Left.* 1961. Reprint. New York: Oxford University Press, 1977.
Adamic, Louis. "What the Proletariat Reads." In *1935 Essay Annual,* edited by Erich A. Walter, pp. 213–21. Chicago: Scott, Foresman and Co., 1935.
Agee, James, and Walker Evans. *Let Us Now Praise Famous Men.* 1941. Reprint. New York: Ballantine Books, 1966.
Alexander, William. *Film on the Left: American Documentary Film from 1931 to 1942.* Princeton, N.J.: Princeton University Press, 1981.
Allen, Frederick Lewis. *Since Yesterday: 1929–1939.* 1940. Reprint. New York: Bantam Books, 1965.
Althusser, Louis. *For Marx.* Translated by Ben Brewster. London: New Left Books, 1977.
———. *Lenin and Philosophy.* Translated by Ben Brewster. London: New Left Books, 1971.
"Appealing to the American Girl with the Program of the YCL." *Daily Worker,* May 29, 1937, p. 6.
Armstrong, Nancy. *Desire and Domestic Fiction: A Political History of the Novel.* New York: Oxford University Press, 1987.
———. "Literature as Women's History." *Genre* 19 (Winter 1986): 347–69.

Armstrong, Nancy, and Leonard Tennenhouse. "Gender and the Work of Words." *Cultural Critique* 13 (Fall 1989): 229–78.

Arvin, Newton. "A Letter on Proletarian Literature." *Partisan Review* (February 1936): 12–14.

Arvon, Henri. *Marxist Esthetics.* Introduction by Fredric Jameson. Translated by Helen Lane. Ithaca, N.Y.: Cornell University Press, 1973.

"Authors' Field Day: A Symposium on Marxist Criticism." *New Masses,* July 3, 1934, pp. 27–32.

Baird, Irene. *Waste Heritage.* 1939. Reprint. Toronto: Macmillan, 1973.

Bakhtin, Mikhail. *The Dialogic Imagination: Four Essays.* Edited by Michael Holquist. Translated by Caryl Emerson and Michael Holquist. Austin: University of Texas Press, 1981.

———. *Rabelais and His World.* Translated by Helene Iswolsky. Cambridge, Mass.: MIT Press, 1968.

Barrett, Michèle. *Women's Oppression Today.* London: Verso, 1980.

Barton, Ann. "Our Readers' Forum." *New Masses,* January 1, 1935, p. 35.

Baym, Nina. "Melodramas of Beset Manhood: How Theories of American Fiction Exclude Women Authors." *American Quarterly* 33 (1981): 123–39.

———. *Woman's Fiction: A Guide to Novels By and About Women in America, 1820–1870.* Ithaca, N.Y.: Cornell University Press, 1978.

Bell, Thomas. *All Brides Are Beautiful.* Boston: Little, Brown, 1936.

Benjamin, Walter. *Charles Baudelaire: A Lyric Poet in the Era of High Capitalism.* Translated by Harry Zohn. London: Verso, 1983.

———. "The Work of Art in the Age of Mechanical Reproduction." In *Illuminations: Essays and Reflections,* edited by Hannah Arendt, translated by Harry Zohn, pp. 217–52. New York: Schocken Books, 1969.

Bennett, Tony. *Formalism and Marxism.* London: Methuen, 1979.

Benton, Jane, and A Group of Workers. "Stockyard Stella." *Working Woman* 6, nos. 1–4 (January–April 1935): 4–5, 4–5, 5–6, 45.

Bercovitch, Sacvan. *Puritan Origins of the American Self.* New Haven, Conn.: Yale University Press, 1975.

Berger, John. *Ways of Seeing.* Hammondsworth, Eng.: Penguin, 1972.

Bergman, Andrew. *We're in the Money: Depression America and Its Films.* New York: Harper and Row, 1971.

Biagi, Shirley. "Forgive Me For Dying." *Antioch Review* 35 (Spring/Summer 1977): 224–36.

Bird, Caroline. *The Invisible Scar.* New York: David McKay Co., 1966.

Blake, Fay M. *The Strike in the American Novel.* Metuchen, N.J.: Scarecrow Press, 1972.

Bloch, Ernst, Georg Lukács, Bertolt Brecht, Walter Benjamin, and Theodor Adorno. *Aesthetics and Politics.* London: New Left Books, 1977.

Blotner, Joseph. *The Modern American Political Novel: 1900–1960.* Austin: University of Texas Press, 1966.

Bodenheim, Maxwell. "Revolutionary Girl." *New Masses,* April 3, 1934, p. 16.

Bonner, Marita. *Frye Street and Environs: The Collected Works of Marita Bonner.* Edited with introduction by Joyce Flynn and Joyce Occomy Stricklin. Boston: Beacon Press, 1987.

Brecht, Bertolt. "The Exception and the Rule." Translated by Eric Bentley. *New Directions* 15 (1955): 45–69.

Buhle, Mari Jo. *Women and the American Left: A Guide to Sources*. Boston: G. K. Hall, 1983.

Bunyan, John. *The Pilgrim's Progress*. 2d ed. Edited by James B. Wharey and revised by Roger Sharrock. Oxford: Oxford University Press, 1960.

Burkom, Selma, and Margaret Williams. "De-Riddling Tillie Olsen's Writings." *San Jose Studies* 2 (1976): 65–83.

Calmer, Alan, ed. *Get Organized*. New York: International Publishers, 1939.

———. "The Proletarian Short Story." *New Masses*, July 2, 1935, pp. 17–18.

———. "Reader's Report." *New Masses*, September 10, 1935, p. 25.

Calverton, V. F. "Leftward Ho!" *Modern Quarterly* 6 (Summer 1932): 26–32.

———. *The Liberation of American Literature*. New York: Charles Scribner's Sons, 1932.

Campbell, Russell. *Cinema Strikes Back: Radical Filmmaking in the United States, 1930–1942*. Studies in Cinema, no. 20. Ann Arbor, Mich.: UMI Research Press, 1982.

Cantwell, Robert. *The Land of Plenty*. New York: Farrar and Rinehart, 1934.

———. "A Town and Its Novels." *New Republic*, February 19, 1936, pp. 51–52.

"Capitalism Kills Women." *Daily Worker*, December 1, 1931, p. 4.

Carby, Hazel. *Reconstructing Womanhood: The Emergence of the Afro-American Woman Novelist*. New York: Oxford University Press, 1989.

Carmon, Walt. "Away from Harlem." *New Masses*, October 1930, p. 18.

Casciato, Arthur D. "Citizen Writers: A History of the League of American Writers, 1935–1942." Ph.D. diss., University of Virginia, 1986.

Chafe, William. *The American Woman: Her Changing Social, Economic and Political Roles, 1920–1970*. New York: Oxford University Press, 1972.

Chambers, Whittaker. "Editorial Note." *New Masses*, January 1932, p. 7.

Clurman, Harold. *The Fervent Years: The Story of the Group Theatre and the Thirties*. New York: Hill and Wang, 1957.

Coiner, Constance. "'Pessimism of the Mind, Optimism of the Will': Literature of Resistance." Ph.D. diss., University of California, Los Angeles, 1987.

Colman, Louis. *Lumber*. Boston: Little, Brown, 1931.

Conroy, Jack, and Curt Johnson, eds. *Writers in Revolt: The Anvil Anthology, 1933–1940*. Westport, Conn.: Lawrence Hill, 1973.

Cook, Sylvia Jenkins. *From Tobacco Road to Route 66: The Southern Poor White in Fiction*. Chapel Hill: University of North Carolina Press, 1976.

Cott, Nancy F. *The Grounding of Modern Feminism*. New Haven, Conn.: Yale University Press, 1987.

Coward, Rosalind. "Female Desire and Sexual Identity." In *Women, Feminist Identity, and Society in the 1980s*, edited by Myriam Diaz-Diacoretz and Iris Zavala, pp. 25–36. Philadelphia: John Benjamins, 1985.

Coward, Rosalind, and John Ellis. *Language and Materialism*. London: Routledge and Kegan Paul, 1977.

Cowley, Malcolm. "Bad Company." *New Republic*, May 25, 1942, p. 737.

———. "A Farewell to the 1930's." *New Republic*, November 8, 1939, pp. 42–44.

Dahlberg, Edward. *Bottom Dogs*. 1930. Reprint. New York: Minerva Press, 1976.

Davidman, Joy. *Letter to a Comrade.* New Haven, Conn.: Yale University Press, 1938.
Davies, James. "How About That 'Safe Period'?" *Working Woman* 6 (July 1935): 12.
Davis, Rebecca Harding. *Life in the Iron Mills: Or, the Korl Woman.* 1859. Reprint. Old Westbury, N.Y.: Feminist Press, 1972.
De Lauretis, Teresa. *Alice Doesn't: Feminism, Semiotics, Cinema.* Bloomington: Indiana University Press, 1984.
———. *Technologies of Gender: Essays on Theory, Film, Fiction.* Bloomington: Indiana University Press, 1987.
———, ed. *Feminist Studies/Critical Studies.* Bloomington: Indiana University Press, 1986.
Deleuze, Gilles, and Felix Guattari. *Anti-Oedipus: Capitalism and Schizophrenia.* Translated by Robert Hurley, Mark Seem, and Helen R. Lane. Preface by Michel Foucault. Minneapolis: University of Minnesota Press, 1983.
———. *Kafka: Toward a Minor Literature.* Translated by Dana Polan. Minneapolis: University of Minnesota Press, 1986.
Dennis, Peggy. *The Autobiography of an American Communist: A Personal View of a Political Life, 1925–1975.* Westport, Conn.: Lawrence Hill, 1977.
Derrida, Jacques. "The Law of Genre." *Glyph* 7 (1980): 202–32.
Derrida, Jacques, and Christie V. MacDonald. "Choreographies." *Diacritics* 12 (Summer 1982): 66–76.
Dixler, Elsa Jane. "The Woman Question: Women and the American Communist Party, 1929–1941." Ph.D. diss., Yale University, 1974.
Doane, Mary Ann. "Film and the Masquerade: Theorising the Female Spectator." *Screen* 23 (September/October 1982): 74–87.
Dooley, Roger. *From Scarface to Scarlett: American Films in the 1930s.* New York: Harcourt Brace Jovanovich, 1979.
Dos Passos, John. *U.S.A.* New York: Modern Library, 1937.
DuPlessis, Rachel Blau. *Writing Beyond the Ending: Narrative Strategies of Twentieth-Century Women Writers.* Bloomington: Indiana University Press, 1985.
Eagleton, Terry. *Criticism and Ideology.* London: Verso, 1976.
———. *Literary Theory.* Minneapolis: University of Minnesota Press, 1983.
Eastman, Max. "Artists in Uniform." *Modern Monthly*, August 1933, pp. 397–404.
Eddy, Simon. "Ballad of a Slightly Addled Cultural Worker on the United Front." *New Masses*, June 8, 1937, p. 19.
Eisler, Benita, ed. *The Lowell Offering: Writings by New England Mill Women, 1840–1845.* Philadelphia: Lippincott, 1977.
Engel, Barbara Alpern, and Clifford Rosenthal, eds. *Five Sisters: Women against the Tsar.* New York: Knopf, 1975.
Fanon, Frantz. *Black Skin, White Masks.* New York: Grove Press, 1967.
Farrell, James T. *Judgment Day.* 1935. Reprint. New York: World Publishing Co., 1946.
———. *A Note on Literary Criticism.* New York: Vanguard Press, 1936.
———. *The Young Manhood of Studs Lonigan.* 1934. Reprint. New York: Avon, 1973.
Faue, Elizabeth. "Women, Work, and Community: Minneapolis, 1929–1945." Ph.D. diss., University of Minnesota, 1987.

Felski, Rita. *Beyond Feminist Aesthetics: Feminist Literature and Social Change.* Cambridge, Mass.: Harvard University Press, 1989.

Fleischhauer, Carl, and Beverly W. Brannan. *Documenting America: 1935–1943.* Berkeley: University of California Press, 1988.

Foley, Barbara. *Telling the Truth: The Theory and Practice of Documentary Fiction.* Ithaca, N.Y.: Cornell University Press, 1986.

———. "Women and the Left in the 1930s." *American Literary History* 2 (Summer 1990): 150–69.

Fortini, Franco. "The Writer's Mandate and the End of Anti-Fascism." *Screen* 15 (Spring 1974): 33–70.

Foucault, Michel. "Truth and Power." In *Power/Knowledge: Selected Interviews and Other Writings, 1972–1977,* translated by Colin Gordon, pp. 109–33. New York: Pantheon, 1980.

Frye, Northrop. *Anatomy of Criticism: Four Essays.* Princeton, N.J.: Princeton University Press, 1957.

Gale, Zona. "A College Girl in the Pennsylvania Mines." *New York Herald Tribune,* March 4, 1934, pp. 1–2.

Garrison, Dee. *Mary Heaton Vorse: The Life of an American Insurgent.* Philadelphia: Temple University Press, 1989.

Gauthier, Xavière. "Is There Such a Thing as Women's Writing?" In *New French Feminisms: An Anthology,* edited by Elaine Marks and Isabelle de Courtivron, pp. 161–64. New York: Schocken Books, 1981.

Gilbert, James Burkhart. *Writers and Partisans: A History of Literary Radicalism in America.* New York: John Wiley and Sons, 1968.

Gilbert, Sandra M., and Susan Gubar. *The Madwoman in the Attic: The Woman Writer and the Nineteenth-Century Imagination.* New Haven, Conn.: Yale University Press, 1979.

———. *No Man's Land: The Place of the Woman Writer in the Twentieth Century.* Vol. 1, *The War of the Words.* New Haven, Conn.: Yale University Press, 1988.

———. "Sexual Linguistics: Gender, Language, Sexuality." *New Literary History* 16 (Spring 1985): 515–43.

Gilfillan, Lauren. "Why Women Really Might as Well Be Communists as Not, or Machines in the Age of Love." *Modern Monthly,* February 1935, pp. 747, 753.

Girls' Commission of the YCL. "Appealing to the American Girl with the Program of the YCL." *Daily Worker,* May 29, 1937, p. 6.

Gold, Michael. "Go Left, Young Writers!" *New Masses,* January 1929, pp. 3–4.

———. *The Hollow Men.* New York: International Publishers, 1941.

———. *Jews without Money.* 1930. Reprint. New York: Carroll and Graf, 1984.

———. "Notes of the Month." *New Masses,* September 1930, pp. 3–5.

———. "Wilder: Prophet of the Genteel Christ." *New Republic,* October 22, 1930, pp. 266–67.

Golden, Paula. "A 'Capitalist' Speaks." *New Force* 1 (February 1932): 2.

Goldman, Emma. *Living My Life.* 2 vols. 1931. Reprint. New York: Dover, 1970.

Gordimer, Nadine. *Burger's Daughter.* New York: Viking Press, 1979.

Gornick, Vivian. *The Romance of American Communism.* New York: Basic Books, 1977.

Gramsci, Antonio. "The Intellectuals." In *Selections from the Prison Notebooks,* edited and translated by Quintin Hoare and Geoffrey Nowell Smith, pp. 3–23. New York: International Publishers, 1971.

Hart, Henry, ed. *American Writers' Congress*. New York: International Publishers, 1935.

———. *The Writer in a Changing World*. London: Lawrence and Wishart, 1937.

Heilbrun, Carolyn. *Reinventing Womanhood*. New York: W. W. Norton, 1979.

Herbst, Josephine. "Feet in the Grass Roots." *Scribners Magazine* 9 (January 1933): 46–51.

———. "The Starched Blue Sky of Spain." *The Noble Savage* 1 (1960): 76–117.

———. "Yesterday's Road." *New American Review* 3 (1968): 84–104.

Hicks, Granville. *The Great Tradition*. New York: Macmillan, 1933.

———. "Revolution and the Novel: Complex and Collective Novels." *New Masses*, April 10, 1934, pp. 23–25.

———. "Revolution and the Novel: Drama and Biography as Models." *New Masses*, April 17, 1934, pp. 24–25.

———. "Revolution and the Novel: The Problem of Documentation." *New Masses*, May 15, 1934, pp. 24–25.

———. "Writers in the Thirties." In *As We Saw the Thirties*, edited by Rita James Simon, pp. 76–101. Urbana: University of Illinois Press, 1967.

Hicks, Granville, Michael Gold, Isidor Schneider, Joseph North, Paul Peters, and Alan Calmer, eds. *Proletarian Literature in the United States*. New York: International Publishers, 1935.

Hill, Vicki Lynn. "Strategy and Breadth: The Socialist-Feminist in American Fiction." Ph.D. diss., State University of New York at Buffalo, 1979.

Homberger, Eric. *American Writers and Radical Politics, 1900–1939*. New York: St. Martin's Press, 1986.

———. "Proletarian Literature and the John Reed Clubs, 1929–1935." *Journal of American Studies* 13 (1979): 221–44.

Hourwich, Andria Taylor, and Gladys L. Palmer, eds. *I Am a Woman Worker: A Scrapbook of Autobiographies*. 1936. Reprint. New York: Arno Press, 1974.

Howard, June. *Form and History in American Literary Naturalism*. Chapel Hill: University of North Carolina Press, 1985.

———. "Jameson and the Dialectical Use of Genre Criticism." *Critical Exchange* 14 (Fall 1983): 70–80.

Howe, Irving, and Lewis Coser. *The American Communist Party: A Critical History*. New York: Da Capo Press, 1974.

Hull, Gloria. *Women, Color, Poetry: Three Women Writers of the Harlem Renaissance*. Bloomington: Indiana University Press, 1987.

Hurston, Zora Neale. *Their Eyes Were Watching God*. 1937. Reprint. Urbana: University of Illinois Press, 1978.

Hutchins, Grace. "Birth Control." *Working Woman* 6 (August 1935): 13.

———. "Feminists and the Left Wing." *New Masses*, November 20, 1934, pp. 14–15.

———. *Women Who Work*. New York: International Publishers, 1934.

Huyssen, Andreas. *After the Great Divide: Modernism, Mass Culture, Postmodernism*. Bloomington: Indiana University Press, 1986.

Inman, Mary. *In Women's Defense*. Los Angeles, Calif.: Committee to Organize the Advancement of Women, 1940.

"In Reply to Authors." *New Masses*, July 3, 1934, p. 32.

Isserman, Maurice. *Which Side Were You On?: The American Communist Party during the Second World War*. Middletown, Conn.: Wesleyan University Press, 1982.

Jacobs, Harriet. *Incidents in the Life of a Slave Girl*. Edited by Jean Fagan Yellin. Cambridge, Mass.: Harvard University Press, 1987.

Jacobus, Mary. "Is There a Woman in This Text?" *New Literary History* 14 (1982): 117–41.

———. "The Question of Language: Men of Maxims and *The Mill on the Floss*." *Critical Inquiry* 8 (Winter 1981): 207–22.

———. *Reading Woman: Essays in Feminist Criticism*. New York: Columbia University Press, 1986.

Jameson, Fredric. *The Political Unconscious: Narrative as a Socially Symbolic Act*. Ithaca, N.Y.: Cornell University Press, 1981.

Jardine, Alice. *Gynesis: Configurations of Women and Modernity*. Ithaca, N.Y.: Cornell University Press, 1985.

Jehlen, Myra. "Archimedes and the Paradox of Feminist Criticism." *Signs* 6 (Summer 1981): 575–601.

Johnson, Barbara. *The Critical Difference*. Baltimore, Md.: Johns Hopkins University Press, 1980.

———. "Gender Theory and the Yale School." In *Rhetoric and Form: Deconstruction at Yale*, edited by Robert Con Davis and Ronald Schleifer, pp. 101–12. Norman: University of Oklahoma Press, 1985.

Kaplan, Cora. "Pandora's Box: Subjectivity, Class, and Sexuality in Socialist Feminist Criticism." In *Making a Difference: Feminist Literary Criticism*, edited by Gayle Greene and Coppélia Kahn, pp. 146–76. London: Methuen, 1985.

Kempthorne, Dion. "Josephine Herbst: A Critical Introduction." Ph.D. diss., University of Wisconsin, 1973.

Kempton, Murray. *Part of Our Time*. New York: Simon and Schuster, 1955.

Kessler-Harris, Alice, and Paul Lauter. Introduction to *Call Home the Heart*, by Fielding Burke. New York: Feminist Press, 1985.

Klehr, Harvey. *The Heyday of American Communism*. New York: Basic Books, 1984.

Kristeva, Julia. "A New Type of Intellectual: The Dissident." In *The Kristeva Reader*, edited by Toril Moi, pp. 292–300. New York: Columbia University Press, 1986.

———. *The Revolution in Poetic Language*. Translated by Leon Roudiez. New York: Columbia University Press, 1984.

———. "Stabat Mater." Translated by Arthur Goldhammer. In *The Female Body in Western Culture*, edited by Susan Rubin Suleiman, pp. 99–118. Cambridge, Mass.: Harvard University Press, 1986.

Lacey, Candida Ann. "Engendering Conflict: American Women and the Making of a Proletarian Fiction." Ph.D. diss., University of Sussex, 1985.

———. "Striking Fictions: Women Writers and the Making of a Proletarian Realism." *Women's Studies International Forum* 9, no. 4 (1986): 373–84.

Langer, Elinor. "If in Fact I Have Found a Heroine . . ." *Mother Jones* 6 (May 1981): 36–46.

————. *Josephine Herbst: The Story She Could Never Tell.* Boston: Little, Brown, 1984.

Lapsley, Mary. "Scaffolding." *Modern Monthly*, May 1933, p. 209.

Lasch, Christopher. *The New Radicalism in America, 1889–1963: The Intellectual as a Social Type.* New York: Vintage, 1967.

Lauter, Paul. "Working-Class Women's Literature: An Introduction to Its Study." *Radical Teacher* 15 (1979): 16–26.

Lawrence, David. "Who Slew Proletcult?" *Vanguard* 4 (November 1937): 8–12.

Le Bon, Gustave. *The Crowd: A Study of the Popular Mind.* 1895. Reprint. Dunwoody, Ga.: N. S. Berg, 1968.

Lechlitner, Ruth. *Tomorrow's Phoenix.* New York: Alcestis Press, 1937.

Leknorf, Zelda. "Our Readers' Forum." *New Masses*, October 2, 1934, p. 40.

"Lens" [pseud.]. "Flashes and Close-Ups." *Daily Worker*, August 23, 1933, p. 5.

Lentricchia, Frank. *Criticism and Social Change.* Chicago: University of Chicago Press, 1983.

LeSueur, Meridel. "The Derned Crick's Rose." *New Masses*, February 1941, pp. 37–38.

————. "The Fetish of Being Outside." *New Masses*, February 14, 1935, pp. 22–25.

————. *Ripening.* Edited and with an introduction by Elaine Hedges. Old Westbury, N.Y.: Feminist Press, 1982.

————. *Salute to Spring.* New York: International Publishers, 1940.

————. "Sequel to Love." *The Anvil*, January–February 1935, pp. 3–4.

————. "They Follow Us Girls." *The Anvil*, July–August 1935, pp. 5–7.

————. "Women on the Breadlines." *New Masses*, January 1932, pp. 5–7.

Lewis, H. H. "Down the Skidway." In *Writers in Revolt: The Anvil Anthology, 1933–1940*, edited by Jack Conroy and Curt Johnson, pp. 120–24. Westport, Conn.: Lawrence Hill, 1973.

————. "The Man from Moscow." In *Thinking of Russia*, n.p. Holt, Minn.: Haaglund Press, 1932.

Lieberman, Robbie. *"My Song Is My Weapon": People's Songs and the Politics of Culture, 1946–1949.* Urbana: University of Illinois Press, 1989.

Loader, Jayne. "Women in the Left, 1906–1941: A Bibliography of Primary Sources." *University of Michigan Papers in Women's Studies* 2 (1975): 9–82.

Logan, Gertrude. "A Tennessee Woman's Auxiliary of the National Miners Union in Action." *Daily Worker*, March 5, 1932, p. 4.

Lone, Dr. "What Women Should Know." *Working Woman* 5 (February 1934): 15.

Luccock, Hulford E. *American Mirror: Social, Ethical, and Religious Aspects of American Literature, 1930–1940.* New York: Macmillan, 1941.

Lukács, Georg. *History and Class Consciousness.* Translated by Rodney Livingstone. Cambridge, Mass.: MIT Press, 1968.

————. *Studies in European Realism.* New York: Grosset and Dunlap, 1964.

————. *The Theory of the Novel.* Translated by Anna Bostock. Cambridge, Mass.: MIT Press, 1971.

————. *Writer and Critic and Other Essays.* Edited and translated by Arthur D. Kahn. New York: Grosset and Dunlap, 1970.

Lumpkin, Grace. "Southern Woman Bares Tricks of Higher-Ups to Shunt Lynch Blame." *Daily Worker*, November 27, 1933, p. 3.

McCarthy, Mary. "Saint Francesca of the Pacific Northwest." *The Nation*, January 15, 1936, p. 82.

McHenry, Beth. "A Catholic Mother Hears the Truth about Spain." *Daily Worker*, May 25, 1937, p. 7.

———. "Mothers Join Fight for Peace and Security." *Daily Worker*, May 7, 1937, p. 7.

———. "The Nation's Finest—Those YCL Girls." *Daily Worker*, May 6, 1937, pp. 1, 4.

———. "Women Mass in Capital to Ask Added WPA." *Daily Worker*, May 17, 1937, p. 1.

Macherey, Pierre. *A Theory of Literary Production*. Translated by Geoffrey Wall. London: Routledge and Kegan Paul, 1978.

MacKinnon, Janice R., and Stephen R. MacKinnon. *Agnes Smedley: The Life and Times of an American Radical*. Berkeley: University of California Press, 1988.

Madden, David, ed. *Proletarian Writers of the Thirties*. Carbondale: Southern Illinois University Press, 1968.

———. *Tough Guy Writers of the Thirties*. Carbondale: Southern Illinois University Press, 1968.

Margaret, Helene. "Our Readers' Forum." *New Masses*, April 1930, p. 16.

Martin, Emily. *The Woman in the Body: A Cultural Analysis of Reproduction*. Boston: Beacon Press, 1987.

Marx, Karl, Friedrich Engels, V. I. Lenin, and Joseph Stalin. *The Woman Question*. New York: International Publishers, 1951.

Meese, Elizabeth. *Crossing the Double-Cross: The Practice of Feminist Criticism*. Chapel Hill: University of North Carolina Press, 1986.

Miller, Nancy K. "Emphasis Added: Plots and Plausibilities in Women's Fiction." *PMLA* 96 (January 1981): 36–48.

Millet, Fred B. *Contemporary American Authors*. New York: Harcourt, Brace and Co., 1940.

Millet, Martha. "Drawn into Life." *Daily Worker*, January 19, 1935, p. 11.

———. "Last Night." *New Masses*, June 19, 1934, p. 17.

Mitchison, Naomi. "We're Writing a Book." *New Masses*, September 15, 1936, pp. 15–17.

Mitford, Jessica. *A Fine Old Conflict*. New York: Knopf, 1977.

———. *Hons and Rebels*. London: Victor Gollancz, 1960.

Moers, Ellen. *Literary Women*. Garden City, N.Y.: Anchor Books, 1977.

Moi, Toril. *Sexual/Textual Politics: Feminist Literary Theory*. London: Methuen, 1985.

Morrison, Toni. *Beloved*. New York: Knopf, 1987.

Naison, Mark. *Communists in Harlem during the Depression*. New York: Grove Press, 1983.

Nekola, Charlotte, and Paula Rabinowitz, eds. *Writing Red: An Anthology of Women Writers, 1930–1940*. New York: Feminist Press, 1987.

Nelson, Bruce. *Workers on the Waterfront: Seamen, Longshoremen, and Unionism in the 1930s.* Urbana: University of Illinois Press, 1988.

Nelson, Helen Clare. "A Clinical Study: Review of *The Company She Keeps.*" *New Masses,* July 21, 1942, p. 26.

Neruda, Pablo. "To the Mothers of the Dead Militia." *Daily Worker,* May 8, 1937, p. 7.

Newton, Judith, and Deborah S. Rosenfelt, eds. *Feminist Criticism and Social Change.* New York: Methuen, 1985.

North, Joseph. "College Men and Men." *New Masses,* October 1929, pp. 14–15.

———, ed. *New Masses: An Anthology of the Rebel Thirties.* New York: International Publishers, 1969.

"Not Sunny for Girl Slaves in 'Sunny' Florida." *Daily Worker,* January 4, 1929, p. 4.

Nuhn, Ferner. "The Lost Generation and the New Morality." *The Nation,* May 23, 1934, pp. 597–98.

Olsen, Tillie. "Afterword: A Biographical Interpretation." In *Life in the Iron Mills and Other Stories,* by Rebecca Harding Davis, pp. 67–174. New York: Feminist Press, 1986.

——— [Tillie Lerner]. "The Iron Throat." *Partisan Review,* May–June 1934, pp. 3–9.

———. *Silences.* New York: Delacorte Press/Seymour Lawrence, 1978.

——— [Tillie Lerner]. "The Strike." *Partisan Review,* September–October 1934): 3–9.

——— [Tillie Lerner]. "Thousand Dollar Vagrant." *New Republic,* August 29, 1934, pp. 66–70.

Page, Myra. "The Revolution Made a Person out of Me." *Daily Worker,* February 12, 1932, p. 4.

———. "Women Heroes of Socialist Construction." *Daily Worker,* April 16, 1932, p. 4.

Papke, Mary E. "An Analysis of Selected American Marxist Criticism, 1920–1941: From Dogma to Dynamic Strategies." *Minnesota Review* 13 (Fall 1979): 41–69.

Peck, David. "The Development of an American Marxist Literary Criticism: The Monthly *New Masses.*" Ph.D. diss., Temple University, 1968.

Pells, Richard H. *Radical Visions and American Dreams.* New York: Harper and Row, 1973.

Piercy, Marge. *Vida.* New York: Summit Books, 1979.

Pitts, Rebecca. "Women and Communism." *New Masses,* February 19, 1935, pp. 14–18.

Pizer, Donald. "The Camera Eye in *U.S.A.:* The Sexual Center." *Modern Fiction Studies* 26 (Autumn 1980): 417–30.

Porter, Katherine Anne. "Correspondence." *Partisan Review,* March 1938, p. 62.

Prichard, Katharine. "The Cooboo." In *Women and Fiction II,* edited by Susan Cahill, pp. 62–66. New York: New American Library, 1978.

Rabine, Leslie. *Reading the Romantic Heroine.* Ann Arbor: University of Michigan Press, 1986.

Ragon, Michel. *Histoire de la Littérature Prolétarienne en France.* Paris: Albin Michel, 1974.

Rahv, Philip. "An Open Letter to Young Writers." *Rebel Poet* (September 1932): n.p.
———. "Proletarian Literature: A Political Autopsy." *Southern Review* (Winter 1939): 616–28.
———. "A Variety of Fiction." *Partisan Review*, March 1939, pp. 110–11.
Rahv, Philip, and Wallace Phelps. "Recent Problems of Revolutionary Literature." In *Proletarian Literature in the United States*, edited by Granville Hicks et al., pp. 367–72. New York: International Publishers, 1935.
Rhinehart, Irene. "Another Baby?" *Working Woman* 6 (May 1935): 13.
Rich, Adrienne. "Compulsory Heterosexuality and Lesbian Existence." *Signs* 5 (Summer 1980): 62–91.
———. *Of Woman Born: Motherhood as Experience and Institution*. New York: W. W. Norton, 1976.
Rideout, Walter. "Forgotten Images of the Thirties: Josephine Herbst." *The Literary Review* 27 (Fall 1983): 28–36.
———. *The Radical Novel in the United States, 1900–1954: Some Interrelations of Literature and Society*. Cambridge, Mass.: Harvard University Press, 1956.
Robinson, Lillian S. *Sex, Class, and Culture*. Bloomington: Indiana University Press, 1978.
Rolfe, Edwin. "A College Girl Writes about Western Pennsylvania Miners." *Daily Worker*, March 3, 1934, p. 7.
Rosaldo, Michelle, and Louise Lamphere, eds. *Women, Culture, and Society*. Palo Alto, Calif.: Stanford University Press, 1974.
Rosenfelt, Deborah S. "Divided Against Herself." *Moving On* 4 (April/May 1980): 15–23.
———. "From the Thirties: Tillie Olsen and the Radical Tradition." *Feminist Studies* 7 (Fall 1981): 370–406.
———. "Getting into the Game: American Women Writers and the Radical Tradition." *Women's Studies International Forum* 9, no. 4 (1986): 363–72.
Ross, Andrew. *No Respect: Intellectuals and Popular Culture*. New York: Routledge, 1989.
Roth, Henry. *Call It Sleep*. 1934. Reprint. New York: Avon, 1964.
Rowbotham, Sheila. *Women, Resistance, and Revolution*. New York: Pantheon, 1972.
Rukeyser, Muriel. *Theory of Flight*. New Haven, Conn.: Yale University Press, 1935.
Russo, Mary. "Female Grotesques: Carnival and Theory." In *Feminist Studies/Critical Studies*, edited by Teresa de Lauretis, pp. 213–29. Bloomington: Indiana University Press, 1986.
Salzman, Jack, and Barry Wallenstein, eds. *Years of Protest*. New York: Pegasus, 1967.
Salzman, Jack, and Leo Zanderer, eds. *Social Poetry of the 1930s: A Selection*. New York: Burt Franklin and Co., 1978.
Samuelson, Joan Wood. "Patterns of Survival: Four American Women Writers and the Proletarian Novel." Ph.D. diss., Ohio State University, 1982.
Sanger, Margaret. *Margaret Sanger: An Autobiography*. New York: Dover, 1971.
Schachner, E. A. "Revolutionary Literature in the United States Today." *Windsor Quarterly* 2 (Spring 1934): 27–64.
Scharf, Lois. " 'The Forgotten Woman': Working Women, the New Deal, and Women's Organizations." In *Decades of Discontent: The Women's Movement, 1920–*

1940, edited by Lois Scharf and Joan M. Jensen, pp. 243–60. Boston: North-eastern University Press, 1987.

Schofield, Ann, ed. *Sealskin and Shoody: Working Women in American Labor Press Fiction, 1870–1920.* Westport, Conn.: Greenwood Press, 1988.

Schwartz, Lawrence H. *Marxism and Culture: The CPUSA and Aesthetics in the 1930s.* Port Washington, N.Y.: Kennikat Press, 1980.

Scott, Joan Wallach. *Gender and the Politics of History.* New York: Columbia University Press, 1988.

———. "On Language, Gender, and Working-Class History." *International Labor and Working-Class History* 31 (Spring 1987): 1–13.

Shaffer, Robert. "Women and the Communist Party U.S.A., 1930–1940." *Socialist Review* 45 (May/June 1979): 73–118.

Sharistanian, Janet. Afterword to *The Unpossessed*, by Tess Slesinger. 1934. Reprint. Old Westbury, N.Y.: Feminist Press, 1984.

———. "Tess Slesinger's Hollywood Sketches." *Michigan Quarterly Review* 18 (Summer 1979): 429–54.

Showalter, Elaine, ed. *The New Feminist Criticism: Essays on Women, Literature, and Theory.* New York: Pantheon, 1985.

Shulman, Alix Kates. *Burning Questions.* 1978. Reprint. New York: Thunder's Mouth Press, 1990.

Silverman, Kaja. *The Acoustic Mirror: The Female Voice in Psychoanalysis and Cinema.* Bloomington: Indiana University Press, 1988.

———. *The Subject of Semiotics.* New York: Oxford University Press, 1983.

Slesinger, Tess. *Time: The Present.* New York: Simon and Schuster, 1935.

Smedley, Agnes. "Shan-Fei, Communist." *New Masses*, May 1931, pp. 3–5.

Snitow, Ann, Christine Stansell, and Sharon Thompson, eds. *Powers of Desire.* New York: Monthly Review Press, 1983.

Solomon, Maynard, ed. *Marxism and Art: Essays Classic and Contemporary.* New York: Knopf, 1973.

Solow, Herbert. "Minutiae of Left-Wing Literary History." *Partisan Review*, March 1938, pp. 59–63.

Spillers, Hortense J. "Mama's Baby, Papa's Maybe: An American Grammar Book." *Diacritics* (Summer 1987): 65–81.

Spivak, Gayatri Chakravorty. *In Other Worlds: Essays in Cultural Politics.* New York: Methuen, 1987.

Stanton, Domna C. "Autogynography: Is the Subject Different?" In *The Female Autograph*, edited by Domna C. Stanton, pp. 3–20. New York: Literary Forum, 1984.

Stott, William. *Documentary Expression and Thirties America.* New York: Oxford University Press, 1973.

Suggs, Jon Christian. "The Influence of Marxist Aesthetics on American Fiction: 1929–1940." Ph.D. diss., University of Kansas, 1978.

Suleiman, Susan Rubin. *Authoritarian Fictions: The Ideological Novel as a Literary Genre.* New York: Columbia University Press, 1983.

———. "(Re)Writing the Body: The Politics and Poetics of Female Eroticism." In *The Female Body in Western Culture*, edited by Susan Rubin Suleiman, pp. 7–29. Cambridge, Mass.: Harvard University Press, 1986.

Susman, Warren I. "The Thirties." In *The Development of an American Culture*, edited by Stanley Coben and Lorman Ratner, pp. 179–218. Englewood Cliffs, N.J.: Prentice-Hall, 1970.

Swados, Harvey, ed. *The American Writer and the Great Depression*. Indianapolis: Bobbs-Merrill, 1966.

Taggard, Genevieve. *Calling Western Union*. New York: Harper and Brothers, 1936.

———. "Life of the Mind, 1935." *New Masses*, January 1, 1935, p. 16.

———. "Romanticism and Communism." *New Masses*, September 25, 1934, pp. 18–20.

Terkel, Studs. *Hard Times: An Oral History from the Great Depression*. New York: Pantheon, 1970.

Theweleit, Klaus. *Male Fantasies*. Vol. 1, *Women, Floods, Bodies, History*. Translated by Stephen Conway with Erica Carter and Chris Turner. Minneapolis: University of Minnesota Press, 1987.

Trent, Lucia, and Ralph Cheyney. *More Power to Poets!: A Plea for More Poetry in Life, More Life in Poetry*. New York: Henry Harrison, 1934.

Trilling, Lionel. "Young in the Thirties." *Commentary* 41 (May 1966): 43–51.

Trimberger, Ellen Kay. "Women in the Old and New Left: The Evolution of a Politics of Personal Life." *Feminist Studies* 5 (Fall 1979): 432–50.

Trotsky, Leon. *Literature and Revolution*. 1923. Reprint. Ann Arbor: University of Michigan Press, 1975.

Truth, Sojourner. "Ain't I a Woman?" 1851. Published as part of the "Reminiscences of Frances D. Gage." In *The Feminist Papers: From Adams to Beauvoir*, edited by Alice Rossi, pp. 416–19. New York: Columbia University Press, 1973.

Urgo, Joseph R. "Proletarian Literature and Feminism: The Gastonia Novels and Feminist Protest." *Minnesota Review* 24 (Spring 1985): 64–84.

Vance, Carole, ed. *Pleasure and Danger*. Boston: Routledge and Kegan Paul, 1984.

Vorse, Mary Heaton. *Labor's New Millions*. New York: Modern Age Books, 1938.

———. "Lauren Gilfillan's Education." *New Masses*, April 10, 1934, p. 16.

Wald, Alan. *James T. Farrell: The Revolutionary Socialist Years*. New York: New York University Press, 1978.

———. "The Menorah Group Moves Left." *Jewish Social Studies* 38 (Summer/Fall 1976): 289–320.

———. *The New York Intellectuals: The Rise and Decline of the Anti-Stalinist Left from the 1930s to the 1980s*. Chapel Hill: University of North Carolina Press, 1987.

———. *The Revolutionary Imagination: The Poetry and Politics of John Wheelwright and Sherry Mangan*. Chapel Hill: University of North Carolina Press, 1983.

———. "Revolutionary Intellectuals: *Partisan Review* in the 1930s." In *Literature at the Barricades: The American Writer in the 1930s*, edited by Ralph F. Bogardus and Fred Hobson, pp. 187–203. Tuscaloosa: University of Alabama Press, 1982.

Walker, Alice. *Meridian*. New York: Harcourt Brace Jovanovich, 1976.

———. "One Child of One's Own: A Meaningful Digression within the Work(s)— an Excerpt." In *But Some of Us Are Brave*, edited by Gloria T. Hull, Particia Bell Scott, and Barbara Smith, pp. 37–44. Old Westbury, N.Y.: Feminist Press, 1982.

Ware, Susan. *Holding Their Own: American Women in the 1930s*. Boston: Twayne Publishers, 1982.

Warshow, Robert. "The Legacy of the 30's." In *The Immediate Experience: Movies*,

Comics, Theatre, and Other Aspects of Popular Culture, pp. 33–48. Garden City, N.Y.: Doubleday, 1962.

Weedon, Ann. "Correspondence." *New Masses*, July 16, 1935, p. 22.

West, Don. "Our Readers' Forum." *New Masses*, May 19, 1936, p. 22.

Westin, Jeanne. *Making Do: How Women Survived the '30's*. Chicago: Follett Publishing Co., 1976.

"What Can a Woman Do?" *Working Woman* 5 (November 1934): 5.

White, Hayden. *Metahistory: The Historical Imagination in Nineteenth-Century Europe*. Baltimore, Md.: Johns Hopkins University Press, 1973.

Wilk, Mary Beth. "The Inland Woman: Josephine Johnson." Ph.D. diss., University of Massachusetts, 1978.

Williams, Alexander. *Murder in the WPA*. New York: Robert McBride, 1937.

Williams, Raymond. *Marxism and Literature*. Oxford: Oxford University Press, 1977.

Wilson, Harriet. *Our Nig: Or, Sketches from the Life of a Free Black*. Introduction by Henry Louis Gates, Jr. New York: Vintage, 1983.

Winter, Ella. *Red Virtue: Human Relationships in the New Russia*. London: Victor Gollancz, 1933.

———. "What Fascism Means to Mothers." *Working Woman* 4 (August 1933): 6.

Wittig, Monique. *Les Guérillères*. Translated by David Le Vay. New York: Avon, 1973.

———. "The Mark of Gender." *Feminist Issues* 5 (Fall 1982): 3–12.

"Women Slave in Steel Mill." *Daily Worker*, September 23, 1929, p. 3.

Woolf, Virginia. *A Room of One's Own*. New York: Harcourt, Brace and World, 1929.

———. *Women and Writing*. Edited and with an introduction by Michèle Barrett. New York: Harcourt Brace Jovanovich, 1979.

"Work among Women." *Party Organizer* 1 (January 1932): 26–27.

Wright, Richard. *American Hunger*. New York: Harper and Row, 1977.

———. "Between Laughter and Tears." *New Masses*, October 5, 1937, pp. 22, 25.

Yount, Neala J. S. " 'America—Song We Sang without Knowing': Meridel Le Sueur's America." Ph.D. diss., University of Minnesota, 1978.

Zetkin, Clara. *My Recollections of Lenin*. Moscow: Foreign Languages Publishing House, 1956.

Zugsmith, Leane. *Home Is Where You Hang Your Childhood*. New York: Random House, 1937.

Index